FORTY SHADES of GREEN: THE JUNKMAN OF BROOKLYN

by
Joan Flynn Beesley

Winchester Park Press

40 Shades of Green: The Junkman of Brooklyn

Cover collage of Flynn family photos and artifacts created and photographed by Kim Beesley Suski.

Winchester Park Press
joanbeesley@gmail.com

Printed in the United States of America

Publishers Cataloging-in-Publication Data
Beesley, Joan
40 Shades of Green: The Junkman of Brooklyn
By Joan Flynn Beesley
ISBN: 9798218322809
1. Historical Novel-Biography-Autobiography

Dedication

This book is dedicated to the Flynns, to all of us, the "40 Shades of Green" especially those mentioned below:

Michael Flynn, his wife Mary Ann Farrell, his parents, Charles and Bridgette Flynn and his uncles Peter, Francis, John and Stephen Flynn and cousin "Oonie" Farrell, all of County Leitrim, Ireland, Amity Street and the Columbia Street Waterfront in Brooklyn. I will never know you all but I've certainly tried.

I thank my grandparents Frank and Mary Flynn and John and Eleanor Dillon of Brooklyn, especially my beloved parents, Joan and Edward Flynn who guided me in the writing of this book. I must include my Flynn brothers and sisters, Michael, Kevin, Marianne, Elizabeth, Maureen, Ed and John, the source of so much joy to my parents and myself.

I wish to acknowledge the help and encouragement of a newly discovered branch of the Brooklyn Flynns: Diane Brook of the U.K., my new "Flynn" fourth cousin, who answered my "Michael Flynn" query on Genforum.com, providing research and leading to an introduction to Carol Langer and her mother Eileen Bagley of Boston, who met Michael Flynn in her youth. These three wonderful women are the descendants of Mary Gilhooley Flynn and Peter Flynn, Michael's uncle, of County Leitrim, Ireland and Amity Street in Brooklyn, the home of so many immigrants named "Flynn".

I wish to thank the love of my life, Ed Beesley, for his support during the writing of this book and the time spent escorting me one summer through the streets near the Brooklyn waterfront where Michael Flynn lived and had his scrap warehouse at Columbia and Congress Streets.

Finally, I wish to thank my children, Robert, Rosemary and Kimberly Beesley, for their constant inspiration and for whom this book is especially written. I can't help but think that we all have a bit of savvy and salt water in our veins, as did their great-great grandfather Michael Flynn. I want them all to know their history, the story of the Flynns, (from what I've heard, it was grand.)

The days of our lives, fluttering
The slow, lazy turning of each page
Like the pages of a book, wavering,
Hesitant to be replaced.
One day the book completed
The story is over
The book is closed
On the tale of our lives.

CONTENTS

PREFACE

    When you visit, the old people will tell you there are 40 shades of green. You can actually look down from the hilltops of Ireland, at the verdant knolls, moss rock, the ivy-covered broken stone walls, the tree-lined lanes, their dark-green canopies a shady, protective cathedral above, as far as the eye can see, a changing, slowly-turning kaleidoscope of green.

    There are 40 shades of green in America, too. Though harder to see, they are there if you listen and look. They are not, however, in the landscape. They are the immigrants themselves and their descendants, each retaining nuances, whisperings of their heritage, a human kaleidoscope, turning and returning, in our own lifetimes, to what is in our blood.

Looking Back

Barnacles of Age
Those cruel crustaceans
Shackle our thoughts and memories
As we soar mid-flight
Looking through the mirror of my memory
Old age tarnishes the quicksilver of life
With encrusted memories that don't rub off,
That protect us and help us
Through Life's Journey.

Joan Flynn Beesley

I see him still. The stiff, sepia cardboard photo, circa 1873, Brooklyn, New York. His posed, formal upper torso only, hands in lap, probably posed on a stool, as was the fashion in photogravure. The handsome young Irishman, peering out, cool blue eyes, proud, clear and direct. His bowler hat, Irish checkered plaid (green, I'd imagine) cravat, arranged and anchored stiffly at his neck by the gold tie-pin. A formal and dignified posture. Proudly posing in his wainscot, gold watch fob and chain, draped fashionably across his pocket. Brown hair, aquiline nose, ruddy, handsome features offset by the high, stiff white collar.

Those cool, blue eyes focused firmly on the camera, confident, yet distant, something proudly remote there. A second look sees a boldness, a slight impatience –no, a cold distain-for the photographer and his process. A timeless quality to the young man's fearless, penetrating blue eyes: "Don't be takin' me time. Aye have an agenda."

MICHAEL FLYNN, many years later, in 1905, at Age 52

My Forever

I'll be here forever
I've been here forever
Measuring the length
And breadth of my life.

Part 1: Once Upon a Time: County Leitrim, Ireland, 1845

Joan Flynn Beesley

Charles Flynn

"Plop-plop. Plop-plop."

"Tis not a game, y'know," the mother said, as she sat at a worn wooden table, peeling carrots for the fine Irish stew she was making. The object of her criticism was her nineteen year old son, Charles, carelessly peeling onions and tossing them into the large cast iron pot, hissing with boiling water on the stove in the tidy kitchen of the thatched cottage. The year was 1845. The place was County Leitrim in the northernmost part of Ireland.

"Plop."

"If it's potatoes y'd rather be hav'n me peel, I will," he said amiably. Charles was a handsome young man with dark black curly hair and luminous brown eyes, very proud of his tall, nearly 5'10"frame. Years of working with his father on the small Irish conacre farm had made his arms sinewy and strong, yet he had fine hands, not like a farmer at all.

"I best do the potatoes meself, Charles," the mother sighed. "These ones I dug are surely no prize. Couldn't have been much better durin' the last Famine itself."

"I best be go'in now, Ma," he said, listening intently and suddenly laying his knife on the wooden counter. "Tis trouble again."

"Land O'Jesus. Not again."

Charles hurried out the front door, picking up a large wooden staff. He ran down the gravel driveway to the leafy country lane out front. The lane, bordered by a low stonewall on both sides, was completely shaded by large oaks, forming a cathedral of green as it disappeared over the hill. He could see the telltale cloud of dust atop the hill.

As he ran up the lane, the dull roar increased. Then he saw them. What looked like a white cloud in the road was actually about 100 sheep. They had broken through the stone wall and were running down the lane, bleating and crying in a panicked rush. Big old sheep, ready for shearing, small, frightened newborns bleating, separated from their mothers, panicky ewes parted from their young, born that spring, all heading for Charles down in the lane.

"Goddam sheep will be the death o' me yet," Charles thought as he took the position. Arms spread apart, he stood in the middle of the road with his staff outstretched, slowing down the marauding sheep. It took over two hours to herd them back through the hole in the stone wall where they had broken through. Again.

When Charles returned to the cottage his mother had finished the stew. It was a late spring afternoon. The bubbling aroma filled every cranny of the white cottage with the brown thatched roof. His father had died of pneumonia that winter. His brothers, Francis, Stephen, John and cousin Miles, like so many others, had left to seek their fortunes in America. His older brother Peter had immigrated to Scotland. It was now he and his mother. He hadn't quite mastered the art of repairing the breaks in the stone wall, nor the breaks in his mother's heart.

"Yer poor dear pa had talked about buildin' the wall higher," the mother sighed. She was now baking bread, sitting at the worn wooden kitchen table. There were three chairs still. He noted how the late afternoon sunlight fell through the kitchen curtain, across his mother's grey hair as she kneaded the dough.

"Tis the strength of the wall, not the height."

"But Charles, seems they be gettin' out weekly now, right on their own schedule!" she said, smiling at the earnest, and dusty, young man before her. "Can it be you I see? Covered with the dust again and smellin' like one of the sheep, is it?"

"I be go'in now, Ma. Be back for supper, sure," Charles said as he lowered his lanky form, giving her a hug.

From the front room, the young man collected his easel, brushes and paints and hurried out to capture the afternoon sun from the wonderful vantage point he had found by the stonewall at the top of the lane where he had just repaired the wall. He stole away to this spot whenever he could. What started as a hobby was beginning to consume him. Each of his recent paintings began to beautifully capture the Irish countryside of Leitrim.

Yesterday he managed to rough out his current landscape, the verdant valley below, it's flat meadow swept by wildflowers of every shape and kind, horses, brown and white cows, and the inevitable herds of sheep. Though quite poor, the family managed to get by on their potatoes, several pigs and sheep which their landlord provided in lieu of money. By the standard of the day, they were actually very fortunate, getting by in spite of the frequent, minor potato famines that seemed to strike every other year. Charles' art supplies had come to him through his father.

As he hauled his easel and paints up over the stone wall, he surveyed the valley below, the afternoon sun illuminating the rolling green hills and small mountains. Drifting clouds caressed them with brief shadows as they inched slowly by.

"Indeed," he thought, "the old ones were right. Ireland truly is 40 shades of green and I mean to capture every one of them in me paintin'!"

Charles was quite the picture himself, fine lad that he was. His brow furrowed, black eyes intent, he rushed feverishly to paint the wonderful, ever-changing kaleidoscope that was the Irish countryside in spring. He owned only 4 basic colors and had to experiment laboriously to mix just the right tones of green, blending carefully as he added his yellows, blues and reds.

Suddenly, from the corner of his eye, he saw a figure in white, walking slowly down the lane, from the direction of the neighboring town. It was a young woman. Recently, a band of town boys had ridiculed him, calling him" The Gentleman Painter." Few people in his impoverished village had time to paint the rich landscape. They eked a living by farming potatoes, turnips and raising cows and the ever-present sheep from which the village weaved the beautiful blends of lambskin and wool throws for which it would someday be famous.

Quickly the shy Irishman gathered his pallet and paints, collapsed his easel and hunkered down behind the stone wall between two large boulders that had been discarded, too large to be a part of the wall. He would not be made a fool of twice.

"Soon this pesky person will be on her way. The luck of it t'will be I can paint for another hour into the evenin' light," he thought to himself, waiting for the unwelcome intruder to pass along.

"Baa. Baaaaaa."

Suddenly a small lamb with a tinkling bell crossed the lane. It had squeezed through the troublesome stone wall and was now on a quest to announce the presence of the curious figure, now painfully crouching down between the rocks, clutching his easel and paints.

"Tis a sight ye are now, surely," announced a teasing voice.

And Charles looked up to see a vision that made the luxurious landscape he was painting pale in comparison. She wore a long white dress with smocking, as was the fashion, with a green sash that accentuated her slender waist.

"May I ask, do all the lads of County Leitrim hide in rocks now, waitin' to be liberated?"

She laughed, not so much at him, but at his situation, as Charles slowly lifted his long body from between the boulders, reaching down to retrieve his easel and paints.

"Now I see why! All covered in dust, a sight ye are! No wonder you're hidin' yerself!" she laughed. "Will ye be joinin' me out here on the lane? And land o'God, what *is* that smell?"

"Enough, lass!" Charles tried to sound gruff, but could feel that damnable red blush inflaming his cheeks, as he leapt the stone wall to face the most beautiful girl he had ever seen.

"I am Bridgette Gilhooley, up from Leitrim town to stay with me Gilhooley cousins up the road for the summer," explained the young woman with emerald green eyes and thick chestnut hair the color of fine polished mahogany, gathered in a long thick braid over her starched white collar.

"Pleased I am t' meet you," he said, taking off his cap. His artist's eyes were filled with the beauty of her extraordinary white porcelain skin, high cheekbones and lovely smile.

"And do ye have a name, perhaps?" she laughed.

"I do. 'Tis Charles. Charles Flynn."

And so it began. After talking a while by the stone wall he showed her the landscape he was working on.

"Tis grand, Charles Flynn. A talented artist ye are surely."

"Tell me now, Bridgette Gilhooley, do ya see what's missin' in me paintin'?" he asked in his quiet way, amazing himself with his boldness.

"Is it the river itself below, for I'm not see'in it quite yet, in yer fine paintin'."

"The fine thing I'm missin' is yerself, Miss Bridgette. Can ye come back tomorrow, say 5 o'clock when the light is golden?" he asked, pulling out a watch fob, more functional than ornate, about 3 inches long, criss-crossed into an intricate inter-locking pattern, chain-like, that folded neatly on itself, supporting a gold watch.

"What a lovely watch," she observed.

"Twas about all me father left me, and his paints," he said softly.

"If you'll sit here on the wall I'll paint ye into my landscape and t'will be as fine a landscape as any in th' county, with you in it, I mean."

And so, that's exactly the story of how Charles and Bridgette met. Every day in the late afternoon, he would meet her down the lane, where he would pose her sitting on the wall, capturing her delicate beauty in the light of the fading day, stroke by stroke, adding her into his magnificent landscape, adding her into his life. The finished landscape was magnificent, the 40 shades of green surrounding the portrait of

Bridgette with her emerald green eyes smiling out at the viewer, much as she first smiled down at the cowering artist when she discovered him hiding in the rock wall.

They married the following spring, Bridgette leaving her family, to join Charles and his mother in their family cottage.

Reflections

Stir the ashes of the past
The tea-leaves of time
Fluttering pages
Softly lifting, turning,
Pausing for an instant,
Hesitating,
Then moving forward.

Part 2: Somewhere in Time: Denver, Colorado,1995

Joan Flynn Beesley

Joan Flynn Beesley

She had been to Ireland. She had spent time in Limerick, Tipperary, Dublin and Carrick-on-Shannon, only five minutes from Leitrim, had they known. She visited there with her parents, Joan and Ed Flynn, who opened the first authentic Irish Import stores in Cleveland in the early 1990's.

Staying in remote cottages with several Irish families in the country, she had many memories: the wonderful hearty breakfasts, the cold, damp nights warmed by peat in the stone fireplaces, the mysterious dolmen mounds, the late afternoon she watched her teenage son venture far down in a valley amid a large herd of brown and white cows.

At first he had approached the herd cautiously. She held her breath as the curious seventeen year-old cautiously walked among them. Their warm cow-breath hovering in the chilly air, they scattered slowly, acknowledging his presence with low, communal mooing. It was a timeless moment, the newly-minted, meeting the very old and ancient.

She loved that time in Ireland. Her last name being "Flynn", the two week vacation had been more like a homecoming. Asking directions back to the bed and breakfast after a day of sight-seeing the old Gaelic road signs were mystical at best: she found the Irish absolutely loved giving directions. As she looked into the faces of the Irish folk she encountered, she saw the expressions of old aunts and uncles, her beloved grandparents Mary and Frank Flynn, now deceased and at rest in Brooklyn's Holy Cross cemetery. The Irish she met would say this or that "was grand", a phrase she often heard her Grandmother Flynn say long ago in her childhood in Brooklyn.

These faces were familiar, accepting her with an immediate recognition as well. They were eager to make sure she understood at least half of what she would actually remember about their elaborate instructions, embellished with local tales and fables about this corner or that fork in the road. It was like a homecoming. Like her, these people all loved history, music, writing, poetry and the ever-changing forty shades of green around them, changing focus with the mist or rain. Unlike them, however, she made her living far away in the telecommunications business.

Nothing in life prepared her for what would happen early that crisp, fall afternoon in Denver. Nothing. The Dow was up, Nasdaq down, much to the detriment of her tech mutual funds. For the third time that morning, she clicked idly away on her web browser, accessing Yahoo Finance, logging in to check her diminishing positions on Charles Schwab.

"There must be more to life than this," she thought. From her corner office on the ninth floor of the mammoth telecommunications building, she looked beyond the glass-mirrored sky-scrapers, the shining buildings reflecting each other, MCI, QWEST and the other telco titans. The old and venerable was reflected there as well: the historic Brown Palace, Trinity Church, the Petroleum Building, a reminder of Denver's free-wheeling oil and gas heydays in the 70's. And there beyond, lay the snow-capped Rockies, the whole frosted front range as far as they eye could see, running north to south, their peaks rising elegant and majestic against the bright blue western afternoon sky, a picture right out of Zane Grey's Old West.

Through Ancestry.com she had verified family lore that her great grandfather Michael Flynn had come from Ireland when he was three years old. Tenderly she had researched and found his name late one night on the 1900 Brooklyn Census, found him there, living in a brownstone, occupation "Paper stock", whatever that meant, at 230 Baltic Street with his wife Mary Anne Farrell, several blocks from Brooklyn Harbor. Years earlier he had written "Newsagent" on a Census line. She later learned from his obituary that early on he specialized in the processing of scrap rope which was sold to the paper mills. At 230 Baltic they also had Irish boarders with quaint titles such as "shirt maker" and "button maker," occupations that no longer existed. A cousin with the name of John Farrell lived there as well.

She knew the stories about the man-in his late forties in 1900- who would soon become the famous patriarch of the Flynn's in Brooklyn, a shrewd tycoon rising from "Junkman" to own a massive steel and aluminum window business, with deals in Florida and Peru, whose company would someday win the bid for the Hyatt Regency in New York among many others.

Michael Flynn died in 1942, four years before she was born. She thought there was a strange silence about the last years of life. He died at age 88, a very long life for someone born in the 1850's. A master entrepreneur, confined to his bed with painful arthritis for his last thirteen years, he had been the friend of Brooklyn Democratic politicians and statesmen, according to his obituary. "Friend of major political leaders including James Kane, James Dunne, James Innis, Michael Coffey and State Senator Bart Cronin" it read.

Researching the names, she learned they were all associated with the tumultuous "Brooklyn Ring" Democratic Party run by Boss McLaughlin from 1862 to 1903, Brooklyn's equivalent of New York's Tammany Hall. The powerful Irish political machine was most influential in awarding contracts to their own for the paving of streets and most public works and helped finance the building of The Brooklyn Bridge and Prospect Park. Colorful scandals, elections day shoot-outs, creative land valuations, brawls and truly ingenuous political mayhem were all chronicled with delicious fervor by The New York Times across the East River in Manhattan, in biased support of their own slate of politicians. In scrupulous detail they reported the Ring's involvement in the Coney Island Athletic Club's Prizefighting Exhibition and how he Ring, prior to an election night, would arrange accelerated and "loose" naturalization of "immigrant thugs" in key wards, to increase the vote.

She read these accounts of the Ring's celebrated political shenanigans late at night, glowingly positive versions of these exploits reported in proud detail by The Brooklyn Eagle, in contrast to The New York Times. She never knew the part her great-grandfather might have played in all this but he obviously made his fortune, connected with the Democratic machine of Irishmen like himself. The Irish statesmen referred to in his obituary had risen from dire squalor as well. Boss McLaughlin himself was from County Cork, a rope-maker, then a civilian-contractor for The Brooklyn Navy Yard, a position of patronage from which he awarded work and livelihood in exchange for votes and political loyalty to the Irish Democratic leaders. Except for the names cited in his obituary by her grandfather, Michael Flynn's son, this was the only mention of any association. The obituary stated he was also active in The Brooklyn Lodge of Elks, The Emerald Association, The St. Patrick Society of Brooklyn and was a life member of Columbus Council 126, Knights of Columbus.

Certainly, she reasoned, Michael John Flynn was a man of his times and thus supportive of Irish politics, so radical due to the not-too-distant memory of near extinction of the Irish, both by Famine and the British. She read with anger how the British cruelly raised the rent of the struggling sharecroppers, then took their cattle for payment, exporting Irish beef in ships to England. How the predatory "gombeen men" then loaned the starving and desperate Irish money at impossible interest rates.

Having stolen massive amounts of land from the O'Neil Clan in the 1600's under Cromwell, how the Crown settled these areas with radical Orange Protestants from Ulster. How the English Empire, having exhausted Europe's agriculture to feed British soldiers in their Indian and African colonies, systematically converted Irish pastureland to farmland, focusing on only one crop, the potato. How they eventually cancelled the "croppies'" leases altogether, consolidating the land once again back to profitable pastureland, saving extravagant absentee landlords from defaulting on their heavily-mortgaged mansions and land. How they cruelly "tumbled" thousands of Irish cottages, leaving families to die in ditches.

So, was Michael Flynn truly associated with The Brooklyn Ring? Did he contribute any of his money to advance Irish Democratic politics?

"I certainly hope so!" was his great-granddaughter's conclusion, mentally comparing a shattered Dublin of 1873 with the advances of steam turbines, railroads, ship-building and steel-making factories that comprised Northern Ireland's Belfast in the same year. How, in comparison with all the wages created by the Industrial Revolution in other cities, the Irish were economically impoverished, the croppies bravely subsisting, they boasted, on only potatoes and "turf bogs for me fire!"

She could only guess at his role, as her grandparents and father never really spoke much at all about the mystery man responsible for the very comfortable life they all enjoyed. She guessed he was not understood or really appreciated by those around him, at the end of his life. Invalids in pain can be inadvertently avoided over time, that thus, he was probably somewhat isolated during those last thirteen years of his life. They simply referred to him as "Grandpa Flynn". He belonged to a much older, turbulent, far richer world. She surmised he missed his wife and above all, the art of rope salvage and much later, the scrap metal salvage business which he pioneered. Again the obituary stating he salvaged the USS Huntington, USS St. Louis WWI cruisers, as well as many submarines and the "Fulton Elevated Line." He actually dismantled and salvaged the early overhead "L" trains and bridges!

The young telco middle manager knew much more about Michael Flynn's son, Frank Fergus Flynn, her grandfather, who recounted tales about the family business during their long walks along the beach at Breezy Point Surf Club near Jones Beach when she was a child. She would walk by his side every summer, his bleached white tennis shoes next to her tiny sandals, walking the windy mile to the jetty where he would point out Coney Island and the Queen Mary-the First-, grandly sailing from New York Harbor for Europe.

The seagulls would swoop noisily down as they walked, plucking small tidbits from the shoreline and tidal pools. Every summer through her teenage years she accompanied him, steadfast in his routine, as they took in the salt air and all he could tell her about The Michael Flynn Manufacturing Company of which he was president. At times he would refer formally to "my father", and his brother Charlie, but all the great facts he could have told her about the people who made up her heritage, he kept to himself.

One summer, he confided to her with a bit of surprise and quiet astonishment, "You know, they call me 'The Old Man' now," he said, referring to much younger passersby who also made the daily trip to the jetty. Approaching his eighties, this would be their last summer together. There was a certain unspoken tenderness between them. They both enjoyed each other's company, the way a grandfather dotes on his granddaughter, in his quiet, restrained way. As Isis' smiles of heat confront the moon, she soon lost her old man and the sea, but she continued to think of him and the things he had told her, all throughout her life.

Sitting at her flat screen that late morning, she thought of this grandfather, Frank Flynn, of all that was alive and real from those days, of her heritage, known only from those walks, or fragments from stories told around dinner tables in Brooklyn and Philadelphia.

"If only I could have known them better," she reflected. Her next staff meeting was at one o'clock, the same old issues with the same old people. She allowed her mind to drift as she absently fingered the letters on her keyboard. She launched her web-browser, accessing Yahoo.Travel.Ireland. She had even read "Angela's Ashes" that summer, to better understand why these people had left Ireland in such haste and in such massive numbers. A better understanding would have come from reading "Trinity", an old edition she once saw lying forgotten in her parent's basement after they had closed their Irish stores. Even so, she was appalled by the shocking misery and squalor she did read about. These were stories her relatives never shared. www.yahoo.travel.ireland.com was the last thing she remembered.

The floor was damp, her navy blue business suit rumpled, her black suede pumps stained with cow dung. She lay in the dingy corner of the straw-covered barn floor. A rainy, early morning mist hovered in the dank barn air. An old leather harness and pitchfork hung on the wall behind her. Something was terribly wrong: she must be dreaming.

She pulled herself up, picking the straw from her navy wool suit, and looked around to find herself in a very real stable. The warm breath of several startled horses permeated the cold, damp air as she passed gingerly behind them.

"Whoa, take it easy," she said, passing their stalls. The horses were all brown and their size enormous compared to horses she had ridden, growing up in Philadelphia. These huge, muscular animals were like those she had seen in Brooklyn as a child, pulling merchants' wagons of pots and pans or vegetables through the morning streets of Brooklyn, the vendors calling "Veg-tables, fresh veg-tables!" The horses before her were like the great, muscular, working draft horses of Brooklyn.

Peering out of the stable, she could make out nothing in the darkness of early morning. She was now desperately cold as she made her way over the clodded, frozen earth. It appeared to be a field of sorts, with the frozen remnants of some type of crop. Then she saw it.

A stone wall, about two feet high, actually a wall made from piles of un-mortared stones and beyond it a road and what appeared to be countryside as the bone-chilling mist lifted. It was a dirt road with an old grey stone wall on either side, massive trees, probably oaks, now bare and black in the depth of winter.

Making her way over the wall, she peered through the icy mist seeing nothing. She headed down the dirt road-more like a lane-about a hundred feet-then sat on the grey wall, listening to an unfamiliar sound, that of several country roosters, each competing proudly to announce the arrival of morning. Then another sound broke the frozen silence. Very vague and indistinct, she thought she heard a low, baying sound. She sprung from the wall and as she made her way down the lane, the sound grew louder. It was the unmistakable sound of sheep, baaing to each other, as if in acknowledgement, as they woke. Not several sheep, but a great many, she thought. Still, she could not see them, but she knew they were out there, probably settled on the side of the rolling hills she could barely make out, as the fog and dense mist began to lift.

Then she saw it. As the road turned the bend, she could see the lights of a farmhouse, back off the road about fifty feet. Climbing over the wall, she made her way up the slight incline. There was a dirt path, with large oak trees, but as she approached, she noticed it wasn't a farmhouse at all, but a white-washed cottage with a thick, brown thatched roof neatly held down with pegs.

It must have been about 5 am, she reasoned, yet all the lights, or lamps were shining brightly from the windows. Slowly she walked through the mist and peered through a deep-set window into an old, country kitchen: black, cast-iron stove, a wooden table and chairs, fireplace and straw on the floor. Folks seemed to be running everywhere. There was evidently a family crisis and someone named Maureen was clearly running the show. She wore a long dress, white apron and was running back and forth with steaming pots of water from the old iron stove.

"Mother o' God! If we don't find more peat for this fire, we'll be out of hot water surely in no time! 'Tis no Flynn baby came into this world without plenty o' hot water, I can tell ye that! Outa me way!"

A young boy about two yawned, then toddled safely to an alcove at the end of the large kitchen. Maureen found a stack of four inch bricks of peat and threw them into the oven's hold, the fire flaring brightly, the smell of pungent peat bog filling the room.

Maureen's red face was very flushed. Her green eyes flashed. She seemed to be shouting at no one in particular as she whirled her heavy frame back and forth, her thick brown braid unraveling, putting on yet another pot of water to boil as she ran out of the kitchen and up the stairs of the cottage. She repeated this maneuver several times.

Two men dressed in black sat impassively by the fire in rocking chairs. Neither spoke despite Maureen's carrying on. The older man, clenching a black pipe tightly in his bad teeth, wore suspenders and a tattered black wool jacket and boots, rocking and nodding in half-sleep in spite of all the commotion. The younger man, also dressed in black, was silent as well, yet tense and alert. He had thick, wavy black hair, a mustache, black wool sweater and cap. He stared into the fire, his tapered fingers gripping the arms of his rocking chair, for he could hear the screams of his wife in their bedroom above the kitchen. He was twenty-one years old.

Then all was quiet. The old man started from his sleep and stopped rocking. Maureen's frantic runs for hot water had ceased.

Cold as it was outside the cottage, the young woman in the ruined navy wool suit and muddy heels stood by the window and held her breath as a very old woman slowly made her way down the creaking wooden steps from the room above the kitchen. The two men by the hearth rose tentatively as she approached them. Slowly, she held out a wrinkled hand formally to the younger of the men and touched his arm softly.

"Charles, 'tis blessed ye are today with a baby boy. Wee wain, seems to be just fine, but feisty he is, loudest young lad in County Leitrim, God help us, this mornin!" his mother informed him, smiling tiredly.

'Tis grand! But she herself, well, she's had a hard time of it. She's callin' for ye now. Go to her, lad."

The new father kissed his mother and raced up the wooden stairs, almost knocking over Maureen, whose ever-escaping hair was now completely undone, cascading down her long shift. Out of breath, her large bosom heaved as she washed her hands at a large basin.

"Mother o'God, he was a fighter, that new brother of yours, Frank," she said to the sleepy toddler, now sitting in the peat alcove at the far end of the kitchen. "Couldn't make up his mind if he were stay'n or go'n!"

Maureen reached down and hugged the little boy to her chest. "A real fighter, that one," she whispered as she began to search in vain for more peat bricks to put on the fire.

"Ah, well. Guess we've used the last of the peat. You and your proud father will need to go out to the bog and cut me more bricks. Can't have a cold house for the little one, Frank. Be a good boy and fetch me Grandpa 's old papers by the rocker and we'll have one last roarin' go of it!"

The woman in corporate navy blue by the cottage window suddenly grasped the worn window sill. She was in a position to glimpse over Maureen's shoulder as the new midwife crumpled it in her large capable hands before stuffing it in the brick hearth:

IRISH GAZETTE
March 15, 1853

Charles took off his cap and slowly opened the door to his bedroom. Crossing the floor, he stepped gingerly over puddles of water, empty basins and bloody rags at the base and sides of the bed. There, wrapped tightly in a sheet beside his lovely Bridgette-weak, yet radiant and beautiful-was his newborn son, all wavy wet black hair and tiny clenched fists. His wife cried with happiness as he leaned down and tenderly kissed them both.

"'Tis a wonderful day for us all!" exclaimed Bridgette softly, gathering the bloodied sheets at her side. "Just imagine: little Mickey!"

"Be still there, Biddy, my girl! Surely now you can see 'tis not little Mickey at all. He's Michael Flynn, sure as I'm standin' here. Isn't he grand?"

"Joan, are you coming? I've given out your Agenda. Everyone's here and they're ready to start! You need to call into the Conference Operator to bridge on the folks from Minneapolis and Seattle. There's going to be a real priority fight about whose enhancements we want in the second Release! They'll want your cost/benefit!"

The spell was once again broken. "If only I could just go back for a day," she thought wistfully.

"If I could just write about them. There's so much I don't know. But there's so much I *do* know. All the things I've heard from my childhood. I could go *back*, but they won't be there! But that's exactly what I'll do. I'll go back to where they were in Brooklyn, where they lived and spent their lives, and listen, maybe see what they saw. It's the closest I can get to them. I want to tell their story and I will."

She had been to several funerals and knew when people died their belongings were passed down through the family. "But then what?" she thought. "All you really have left were some pictures, the memories, but you also have the places they lived and loved. You had that. Maybe that was the key to knowing better the people you only heard of but would have loved to meet."

"Joan???"

With that she hurried off to her meeting. Life was calling. Her passion, the one she dreamed of at night, the magic times in Ireland and Brooklyn at the turn of the century, the dreamtime she so imagined and started talking about whenever she had a drink with family or her husband, would have to wait.

Part 3: Exodus:
County Leitrim, Ireland, 1854

Charles Flynn

'Tis an abomination. I heard the English soldiers are startin' now in the next town over, tippin' cottages, turnin' out starvin' families who now live in ditches or the remains of their homes.

"And don't any of you take this family in or *your* dwelling will be next!" they proclaim.

Bastards. Mustn't tell Bridgette. I've seen skeletons in rags hoverin' near death in the rain by the roads or livin' under the rubble of their own homes. Truly God has forsaken Ireland. Me Bridgette and I have some seed potatoes left. Might as well eat them.

No sense in plantin' again. 'Tis all rot and mush in the fields. My God, what are we goin' to do? And little Frank and now Mike. With the cold and rain and himself coughin 'so, I fear fer me life just goin' out on the bog to cut peat now for the fire.

Bridgette Flynn

Mrs. Kelly, she herself said she saw English soldiers tip a cottage along the road into Leitrim today. Don't want to tell Charles. He hates the English. I myself am more afraid. Mrs. Kelly said she saw dogs rippin' a carcass apart in the church courtyard, so many waitin' to be buried, the dogs are now settin' upon them.

So cold now, not enough turf for me hearth, let alone for cookin'. So fearful to send little Frank out to the bogs again. No tellin' who might set upon a four year old. But I need a fire for Mike, he with the coughin'. He's a brave little lad. I almost wish we hadn't a brought this wee one into the world.

Still, they've always said the more children we're blessed with, the more land will be given by the landlord to work it!

Michael Flynn

Ma is cryin. Da is angry. 'Tis so very cold here.

Frank Flynn

Bad things I see. But I'm not afraid. Me cousin Oonie Farrell says the soldiers are comin' to our town next. Oonie's fourteen. I may be only four, but Oonie's always been a storyteller God love 'em.

Oonie Farrell

Me God, 'twas terrible. They came this mornin'. Ma sent me out to the bog for peat and when I came back the soldiers were lined up outside our cottage!

"By proclamation of the Queen Victoria all those within are hereby summoned to stand aside this dwelling."

Da was carryin' Grandpa out and laid him by the road. Ma she was cryin'. She tried to run back in to get her china, but the soldiers held her. Grandpa cursed the soldiers and they struck him with the whip. I myself couldn't move, so scared I was, just hid behind a rock. I'm so ashamed. Then the soldiers tied ropes around the side posts and rafters and had their horses pull. They all pushed on the walls. Our cottage just slid over, our fine thatched roof all afire it was, from the hearth. Our Da tried to run inside to get our clothes. They beat him with the whip. And the neighbors, they all stood by, frozen-like.

Before they left the cruel English sergeant read again from his paper:

"Let this be a warning: Anyone whosoever gives shelter or food to this family will suffer the same fate. God save the Queen."

Bastards.

35

Queenstown, Ireland: Cork Harbor
November, 1854

Charles Flynn

Somehow we've made our way all the way down here to Cork, me Bridgette, Frank and Michael. We had no choice in th' matter. The English they came and tilted me cottage. And me poor mother's cottage, by God. No one would take us in but Mrs. Kelly. I had to leave me dear mother, God bless her soul, with Mrs. Kelly. 'Tis hard for her to walk now.

Guess the soldiers heard we had taken in Oonie Farrell and *his* parents. What else could we do? Lucky I had set aside some money under the stone wall from me paintin's.

Bridgette Flynn

No, we'll not go to th' Poorhouse! Mrs. Kelly said t'was that or goin' to America. They that go to the Poorhouse become separated and don't come out...Whatever happens, we stay t'gether, Charles, Frank, poor little Mike and meself. Mrs.Kelly, she made us all packets of ginger snaps for the trip. "For the stomach!" she says.

Wonder what she means?

Frank Flynn

We're goin' to America! Oonie says the streets, they're paved with gold there. Imagine that! Cousin Oonie's comin' with us. They said his parents died in the Poorhouse from typhus.

Michael Flynn

Mother says we're goin' to America, whatever that is. They are all excited. She said even tho I'm only two, t'will be a "great adventure" for us all. We're in the long line now. They've wrapped me all up in the wool blanket in Oonie's arms.

I cough a lot. It's hurtin' me throat.

Oonie Farrell

We all almost made it on board the "Emerald Isle". And such a ship it was, a proud clipper ship, tall sails and all. People sayin' goodbye. Cryin'. Then the crowd tried to rush the boat. Before we knew it, the damned English Captain said,

"That's all! I said that's *all*, ye dam Irish hooligans!"

The sailors fought off the crowd. Some folks fell into the harbor. I was behind Uncle Charles and Aunt Bridgette but folks cut in front o' me. Before I knew it they was shovin' us off the boat and pullin' up the gangplank. Aunt Bridgette was like a wild woman. She sobbed and I saw Uncle Charles tryin' to show the Captain the tickets he bought for Mike and me.

"Get back! I said get *back*! It's oversold, same as last time. Nothin' I can do!" he shouted at Uncle Charles and the angry crowd.

"Damn Irish!"

The Captain refused to let any more family members board and ordered his men to cast off. Uncle Charles was runnin' along the deck. He threw me the tickets in a small leather drawstring bag. I caught it.

"Take it, Oonie," he was yelling.

"Get on the next passage! There's $100 to care for Michael. Bring him safely to us in New York, boy. Get to Brooklyn. Seek out the families of Flynn and Farrell! There's a good boy!"

An older lad tried to catch it but I was able to get it meself. I saw several women on the boat tryin' to help Aunt Bridgette who had fainted. Little cousin Frank stood by Uncle Charles. Sobbing, he looked smaller by the minute as the lines were cut. The clipper "Emerald Isle" slowly pushed away from the dock, bound for New York.

Losin' no time, I made me way up to the very next ship I could find, getting in line close to a family with three children, hoping to blend in. Perhaps the next Captain would be Irish! Cousin Mike was in me arms, wrapped in his blanket. These days he never stops coughin' and the cold mist in Cork Harbor didn't help. All the wee ones and old folk cough constantly. Finally Captain collected our ticket and on board we were.

"So, goin' ye are to America?" the bearded captain asked, looking at me cousin coughin' under the blanket. Clearly the good man was Irish.

"Aye, sir, we are."

" 'Tis a rough crossin', let me tell you, but 'tis a better place yer goin' to."

"Aye."

"Follow this crowd down the steps into steerage, lad. 'Twil' be warmer down there for the wee one under the blanket. We've some fire pots goin'. Make way there," the Captain said to the folks in front of us.

"He's got a sick little lad under that blanket."

And then it dawned on me, the responsibility I had, to get me cousin Mike safely to New York. All of fourteen, I'm a man now. Yes, they told me ma and pa died in that Poorhouse. A whole other tale. Little Mike's forehead is sweaty and he's callin' for his ma and da.

"Hush now, Mike. You'll be fine. We'll all be fine. Here's a gingersnap from the pack. Why isn't that your name on it now, lad?"

The plan was for us to hook up with my family, the Farrell's and the Flynn's, the others who had left Ireland before us and were now safe in New York, livin' on those golden streets. I could hardly wait to get there, to see that gold! I settled in down in steerage on me bunk, near one of those warm swingin' pots, safe at last on the "North Carolina"!

The "North Carolina"
Somewhere in the Atlantic
November 12, 1854

Michael Flynn

A great many people down here. Steerage, they call it. Very cold. Someone said the ocean's right on th'other side of the wall, and there are fish too. Imagine that.

They are all very nice to me. But the ship rocks back and forth. Back and forth. Oonie said to think of it like a cradle. Oonie said that is what makes the people sick and throw up. Oonie said to stay out of it.

'Tis very dark down here. Sometimes those pots slop over. It smells just awful. I miss the sunlight. People I don't know hold me on their laps. They tell me stories about the fairies. We sing. Sometimes there are games.

Sometimes at night they all sing songs and clap and dance the jig. I like it when that man plays his accordion. They tell me I'm a brave little fellow to be makin' the journey to America where the streets are paved with gold. I wonder what that means. They smile when they tell it.

I miss me ma and dad. Ma was cryin' so at the boat. There are other ma's down here with their wee ones. So lucky to have mothers, they are.

That pretty ma I liked with the red hair... she used to hold me on her lap, sing'n to me, playin' cat 'n th' cradle with her yarn. I went over to her bed yesterday. She had stopped coughing. She didn't move or answer when I called her. Oonie pulled me over to our side. Told me not to touch her. Said she's up in heaven with the angels now. They've covered her up with a blanket.

I liked her. I will miss her.

47

Brooklyn Harbor
November 15, 1854

Bridgette Flynn

T'was a hard crossin', it was, 'specially without me little Michael. But all the good women on board assured me every day that we'll all be back t'gether. Not unusual for a family to be separated for a while when comin' to America, they said.

But the wee lad is so very little. How I wanted to show him all the other ships as they guided us into th' harbor. Charles and little Frank both reassure me that Oonie will show him all the other ships when their ship docks as well.

But we're better off than some. After we sailed into New York harbor and walked down the plank, I saw men carryin' coffins up the plank for those poor souls that died on th' way over, probably gone to th' typhus. But I know we'll see him again with the grace o' God. I know Oonie Farrell will take good care of his little cousin.

Charles Flynn

Ah, 'twas somethin', sailin'into The Great Harbor. Frank, me oldest, me beautiful Bridgette and me. Hard crossin' it was.

But as I myself remind me Bridgette every day, no more rottin' potatoes or rottin' English soldiers. 'Twil be heaven on earth. Streets paved with gold you know. Took us to the waterfront of Brooklyn itself.

What a sight! So many good people searchin for relatives! Why, I said to me Bridgette, "Biddy girl, 'tis more chaotic then when we left Cork!" Families lookin for families and of course, she lookin' for little Michael. Told her he'll be arrivin' after us, of course. Told Oonie to take the next passage they could get on, God help 'em.

Frank Flynn

Keepin' me eyes open for me brother. So many families callin' for relatives, we could barely get down the gangplank.

"Ships arrivin' behind us. Move along, move along, ye hooligans, get off me boat! My job's done now. You micks are here in America now, God help us all!"

Hate that English captain. Hate all them bloody English.

Charles Flynn

We're famished. Not know'in where we'll be stay'n tonight. Yet how grand to have our feet on firm land. And sadly, 'tis not gold, but earth it is, with new cobblestones. And all the stores and tall houses now-tenements-they're called. And families callin' out for families.

Finally I see an older Irish lady callin' "The Family Flynn, The Family Flynn!" and suddenly there are 50 people all crowdin' round her.

"Flynns from County Leitrim only!" she yells.

A persistant family from County Mayo remains with her. All the others slowly walk away.

" I told you once, I'm searchin' for Flynns from The County *Leitrim*, God Help us, not Mayo!" the black-haired woman explains impatiently.

"But are ye not now the cousin of my sister Maggie, bein' she that died of the typhus in the Dublin Workhouse? You do so resemble her!" someone in the crowd asks the woman seeking Flynns.

The Flynn woman is confused, stating, now with compassion, that she does not know of such a person and suddenly, before I can get to her, makes her way through the hundreds of people, disappearing before my eyes.

Imagine, if you will, this scene being played over hundreds of times with so many families 'til one of us is lucky. Which we were.

Bridgette Flynn

We were there in the harbor all day, we were. Brooklyn Flynn families, lookin' for arrivin' Flynns. The other immigrants who were not met, startin' bravely out on foot away from the harbor and up those long Brooklyn streets, crowded with people, dogs, people sellin' things, seekin' lodging for the night, many of them very sick from the passage.

"Tis too bad now that yer King Fergus Flynn of Ireland and Queen Maeve begat so many, and such a large following, of the family Flynn!" I say to Charles and he smiles that wonderful, proud smile, he does.

Charles Flynn

And so it was the crowd thinned out. 'Twas about six o"clock. Cold, tired we were. I left Bridgette and Frank in a booth in a little tavern where they rested and were given water.

Lookin' out over the crowded streets along the waterfront, I recalled how me eldest brother, Peter Flynn, left County Leitrim long ago with his new wife for Scotland.

The story goes a friend of Peter's in Leitrim had been tryin' to attend a secret Mass. English soldiers stopped him on the road home, discoverin' a penal cross - the secret sign used to show each other we were RC - up his sleeve, beat him up and left him in a ditch. That very next day, Peter decided to leave for Scotland. To leave for places unknown, he announced, that things surely would improve, leavin' both the famines and the English behind. But the rumor was they didn't like it much in Scotland and planned to sail with their children to New York.

And so, about we were, to be settin' off from the Harbor with little Frank, crossin' the docks and up into the great streets of Brooklyn. T'was then I again spied the Irish woman with long black hair on the corner holding her sign. "Flynns from Leitrim". I ran over to the small crowd about her which was slowly disbursin'.

"Good evenin'," I said hopefully. "I be Charles Flynn of County Leitrim with me wife Bridgette and young son, Frank."

The woman peered at me carefully and intently. She appeared to be tough, or had been made toughened up. Slowly she gathered the black shawl around her narrow shoulders.

"And would yer wife happen to have the last name "Gilhooley?" she asked softly.

"Aye, she would," I said.

"Then I might be your in-law, oldest cousin of Bridgette Gilhooley, of County Leitrum, wife of your oldest brother Peter," she added quietly.

"Where is that stubborn Irish beauty of a little cousin of mine? Did she finally make the trip? Be she with you?" she asked, her passionless face finally coming to life as she looked excitedly behind me.

Then, before I could respond, I watched her face change as the realization of *why* her cousin may not have been behind me, became clear to her. Her face, much older, but resemblin' Bridgette's, had briefly shown with a long–passed youthful enthusiasm. It now became stoic and fixed in age once more. I watched as she tightened the black wool shawl, tears waitin' in her eyes, bracing for my response.

Suddenly a lovely, familiar voice behind me laughingly said, "And did ye *hear* the one about the man who abandoned his wife and young son after their long crossin' to drink water forever in a Brooklyn pub?"

Words cannot describe to ye the meeting of these two cousins.

"Glory be, Mary, we thought all this time ye be in Scotland with Peter! Where *are* Peter and the wee ones?"

"Welcome to America!" Mary Gilhooley Flynn formally said to me, Bridgette and Frank, as we all embraced, the momentarily youthful enthusiasm now drained from her face and her true age reappearing.

"Please come with me. You must all be very tired. We've lots to speak of."

And now 'twas I who suddenly froze in my place. Mary told us quietly that she was now a widow. My brother Peter had contracted typhus as did two of his children when they arrived in Brooklyn and died six months later.

Frank Flynn

Aunt Mary Gilhooley Flynn took us home to a red "brownstone" house, 54 Amity Street, four floors it is, where a great many people live together, a "boardin'" house they call it. No cottages here! We have our own room up there on the top floor. I discovered there are so many Flynns livin' there. There are young Flynn cousins me own age and also young Farrell cousins.

Ye can throw things down the air vent, ease-drop'n on people, and play on the front stoop. There is a fine alley behind the boardin' house with a fire 'scape where ma hangs the clothes from a clothesline. I found out many of me cousins came over from Ireland in the bottom of a ship just like ours!

From our room on the top floor there's a fine window. We can see the Great Harbor which is only two blocks away. Ma sits by the sill for many hours in her chair, with Aunt Mary, watchin' the great ships slowly arrivin'. Each time a ship pulls in, bringin' folks over, we all run down the block to see if it's a ship from Ireland and if Mike and Oonie are on it. The unloadin' takes a great while, but she is so excited as all the people finally come walkin' down.

We've been here two weeks now. Used to be only 3 ships arrivin' each day. Now there are 5, most of which are comin' from Ireland. So we just come back home. Ma, she cries and prays, waitin' by the window with Aunt Mary for the next ship.

Bridgette Flynn

'Tis often now I go round the corner with me cousin Mary to St. Paul's Church to pray. 'Tis a beautiful Church, where all the Irish go. So large and cavernous it is, like a cathedral, seemin' to take up the entire block, with statues of Mother Mary and St. Patrick himself. There we were, just goin' to Mass and receivin', not lookin' over our shoulders, afraid as we were, of the English soldiers comin', shoutin' and throwin' us out. I kept listen'n for the sound of their horses outside! So many Irish, just like ourselves, poor but smilin' just the same. How I like it here.

I pray for my little Michael every day. Did the ship go down? Did he die a quick death? Did he die from the constant cough or typhus, little man that he was? 'Twil be two weeks now. Surely the next ship they boarded should have arrived the very next day.

I never trusted that Oonie Farrell, somethin' 'bout that lad. Did he take the $100 Charles threw to him and turn back for County Leitrim, cowardly little mischief-maker that he was? No, I never liked Oonie that much, can't say why. If he did dare do such a thing, I can only be hopin' some family would have taken Mike in. Such a fine lookin' little wain, but sickly so. Just three years old, he not knowin' where his da and ma are. That's the worst of it, that he might be thinkin' we meant to just leave him behind back there in Cork. Could that be runnin' through his head? I couldn't bear it that bein' what he thinks.

And so we go down there every day, me watchin' the Harbor from the upstairs window for ships. This mornin' I climbed out onto the fire escape and up onto the roof itself. The view! 'Tis heaven itself! I can see La the clipper ships as they make the great slow turn and come our way, so I know 'twil soon be time again to grab Charles and Frank and run down to the dock. Charles bringin' home the odd bit of rope, paper, tin, this and that, left behind by the big ships.

Charles Flynn

By God I can't be goin' down with her now to meet every ship comin' from Ireland! But each time we go I save some rope, odds and ends cast off by the crew and bring 'em home to sell. God help little Michael. Where can the little lad be? I'm told they took the very next ship to leave Cork, that they were *seen* boardin' the very next ship that left! Did it sink? Did they die on board from typhus? God help them. If I only just be findin' out!

And me Bridgette. Not know'in is drivin' the lass crazy. I told her if our worst fears come true, we'll have another little lad but she'll hear nothin' of it. Says she'll meet every ship that docks 'til she finds Mike. I believe she will. Just stare'n out that window. It's been all of two weeks now. Where could that boy Oonie and Mike be?

We're livin'on top of a grand red brownstone! The buildin' is bustin' with Flynns! Flynns everywhere. Back in Ireland we were told, "Just walk to Amity Street!" when we landed. Sure enough it was 2 blocks from the docks! 'Tis a street of all Flynns and Farrells! No pegged thatched cottages here! More like Queenstown, Cork where we left, but *these* brownstones, narrow and tall they are.

From our walks down to meet the ships I see the big boats leavin' the frayed hawsers on the docks, huge coils of hemp and scrap. I'm told they're no longer needed for the return trip over to New York to pick up passengers headed for England, then back to Ireland to pick up more of us.

I be goin' down tonight. I'll see can I carry some of those heavy hemp ropes back, maybe salvage a bit and sell 'em if I can find a buyer. One of the clippers left a boiler behind, big heavy metal thing it is. Some of the men have a horse and wagon. Might see can we all lift the blessed thing and store it away for salvage. Must be of value to a factory somewhere with all this buildin' goin on.

New construction everywhere! Buildin' rowhouses and boardin' houses up all the streets goin'up Brooklyn as far as you can see! Stores on every corner. Dublin herself, she couldn't be any busier! 'Tis no Farmine here. There are potatoes aplenty and very good ones, I must say, for sure, but certainly not grown around these docks. No landlords, no conacre, no English! Have to make a deal and soon. Two boys and a wife to feed....

Raleigh, North Carolina
November 30, 1854

Oonie Farrell

The rough trip is over! And ye' guessed it. We've landed in North Carolina, not New York! Like I said, Captain Kenny, he was Irish and he's arranged for cousin Mike and I to board a steamer up to New York.

Brooklyn, New York
December 3, 1854

Oonie Farrell

We've just landed in the Great Harbor! Many other big ships there overflowin' with so many people just like us! We've been checked for lice under the eye lids. No fun, that. They force yer upper eye lids up to check. Little Mike's quite improved, but very thin.

We're takin' a ferry across New York Harbor to Brooklyn. I can see the waterfront now! I can't quite make out where those streets paved with gold are yet!

Bridgette Flynn

Jesus, Mary and Joseph. Down I went again to the docks this mornin'. 'Twas bright, about 8 am. I've given up meetin' each and every ship. I just sit across the way from the dock, starin' across the Harbor at New York itself.

So large it is, a great Island as far as you can see, then it drops off to the west and the ocean. Maybe some day Charles, Frank and I will take a boat over to see it. T'wil be grand. I was about to be goin' back to the boardin' house but decided to stay and see a boat arrivin', a small, curious boat not a large clipper like the "Emerald Isle" we came in. More of a "steamship" they called it.

I watched the people startin' down the gangway. Some folks well-dressed. Such pretty suitcases, those colored labels announcin' where they'd been. A fancy woman walked right by me with a large flowered straw hat and beautiful gown. She talked so odd, she did.

"Why, George," she said, in the strangest way, "I just can't *believe* ya'all brought me up here all the way from Noth Carolinah to New York!!"

I watched the fine ladies and gents paradin' down the plank, followed by a crowd of the more plainly clothed, then several poor families like us, who, no doubt, made the trip cramped below deck in steerage. I turned t' go.

'Twas then I saw 'em. That ragged, scrawny cousin I distrust, Oonie Farrell, carryin' somethin' wrapped up in a blanket. Oh, my God, I thought. Can it be themselves after all this time? Oonie was squintin' at the sun, with one hand shieldin' his eyes, the other holdin' the bundle in a blanket over his shoulder. Oh me God, I thought, the darkest thoughts runnin' through me head! Like a wild woman I ran up the gangplank.

"Oonie, Oonie Farrell!!" I cried. Oonie looked pale and thin.

"Aunt Bridgette! Glory be!! The money's all gone. I'm so sorry. I got right on the very next boat, just like Uncle Charles said, but 'twas bound for North Carolina!"

Oonie is all of seventeen years old but he started to cry as he handed over the bundle he was carryin'.

"Aye, there now, Oonie, it's all right."

I lifted the weight under the filthy blanket from Oonie, carefully to me arms. With the greatest of all relief, I heard that familiar little cough, never thinkin' the blasted cough would be so welcome to me ears. I moved the blanket to see sleepy blue eyes blinkin' in the sunlight. 'Twas then I saw a thin, little Michael John Flynn and he lookin' up at me.

"Mommy!

Part 4: Junkman
54 Amity Street, Brooklyn, New York, 1860

And so Charles Flynn, his wife Bridgette and their sons Frank and Michael were safe at last. They stayed for many years on Amity Street with the widow Mary Gilhooley Flynn, in the tall row house two blocks from magnificent New York Harbor with all the bustle and excitement of the immigrant ships arriving daily.

Indeed, as listed in The Brooklyn Directory of 1860, 54 and 56 Amity Street were full of Flynns and Farrells, thanks to the efforts of Mary Flynn. The widow of Peter Flynn relentlessly met all the ships, in all kinds of weather, from Ireland every day, providing food and lodging to the often very sick and frightened Flynn immigrants from County Leitrim.

Perhaps with the tragic loss of her husband and two of her children 6 months after their crossing, she was making sure no more arriving Flynns suffered the same fate. The Flynns owed much to her. Besides Charles and his family, Mary Flynn eventually located Francis, Stephen and John Flynn and their families arriving on cold nights down in the harbor. Early one rainy morning, she hailed down Charles's cousin Miles and his family, and a great many others who came over fleeing the famines and oppression from the British. And, two years later, Bridgette Flynn gave birth to her third child, a little boy named John Flynn.

It was aboard the Emerald Isle that Charles discovered he had quite a knack for locating things other people needed. He bartered for them and in fact, became the informal ship's chandler, a general broker of needed items. In Brooklyn he found work as a junkman and, accompanied by his growing sons Frank and Michael, he would go down to the docks and collect anything left behind by the big immigrant ships after they sailed out into the Harbor and across the Atlantic to bring more immigrants from Cork, then called Queenstown.

Eventually Charles opened up a scrap yard down on the Columbia Street waterfront. There he salvaged hawsers, other kinds of rope and metal, reselling to construction companies who needed all kinds of items. The building boom in row and boarding houses truly exploded in lower Brooklyn to house the tide of immigrants arriving daily. Charles and his family had no way to know that by 1854, when they arrived, already two million Irish, one quarter of the entire Irish population, had already immigrated to New York!

73

Brooklyn, New York, 1872

Michael Flynn's trans-Atlantic cough went away, but even as a boy his joints always ached painfully. But that didn't stop him from growing into the wiry young teenage scrapper that he was. At nineteen he was street smart, having grown up along the docks with his father, learning how to make a buck, buying and selling rope and other materials.

Like his father Charles, Michael saw opportunity in things other men discarded. It was just a matter of understanding the demand for certain things. Charles and Bridgette were now in their fifties and growing more and more dependent on Michael and Frank to help with the family scrap business.

"I'll have me own business someday, Frank, I will!"

Michael was hauling old leather horse harnesses into the back of the small storefront salvage shop run by his father. His older brother Frank was busy with a crowd of children who had salvaged small metal objects, old tin cans, rusty utensils and even old rags that they often brought into the shop to the "Junkman."

"Junkman, Junkman!" they cried.

These were very poor, dirty youngsters, dressed in rags not much better than the ones they brought in for pennies. Frank took their offerings, sometimes giving a penny or two more to the really hungry looking children.

"Go on now!" he told them good naturedly. "'Tis more good rags we be needin' now! Out with the lot of ya! Off you go!"

With the exploding demand for newspapers like The Brooklyn Eagle and The Brooklyn Standard, paper mills were paying more and more for rags, which they turned into newspaper.

The very next week, Frank and Charles were delivering discarded pallets to a construction site. When they returned, they were surprised to see an old wagon pull up in front of the store. There was Michael proudly sitting up front holding the reins of a huge, but very thin, old beige draft horse. These horses were bred as work horses, very large and powerful. Michael beamed as the large animal impatiently stamped the large cobble stones below his hoofs.

"You be salvagin' that animal and cart there, son?" his father joked.

"And where did ye get it now, Mike?" Frank stared at the proud teenager sitting high up in the front seat.

"Made a deal with the blacksmith, I did. He'll let us use his horse and wagon every day in the mornin' for collectin' junk if we give him a cut of all the old iron we can find for him to melt down for horseshoein'."

Michael Flynn had a high forehead, dark blond hair and intense blue eyes, eyes that saw opportunities for making money, money others did not see.

There was something else about Michael. He was very serious, very unemotional when it came to money and deal-making, slightly cold and detached. He seemed to regard it all as the "art of the deal" and he was very efficient, very good at turning a penny.

Brooklyn, New York 1875

Seventeen year-old Mary Ann Farrell was born in Brooklyn and proud of it. She lived on Van Brundt Street with her parents and two younger brothers, Patrick and Michael.

"I _told_ you to get Mama's old rags for the junk man. Do you see him yet? He'll be comin' down the street with his horse and wagon at half-past ten as always! Get now. Be quick, Patrick!" Mary Ann was brushing her long chestnut hair, seated at her mother's mahogany dressing table on the second floor of their brownstone home.

"There's no more rags, Sis. We be givin' him the last of the rags last week!" her little brother informed her.

"Surely they'll be some old newspapers in the basement! Quick, Patrick, go run down there and fetch me some!" Patrick ran down to the cellar while the other brother kept watch at the window of Mary Ann's mother's bedroom.

"Sis, the junkman be com'in, right on time! Here he comes! I can see his horse roundin' the corner. Ah, he's stoppin' to get tin cans and ropes from the Fitzgerald kids."

Mary Ann quickly adjusted the high white collar of her blouse, pinched her cheeks and ran down the stairs of the brownstone house to the first floor.

"Be quick now, Patrick! He himself is down the street! Hurry with those papers!" she called down to her little brother in the cellar.

"I can't find any more newspapers. I brought up the last of them for you yesterday," the little boy called up.

"Land o' Heaven! If I don't have something to give him, he won't pull his wagon over!" she called down to the little boy. Then she saw something beside her father's chair in his study. She grabbed the morning edition of the Brooklyn Eagle, ran down the long dark tiled foyer, sliding and falling as she slid around the corner to open the heavy front door.

A completely transformed, serene young woman appeared on the other side of the door. In the early morning sunlight, a composed young woman of breeding regally took up a graceful position on the concrete stoop by the front door high above the street, arranging her long black taffeta skirt with a flourish, holding the unread Brooklyn Eagle complacently on her lap.

The junkman was seated high up in his wagon pulled by the huge beige yellow draft horse. He looked up to see the graceful beauty arranging herself thoughtfully by her front door.

"Flynn Brothers, Junk (Michael and Frank)" was now proudly painted in gold and black lettering on both sides of the wagon he had soon acquired from the blacksmith.

He stopped the wagon across the street about 3 houses down from the Farrell's. A small crowd of about eight adults and five children were in line, some holding bundles of rags, newspapers, empty tin cans, ropes, old clothes and broken metal utensils. The young man stood about 5' 6" with blondish brown hair, lanky, with a wiry frame. He wore suspenders over a striped shirt and brown pants.

"Ah, Mrs. Duffy, and how are ye and yer Mr. today? And what do I see there? More rags today is it? Would ye take three dollars for the lot of them now?"

Mrs. Duffy was a very old white-haired woman, thin as a grasshopper, with a cane in one hand and the basket of rags in the other.

"Michael, you be givin' your da me regards. And would you also be givin' an old woman a bit more for these clothes? I like me tea and biscuits, you know, and the odd log for me fire is greatly appreciated!"

"For you, Mrs. Duffy, four dollars it is!", the junkman said, taking the money out of his leather pouch and giving her a kiss on the cheek and a hug. Then he felt for his brass watch fob, a gift from his father. More functional than ornate, about 3 inches long, criss-crossed into an intricate inter-locking pattern, chain-like, that folded neatly on itself, supporting a gold watch. He reached for it, prying open the stiff, crusted 24k gold lid enclosing the old watch: "10:30 am".

He jumped up on the heavy spoke wheel of the wagon and tucked the bundle of rags securely in with a huge pile of items he had collected in the neighborhoods starting at 6 am that morning. Restaurants and bars along the dock sold him their tins, bottles and old pots and pans from the night before while neighborhood wives sold things they no longer wanted, increasing their weekly house money for food. Older children would constantly bring him items to buy penny candy; dirty little orphans bringing anything they could find for food.

Young Michael was a shrewd businessman. His livelihood depended on it. On a good day he might haul away old washers or even ovens with the help of his older brother Frank. The brownstone row houses were going up faster than anyone could have ever imagined now, far beyond the waterfront, up Atlantic and Pacific Avenues and Canal Streets. In fact, Brooklyn was growing so fast, due to the flood of immigrants, that they were actually talking about building a bridge connecting Brooklyn with New York across the harbor!

The Flynn junkmen sold the rags to the paper mills that supplied newsprint to The Brooklyn Eagle. The insatiable demand for news was now in its heyday. In fact, Michael once described his occupation very early on as "Newsagent" on a census, a boyhood job that may very well have involved initially selling the newspapers themselves.

While lumber was first used to create pulp, rags were now used as well. Hemp from the hawsers which tied up the ships could also be resold and made into new rope or paper. But the real profit would come later from something else.

The Flynns knew anything made of metal, large or small, could be sold to the foundry and melted down to always create something new. Some families simply wanted old ovens and washers taken away. Some even paid for this service so that Charles Flynn soon had to find an old lot with a small office two streets away down on Columbia Street which he used as a warehouse for the ovens and various metal objects Michael and his brother brought back.

Mary Ann listened eagerly as Michael Flynn made a deal with one of the men on the block. He always left his customers happily thinking they made a good deal.

"I've an old wrought iron fence in the back, rusted and not safe for me kids who like to swing on the creakin' old broken gate. Can ye come and remove it for me now and cart it away, Mr. Flynn?"

"Ay, we'd be glad to salvage it for you if ye can dig it up and leave it by the sidewalk next week. I'll need to bring the wagon empty so we can load it all. What price will you be payin' for us to load it all up and take it off your hands?"

"Am thinkin' $15 dollars," the man replied.

"Call it $20 and you have a deal, Mr. Murphy," said Michael quickly. "Me old horse is spoiled, he is. Prefers rags and rope."

They shook hands, but before Michael climbed up into the seat of his wagon, he noticed two little street children, a girl and her little brother, standing silently by the wagon. They were dirty, thin and dressed in torn traditional Irish peasant clothing.

"Junkman, we've fine things to sell," the little girl called. She opened her apron and to Michael's surprise, he saw a small silver hairbrush and mirror.

"Wee Miss," he said kneeling down on the sidewalk next to the girl and her brother, "tell me, how did ye come by this finery?" he asked gently. From time to time he had come across this sad occurrence, when children were desperate for food.

"Tis our mother's. She has died. There's nothing in the cupboard for us to eat." She replied softly in a hollow voice.

"And who is takin care of ye now?" he asked her.

"Our da. He works on the docks, but there's not so much to eat," she explained.

Mary Ann saw Michael reach into his leather pouch and take out a $5 bill.

"Here. Take yerself and the wee wain home now, Miss. Here's a $5 bill for food. Never part with your mother's belongings. Go and tidy up the place now for when your da comes home from work. Remember, the girl of the family is you now. He'll be countin' on you in his sadness."

Michael looked much older than his nineteen years. By now he was a talented negotiator with a keen eye for value in the salvage business. But he remembered his roots, where he came from and took pity on some of the smaller children who brought rusted tins and utensils to the wagon to sell for food. He gave the little girl a hug, climbed up into the wagon, took the reins sharply, directing the huge draft horse to the Farrell home across the street.

The beautiful creature with the mahogany hair pulled high upon her head was now gracefully descending her steps with a newspaper in hand.

"Whoa," said Michael, lowering himself down from his seat, smiling. "And how are ye today, Miss?"

"Thank you, I am doing well, Mr. Flynn. All I have today is a paper, I'm afraid," she said looking up at Michael from under her thick brown lashes. Born in New York, she prided herself on her diction.

Michael took the paper from her and was about to take .02 from his leather pouch when he looked up at her and said, "But Miss, did ye not see that this is today's paper?"

"Oh, dear, is it really?"

Suddenly the front door of the Farrell home opened revealing Patrick, tumbling down the stoop, his arms loaded with aprons and dish towels.

"Here, Sis! I searched and searched like you said and finally found things you can give the junkman!" the little boy exclaimed proudly.

Mary Ann's face flushed. So did Michael's.

"Patrick, go back in that house before I give you what for," she warned him.

"Mr. Flynn, I've only the newspaper to give you. I've no more rags since last week," she explained softly.

"But this is today's Brooklyn Eagle!"

"So it is," she said softly. Then Mary Ann Farrell turned away, gathered up her skirts regally, climbed up the stoop and quietly closed the door.

Brooklyn, New York, February, 1883

The Brooklyn Bridge was completed in 1883. In fact, Michael Flynn, now a young man, watched its progress to the east every day, as he walked the three blocks from Amity Street down to the Congress Street warehouse, from the first pylons sunk into the East River until the massive cables were finally strung.

He and Mary Ann Farrell, who for several years now, had ceased having to get the young man's attention with newspapers, were married on February 2, 1880 at St. Paul's Church, "The Irish Catholic Church" on Clinton Street. The very one his mother Bridget had gone to every day to pray for his safe arrival.

So cold it was. But all the Flynn's and Farrell's made for a very fine wedding. Nellie Flynn, daughter of Mary Gilhooley Flynn was Michael's first cousin, and served as witness at the wedding. A great crowd it was. Besides Michael's parents, Charles and Bridgette, his brothers Frank and John, there were his uncles Stephen, John and Francis, his cousin Miles and their families, Oonie Farrell and an equal contingent of Farrells from Mary Ann's family.

The young couple had once taken the ferry from Brooklyn to Manhattan on an outing. But now, finally, the great bridge, about 8 blocks from his home, loomed in the distance like a giant sprawling cat.

On Opening Day, Mary Ann and her family and Michael, his parents Charles and Bridget, older brother Frank and younger brother John, all walked down, along the water, past Atlantic, then Pacific Avenue, towards their Brooklyn Bridge.

It was ten o'clock, a beautiful day, an azure sky, with ferries, tug boats, pleasure boats, schooners, clippers, steamers, every kind of ship sailing under the bridge, tooting horns, in its honor. Fire boats sprayed water high into the air in celebration. There were municipal brass bands playing John Phillip Sousa marches, a parade down Canal Street, school bands, people selling ribbons and mementos to mark the event. It looked as if all of Brooklyn turned out for the opening of the Bridge.

The Flynns and the Farrells packed picnic baskets of turkey sandwiches and seltzer which they spread out on a picnic table. After moving speeches by the mayors of both Brooklyn and Manhattan, the ribbon was finally cut by the governor of New York and crowds eagerly thronged to be the first to cross the bridge in the wooden pedestrian lanes.

"Michael, Michael, will you cross with me now?" she called.

Mary Ann had grown into a beautiful young wife, in her high white starched blouse and long billowing black crepe'd chine skirt. Michael had finished his turkey but stood off from the families on the green hill, standing down by the base of the bridge at the waterfront.

"Wait now, will ye, just a moment," he called, thoughtfully transfixed.

She had seen that look before, quietly intent, a certain calculating calmness. All around the foundation of the bridge, below the street were huge abandoned cast iron reels used to house the heavy cables that supported the bridge. Among them were all kinds of metal debris in the form of old soldiering tools, wheel barrows, huge spools of excess cables and wires, planks, even an old engine.

"Why had I not come down here before, I ask you?'" Michael was clearly excited as he ran to get his father and brothers.

"Don't you see it, Mary Ann?" he called back over his shoulder. Mary Ann watched her handsome young husband sprint up the slope below the bridge in his white shirt, striped pants and suspenders, blondish mustache and straw hat.

"All this! Look! Below the Bridge. Just waitin' Why, it's all scrap metal!!"

Later that evening, Mary Ann went back to her parents' house and had dinner as Michael had to work that evening down at the warehouse. She heard a knock at the front door of her parents' brownstone. It was 8 o'clock, a beautiful summer evening. She had just dried the dishes for her parents who were sitting in the front room parlor.

"I'll be goin' back to the Bridge to cross it now that the crowds have cleared. Wondering if a certain young wife would be allowed to walk across it this evening with me?" said the wiry figure at her door. Michael stepped into the parlor, his blue eyes twinkling.

"Evenin', Mrs. Farrell, Mr. Farrell. I am thinkin' I might take Mary Ann back to cross the Bridge, now that the crowds have cleared," he stated. Mary Ann took off her apron eagerly.

"Mother, would you and Dad like to come along?" she asked.

"Lord, no! We've had enough of that bridge for one day. Watch out for the merrymakers," her mother called, "There may be drinkin'!"

Mary Ann and Michael walked down the stoop of her row house, out into the soft night, along the gently sloping Brooklyn streets down to the waterfront. As they walked along the docks in the soft summer night, they were not alone. Many other couples, as well as families, had the same idea, strolling along the cool water. To their left, the East River shimmered in the night, all kinds of boats and parties still celebrating the building of the Bridge. Fireworks lit up the night sky, launched from ships and from the docks of both Manhattan and Brooklyn as well. The lights of Manhattan glowed and flickered across the water.

Finally, the young couple reached the entrance to the Bridge and the endless wooden planks before them. The tiny, thread-like cables Michael had watched on his way to work were now a foot wide as they walked slowly across the Bridge. Everyone walked slowly, taking in the magnificent views of the East River and Manhattan beyond. They paused at the center of the Bridge to watch the exciting panorama under the night stars.

"Ah, look, now, Mary Ann!" Michael Flynn said tenderly. "Tis foggy down there, but you can just make out Battery Park, there in the distance, the very tip of New York itself!" he said pointing to the west. From their vantage point they could see all along the entire Brooklyn and Manhattan waterfronts.

"And do ye remember it, Michael, the end of The Crossing?" she asked softly.

"Ay, as in a dream, I do, bein' carried. I believe I do. They all rushed to the side. I'm told 'twas November 15, 1854. Very foggy and very, very cold. " he said thoughtfully. They both looked wistfully down the River, leaning out on the rail of the Bridge.

"And do ye think things will change, now that we can walk across the River to New York?" she asked in a low tone.

"No, now, not really."

"Why not?"

He turned to face the green-eyed beauty, as her hair, untressed and curling from the moisture of the river, blew softly in the night air, framing her beautiful face. He gathered her in his lean, strong arms, still wearing his best white dress shirt and suspenders.

"Because ay have everything I care about right here in Brooklyn," he breathed into her hair. As he kissed her he reached into his trouser pocket and gave her a small box with two sparkling emerald earings.

"Ay love you, Mary Ann Farrell. The business is growin' and we be standin' on the bridge to our future."

"'Tis not just our future, Mike Flynn. I've been meanin' to tell you. There'll be a wee one joinin' us in the Spring!"

After living briefly with Michael's family on Amity Street, they moved over to the Tower Building, a huge tenement building on Clinton Street. And Michael Flynn, with his sharp eye for salvaging and scrap metal, continued to prosper.

It was well known that the Irish were courted by politicians for their vote and Michael Flynn used this to full advantage to advance his business. As he joined The Brooklyn Lodge of Elks, The Emerald Association, the St. Patrick's Society of Brooklyn, the Columbus Council 126, Knights of Columbus, he made many contacts. His business, which he initially described as "rags and paper stock", became simply "junk".

While his father Charles and brother Frank still worked in the business, it was Michael who looked for greater and more complex opportunities, salvaging and then reselling any and all kinds of discarded material along the docks and up into Brooklyn, which continued to grow at a fantastic rate.

Brooklyn, New York, 1890

Michael, now reasonably well-off, moved his wife and delicate new baby daughter, Anna, from the overcrowded, noisy tenement on Tower Street to a beautiful new dark-red brick row house he purchased on Baltic Street., the Census proudly stating the rare entry, "Homeowner". Their huge tenement house would eventually burn down with a massive fire, common in the days of wooden buildings.

The row house on Baltic was something special. It reminded Michael of his boyhood home on Amity Street. Yet it was not a river-weathered old reddish row house like Amity, the entire street a welcomed haven for exhausted Irish immigrants, arriving literally right off the boats.

230 Baltic was relatively new. Narrow and stately, it was a three-floored residence on a quiet, narrow, leafy street. Up the front stoop and inside the home was a front parlor and yes, one could see the New York Harbor and the newly dedicated Statue of Liberty from the roof-top. Over time, the Flynn's took in two servants and had two more children, Francis Fergus or "Frank", and Charles, named after Michael's brother Frank and father Charles. And still the business flourished.

95

Brooklyn, New York, 1900

Joan Flynn Beesley

And how did Michael Flynn and his family fare at the turn of the century? The 1900 Census found them all living at 230 Baltic Street and doing quite well, except for the eldest child Anna, who was diagnosed with epilepsy. Anna had the same broad forehead, blue eyes and light hair as Michael's. She would die in her late teens.

The Census also found a servant girl Bridget Lynch, 21, a boarder James Nolan, 17, a boarder Mary Quinlan, 25, and another boarder John Farrell, 22, a possible relative of Mary Ann's or Oonie Farrell's. Michael Flynn proudly owned the home, a rarity for Irish immigrants at that time, due to his skill with money, which included income from the boarders.

Around the corner from Baltic Street was a large Irish Catholic school building belonging to the parish of St. Paul's where Michael and Mary Ann were married. A massive building built of large reddish blocks, it had "1880" proudly etched at the top of the building over the street. But now a man of means, Michael chose to send his two sons to St. Francis Military School, where sons of promising families went to learn discipline, social graces and business skills so as to assume their positions in successful New York family businesses.

Michael enjoyed horses and bought Frank and Charlie a pony cart in which they went for rides on Sunday up in Prospect Park. Michael bought a share in a racehorse called "Rataplan", named for the pleasing sound of the horse's hoofs. He had a portrait done of Rataplan, a circular tondo of the handsome brown horse's head, which hung in the dining room of Baltic St. in an ornate gold frame.

Brooklyn, New York, 1905

One summer evening, Mary Ann and Michael were sitting out on the stoop of 230 Baltic, after dinner with their teenage sons, Anna retiring to her room. Michael was now 52 years old.

"I've somethin' to tell all of ye," He suddenly said, quietly.

"Well, I guess you better be tellin' it or we'll never know!" Mary Ann teased. She wore her thick brown hair high on her head now. It was streaked with grey and her girlish figure had turned matronly under her long skirt.

"I've made arrangements to visit Ireland. In fact I went down to J. Lehrenkrauss today and had me passport made. I'll be gone for 4 months. You lads will be runnin' the business with Grandpa Charles while I'm gone."

"Can we go, Dad? Can't we come along?" Frank and Charles asked excitedly.

"No. You boys have school and the scrap business. It'll give you a chance to manage things, see what you can do without me."

Now it was Mary Ann's turn. Born in New York, her parents had come from Ireland. So many stories.

"Can I come along, Michael?" she asked.

"No, dearie. 'Twill be a trip I need to make alone. I am going to the north, to Leitrim, where I'm from, with a first stop in England. I will be buyin' diamonds and bringing them back for the women in the Flynn family, for you and me mother, Bridget."

"Oh, Michael, how wonderful. But I don't know what I'll be doin'without you," she said. Although they were well on the way to making their fortune, she never forgot their roots, especially Michael's.

And so Michael sailed away one day on an ocean liner headed from Manhattan to England and then on to Ireland. Strolling on board one afternoon in his business suit, he noticed a man painting at his easel.

"Good afternoon to ye. Fine weather, we're having," Michael said, his hands in his vest pockets, a handsome gold watch fob hanging gracefully from a loop of gold chain. A wedding gift from his father Charles, the watch fob was more functional than ornate, about three inches long, criss-crossed into an intricate inter-locking pattern, chain-like, that folded neatly on itself, supporting a gold watch.

"Beautiful day. Pleased to make your acquaintance as well," the painter said, looking up from the hazy landscape he was completing.

"My name is Michael Flynn of Brooklyn, paper-stock," Michael explained formally. "I'm making a trip to back Ireland. A far different trip than the one that brought me to America."

"Good afternoon, Mr. Flynn. My name is Cropsey, Jasper Cropsey. I enjoy painting scenes of the Hudson, upper New York. The river is always changing, you know."

"Do ye mind if I sit a while and watch you paint? This damp, cold air, it does bother me legs a bit now," he said, laying his cane by a deck chair.

He presented himself now as a serious, almost stern man, uniquely perceptive in making deals and that included making important relationships. He was a formal man, a gentleman who took pride in his appearance and good manners.

And so the men talked, met for dinner that evening, and by the time they reached England, developed a friendship that lasted a lifetime. In fact, Michael made arrangements to buy many of Cropsey's beautiful Hudson River paintings that hung in his home in Brooklyn for many years.

As promised, he bought large loose diamonds in England which he had made into earrings for Marianne, Bridget and Anna. It was in England he also bought many paintings by Charles Jacques, a French landscape painter of the Barbizon School, noted for their realistic landscapes of the French countryside. His most popular paintings were romantic, yet realistic depictions of sheep and shepardesses, in lush green, misty settings. In fact, Michael hung an exquisite painting of a shepardess with a staff, walking down the road with her sheep, by his fireplace on Baltic Street. If you stared hard enough, the shepherdess actually seemed to be walking the road towards you. Never a painter himself, Michael inherited an appreciation of art from his father, Charles.

After Michael picked the diamonds for the Flynn women in England, he boarded the ship on to Ireland. Now having the means, when the Flynn's made a purchase of any consequence, they bought the very best available.

According to his passport, he "disembarked alone at Queenstown." Now 52, he was trying to go back, to retrace the steps during the Famine which had led him to New York. How moving for him to discover that "Queenstown" was actually the old name for Cork, whose harbor was the main port from which the Irish immigrants fled on "coffin" ships to America.

And yet, as the big cruise ship slowly glided into Cork Harbor, there was something familiar to him, in the cold and rainy mist. In spite of the 50 odd years and all the stories of hardship and pain, he felt a familiarity with the place, that only the Irish experience when visiting Ireland.

When he looked into the eyes of the inn-keepers and hostellers, it was as if they recognized him, a certain acceptance, without even speaking, that the Irish understand when they meet. There, in the eyes of people who had never left Ireland, was such familiarity, as if he were looking and speaking to his own relatives. And, he noticed, when introducing himself as "Mr. Flynn", it always seemed to evoke a certain delightful acceptance, an alliance with whomever he met.

And what did Michael do there in Ireland? Having worked so hard, frantically and intensely, his whole life, he was taking a break, making the trip he always dreamed about. After seeing Dublin, he made his way north, to County Leitrim, where the Flynns had left, fleeing both the tyranny of the Crown and horrors of the Famine.

A quiet older man, well-dressed, with a firmly set jaw and distinguished mustache, he could be seen walking through the villages, stopping to inquire at churches, sitting occasionally on a bench to observe the people or often walking alone in the country, taking in the ever-changing forty shades of green. Listening for his past. Checking the time on his watch fob, more functional than ornate, about 3 inches long, criss-crossed into an intricate inter-locking pattern, chain-like, that folded neatly on itself, supporting a gold watch.

And what did he find there? I believe he found himself.

And he understood, with a certain peace, who he and his parents were, by taking in where they came from, by spending time in the places that had formed them, their experiences and their character. The villagers and peasants were certainly not as cosmopolitan as the Irish of Brooklyn. In their endearing mirth and good-nature, their lack of sophistication, the "quaint folk", Michael could see his parents, and perhaps himself, as they would have been, had fate not intervened and displaced them far from home.

He truly felt at home here, but it was home no more. His life – his family and his prosperous business – was back in Brooklyn. That was where he preferred to be. That was where he, building on the original tough, back-breaking work of his father Charles, had made his luck and his fortune, by looking for larger and larger salvaging opportunities. And yet...

Sometimes in going home to a place, you become "centered", as they say. In County Leitrim, he made peace with himself in going back and discovering the place he had come from. He saw men he might have grown up to be, re-connecting with his past, filling in the blanks. And then was able to move forward, having rediscovered his real heritage first hand.

He actually kind of "shook hands" with a teenage self who he met there, who psychologically embraced and comforted the old man, held him and told him it was OK, to move on now, to go back to his life in America. He also found his very young self there in a sense as well, and that young infant comforted the somewhat stern man who now walked with a cane due to pains in his legs which the doctor said was the beginnings of acute arthritis.

"'Tis all fine now," his younger self told him, "Go back."

And did he find any Flynns or Gilhooley's related to his parents, Charles and Bridget? In searching the villages where they were from, looking for, perhaps, aunts, uncles or cousins, who might remember his parents, he found nothing. So many Flynns and Gilhooley's, yet no one recalling his specific lineage. Only one thought: the ones who stayed had all either died during the Famine or eventually come to America and blended into the Melting Pot. So many records had been burned during the Post Office Rebellion in Dublin that county records, many unkept due to the chaos and oppression of the Famine years, were his only source of research.

And then he reached a point in his journey when he knew it was time to leave, once again from rainy and cold Cork Harbor, but this time in the luxury of a cruise ship, returning to his home, Brooklyn, the love of Mary Ann and his children, Frank, Charles and Anna. And he was right, it was indeed quite a different journey from his original one.

'Tis said Michael Flynn returned to Brooklyn Harbor, a quieter, a more peaceful man.

Brooklyn, New York, 1908

It was dinner time at 230 Baltic. Bridget Lynch, the servant girl, was serving a roast from the kitchen to Mary Ann, Michael, their sons Frank and his younger brother, Charlie, named for Michael Flynn's father. The mahogany paneled dining room glowed with light from a large canopied chandelier hung low over the long dining table, which was covered by a beige embroidered Madeira tablecloth. Mary Ann always used her best sterling silver at meals.

"Bridget, Anna will be dining in her room tonight," Mary Ann instructed Bridget as she brought the sizzling roast to Michael for carving.

Sitting at his place at the head of the table in his grey business suit and vest with his gold timepiece and watch fob, Michael rolled up his sleeves and took the ornate bone carving knife and fork with the silver handles, each engraved with a scrolled "$\mathcal{F}$" for "Flynn".

"Michael, Anna had another fit today, a long one, about three minutes. Just shakin' so. We held her the best we could. I called Dr. Brennan and he came around with some smellin' salts which seemed to calm her. She's been stayin' more and more in her room, afraid to go out on the street in case she might have a fit in public."

Mary Ann addressed Michael from their opposite ends of the table, the boys on each side of them. Still an attractive, but somewhat stout matron, in her high white collared blouse and broach, her voice was low and concerned.

Michael Flynn was now 55 and Marianne was 50.

"If Brennan can't help her we need to find someone who can," Michael Flynn's eyes blazed with impatience.

"It's all right, father. I'll be all right, but I think I'll take dinner in my room tonight." said a soft voice in the doorway.

Anna Flynn was eighteen now, with blondish brown curls, blue eyes, the same high forehead, resembling her father's in his youth. She wore glasses and was dressed in her nightgown and robe. Tonight she had that hollow-eyed look and strange beige and rose skin pallor her distressed parents had come to associate with the days she had her epileptic fits.

She came over to the table and gave her father a hug.
"There now, lass, everythin's goin' to be all right. We'll give Dr. Brennan one more try and if he can't do anything, I'll find the best doctor in

Brooklyn for ye', I will," Michael Flynn said, looking down at his plate.

He was used to controlling things, and the love of his life, Anna with blue eyes just like his, was suffering and he couldn't fix it. It made him angry.

Anna went up to her room and Bridget continued serving the meal. Suddenly the door chimed with its lovely ornamental "Big Ben" sound telling visitors 230 Baltic was a residence of importance.

"Who can it be now?" Michael grumbled impatiently, "That a family can't have an evening meal in peace."

"Bridget, will you answer the door and tell them we are seated, having dinner, please," Mary Anne directed the servant.

"Yes, Mrs. Flynn," said Bridget, who hurried through the front parlor and down the front hall to the door. The chime sounded again before she reached it.

Before long, Bridget returned to the dining room, but she was not alone. At her side was a pretty young girl of in brown braids, dressed plainly in a long dress, boots and soiled white apron. She was holding a large pink striped hatbox tied with a pretty pink satin ribbon.

"Excuse me please, Mrs. Flynn. This is the hat you ordered from the Emporium," the girl announced in a clear, capable voice.

The boys continued eating the roast, taking their cue from their father. Michael Flynn eyed her sternly.

The girl opened the fancy, pink-striped box and carefully lifted out an enormous straw hat adorned with peacock feathers and velvet ribbons.

"Ah," said Mary Ann, "This is my Labor Day hat which I shall wear to the parade in Prospect Park," she exclaimed grandly to the table.

"Here, thank you very much, and please, miss, take this for your trouble," said Mary Ann, taking several dollars from her dress.

"Oh, 'tis no trouble, my father, he takes care of the horses at the Emporium. He gave me the ride over," she explained proudly, brushing her wavy dark brown hair back from her face.

"And what is your name, dear?" Mary Ann asked.

"Mary. Mary Margaret Cummings, Mrs. Flynn," she said, looking directly at Mary Ann with brown eyes, mature for her years. Her clothes were old and a bit disheveled from riding in the wagon with her father, Andrew, making other deliveries from the Emporium.

"Well, Mary Margaret Cummings, 'tis a beautiful hat indeed," said Mary Ann. "Step over here, child," as she beckoned Mary into the ambience of her ornate dining room.

"And which of my sons will you have, my dear?" Mary Ann asked her proudly, while Frank and his younger brother Charles, looked up politely, for they were courteous and well-trained in manners, even if their evening meal was being interrupted by a delivery girl from the Emporium.

"_That_ one!" Mary Cummings said decisively, with great confidence, pointing at the older Frank Flynn.

"And why, my dear?" asked Mary Ann.

"Because he's in _uniform_!" Mary replied , smiling at Frank, still finely outfitted in his military school uniform with shining brass buttons from the afternoon.

"Well, thank you, my dear. I'm sure your father's waiting with the horses," said Mary Ann. "I'm so looking forward to wearing this grand hat!"

As Bridget showed little Mary Cummings out, the younger brother Charlie, mimicked her, "Because he's in _uniform_!" he teased, snapping this napkin at Frank.

It must be said, however, that pretty Mary Cummings, helping her father with deliveries from the Emporium, had made quite an impression on both brothers, Charles, wishing to God he was still wearing his uniform.

Brooklyn, New York, 1919

Mary Margaret Cummings lived on 2nd Street in a poor section of Brooklyn with her parents Ellen and Andrew, who tended horses for the Emporium. Mary was the oldest of 10 children: Helen, Francis, Jim, Elizabeth, John, Edward, William, Tom and her youngest sister, Jenny, who, like Frank Flynn's older sister, Anna, would die in her late teens, "Consumption" being a frequent cause of death in those days, related closely to tuberculosis.

Down in the Red Hook section of Brooklyn, also close to the Brooklyn Harbor and the Gowanus Canal, their row house was very plain in contrast to the Flynn's fine brick home on Baltic Street. Andrew tried to upgrade the appearance with a type of round river rock set in concrete, but his good intentions had the opposite effect.

Was it love at first sight? We'll never know the answer to that one. But what we do know for sure is that Mary Cummings and Frank Flynn were wed in June of 1919. And the new Mrs. Mary Flynn wore a very fine white dress and ornate pearl headdress and veil which did not come from her father's Emporium. And in fact, many of her new and fine belongings found themselves always monogrammed with a beautiful, ornate "MFM" scroll that she proudly used at every opportunity, the rest of her life.

Brooklyn, New York, 1921

During his teens and young adulthood, Frank Flynn, the oldest, was groomed at Michael Flynn's side in the ever expanding and profitable scrap business, to someday take the lead as president, when Michael could no longer work, due to his ever present, painful arthritis.

They say greatness alternates with each generation. While Frank dutifully paid attention to the lessons of running the business, he was not his father. While every inch a gentleman, tall, quiet, with excellent breeding, etiquette and good humor, the young man lacked the hunger and passion - the fire - that drove Michael Flynn in his absolute talent for making money in the scrap metal business.

Michael, while also quiet, was shrewd, somewhat stern, constantly absorbed with business and his growing political contacts in Brooklyn, The Emerald Association and the Knights of Columbus as well as up and coming Democratic leaders of the Brooklyn Ring.

It may have been that outwardly he was never able to demonstrate the love for his sons that most certainly he felt inside. Quite likely, it may have been that common Irish trait, a combination of non-communication, pride and stubbornness, often painfully experienced between Irish fathers and sons. He felt it with his own father Charles, who was also very preoccupied with making a dollar to support his newly arrived-and growing-family.

And so Frank Flynn grew to be a man. Pleasant to all, he had a certain discernible quietness, an aloofness, a formality, as if in his good appearance and manners, he was trying the best he could, to win his father's approval, while sadly it was shrewdness in business, that would have won the respect and approval of Michael Flynn.

While competent, that shrewdness was not Frank Flynn's strong suit. He lacked the talent and, secure in the sizable fortune Michael Flynn was making with his company, may have simply lacked the basic, driving hunger that fuels success, as the family became increasingly wealthy.

119

Brooklyn, New York, 1929

Little Edward Flynn had been taken by his father Frank on several trips to the Michael Flynn Inc. office and salvage yard at Congress and Columbia Avenue, down by the Brooklyn Harbor. The first time Edward went had been a beautiful blue day with seagulls flying above.

"We're going in here, Edward, to visit a very special place," Frank explained to his small son, taking his hand as they walked past lines of desperate, out of work men crowding the docks looking for work. The stock market had collapsed and it was the start of the Great Depression. They entered the door of a store front office with "Michael Flynn, Inc." in gold letters, the door closing with a pleasant little bell announcing their arrival.

"Hello there, Edward," said the old man, his grandfather Michael, sitting behind the counter. He opened up a section of the long, worn wooden counter to let Edward and his father pass through and into his office. He sunk into his worn leather chair, both of which seemed to exhale behind his huge desk.

"And what brings ye men down here today?" he asked kindly of the blond little six year old in knickers and his own son, dressed in a business suit.

"Father said its time for me to see the business and that there are interesting things down here, Grandpa. I want to see them," the little boy said seriously.

"Well 'tis right here I got my start indeed," Michael said proudly. "But first, lad, I'd like to show ye something I've been working on."

Michael wore suspenders, lean and trim as ever in his mustache. Yet the young man who leapt up effortlessly on his old scrap wagon and horse, now moved stiffly around his desk with a cane. He was now 76 and his body was riddled with pain.

"See these brass banks?" he said, pointing to highly polished brass, cone-shaped containers on his desk. Each had a penny-slot drilled into them for coins to be deposited.

"Bet ye don't know where *these* came from!" he asked, excitement in his voice.

"No sir, I don't," said Edward, as his father waited patiently behind him.

"They are left over bomb sites from WWI! The Navy had no use for 'em so they paid me to haul 'em away and now I make banks from them in me spare time. I give 'em out to the folks here in the neighborhood," he exclaimed.

"And now, Edward, I want to show you some really interesting things out in the scrap yard." Little Edward and Frank followed Michael, who walked slowly out the screen door in the back of the office to the scrap yard next door, enclosed by a chain link fence.

It was a fascinating place. Edward looked at old diving helmets, airplane propellers, all kinds of things made of metal that had been discarded and salvaged by Michael Flynn, waiting to be sold as scrap metal to the Navy or companies needing metal. Edward's canny Irish grandfather had actually bought the Normandy when it was decommissioned, had it melted down to scrap metal, and sold it back to the Navy!

Brooklyn, New York, 1930

Moving away from their beginnings near the Brooklyn waterfront, Frank and Mary Cummings Flynn moved briefly to an apartment on the corner of 8th Ave. and 5th Street, in the Park Slope area of Brooklyn near the beautiful Prospect Park. They liked the leafy green neighborhood. Mary shopped along 7th Avenue and they lived a comfortable life dining out frequently at Michel's and Gage 'n Tollner's restaurants on Flatbush and Fulton Avenues.

After an underground spring was discovered under their apartment building, it was vacated and they moved up the block to a residence where they stayed for the next 35 years: 587 5th Street, a half block away from Prospect Park.

After losing his beloved Mary Ann, a now-crippled Michael continued for a time going to the office and warehouse at Columbia and Congress, going home alone to 230 Baltic at night.

But it was in 1930 that Michael Flynn really made his mark. The venerable David E. Lupton Co. Sons Company, the renowned English premier maker of high-end residential casement windows, did not survive The Depression and in 1930 went bankrupt. It was decided to purchase the company's enormous eleven acre factory at Allegany and Tulip Streets in Philadelphia and salvage its window inventory for scrap metal. But the plan changed. A decision was made to simply purchase the business and keep the men employed.

"Let's make windows!" they decided.

And so they purchased the Philadelphia factory and kept the workers employed during The Depression. Mullions, casements and extrusions became the topic of the day as the Flynns learned the window business. The company now made the sought-after "casement windows" made famous in the early 19th century, the "very best you could buy" as advertised to hi-end homeowners. David Lupton and Michael Flynn collaborated and are given credit for designing the circular handle used to open louvered windows in many homes and businesses today. Michael Flynn Inc. now became The Michael Flynn Manufacturing Company with offices in New York, an eleven acre factory and offices in Philadelphia, in addition to the original Michael Flynn, Inc. warehouse at Congress and Columbia.

Early one morning in 1930, Edward, now seven, was awakened to the sound of sawing and chopping in the tiny 2nd floor music room below his room. He and his brother Frank lived on the 3rd floor of the tall brownstone at 587 5th Street. Sleepily, he made his way down to the music room in his pajamas to see workmen, chopping apart the family piano in the small room off the study!

This room was a strange little place, with three steps that lead up to it and then three down to the room itself. It was on the back of the home, with a type of porch with windows that looked out onto the backyard.

"Plink, plink," went the keys of the piano as the men hacked it apart.

"It's all right, Edward," his mother explained gently, arranging his tousled dark blond hair.

"Your Grandfather Michael is coming to live with us now. This will be his room, up here in the music room. We've decided to get rid of the piano to make room for him. Rather than lower it down by ropes into the backyard, we've decided to just chop it up!"

Edward was musically inclined and loved to listen to the piano. It saddened him to hear it was going away, especially in such an undistinguished manner. Yet, how interesting it would be to have his grandfather living there in the house!

And so, Frank Flynn took the helm as president of The Michael Flynn Manufacturing Company, Michael Flynn staying involved in the business as long as he could. He eventually closed his beloved office and warehouse. Over time, the shrewd entrepreneur became an invalid, confined to his bed with painful arthritis, visited each week by his physician, Dr. Brennan, and his good friend, Ignatius, who played checkers with him, tended by a manservant named William. Once, when his room was filled by younger Flynn cousins who came to visit him, he suddenly looked around the room and announced "Huummph!!! Too many people!!!" and memorably shooed everyone from the room.

Brooklyn, New York, 1931

"No, Edward, no! That's <u>not</u> correct!" the old man with the Irish brogue said impatiently to his grandson, Edward.

"Put the pennies back in the can and try again!"

Michael Flynn lay in his bed in the "back room" where he took his meals now. The room was musty from the smell of newspapers. His old companion, The Brooklyn Eagle, which he read religiously every day, lay on the floor by his bed. He sat in his pajamas propped up by his bedrest, a checkered wool blanket and black afghan with colored squares drawn up around his legs.

Suddenly in the doorway, Michael's manservant, William appeared. "I have your bath ready, now, Mr. Flynn," said the muscular man who attended Michael every day, cutting his hair, trimming his mustache and taking care of his personal needs.

"Edward, we'll revisit this tomorrow! Put me can of coins back up on the shelf now," which little Edward was more than happy to do. He knew his buddies were sitting on the front stoop waiting for him to come out and play stickball.

Had he only spent more time with his grandfather, the stories he could have heard about Ireland! But Michael Flynn grew more and more remote due to the arthritic pain coursing through his body and the family seemed to spend less and less time with him as the years sped by.

However, William the manservant, frequently played ball with Edward as his father Frank had little time for him. Edward grew to love William and one of the saddest times of his life was the day William was discharged from the care of Michael Flynn due to "drunkenness".

As said, generations repeat themselves. As Michael Flynn had spent little time with his son Frank, Frank in turn spent little time with his own sons, Frank, Jr. and Edward. Perhaps he just didn't know how. He commuted into New York and to the factory in Philadelphia each week. He raised his sons as he himself had been raised. It is said the Flynn men do not communicate much emotion to their sons, an Irish trait described so well in the book "Trinity" between the characters Conor and his father Tomas in Ballyutogue.

The business continued to prosper. Frank Flynn sent his sons to the finest schools in Brooklyn. Edward went to St. Saviors and then on to the prestigious Brooklyn Prep with other sons of Brooklyn industrialists, in their suit jackets and ties, being groomed and educated to take over family businesses their fathers had done before them. While pampered and well-to-do, Frank and Edward were taught how to work hard. They had good values from a strong Irish Catholic upbringing and lots of good times and encouragement from Mary Flynn's nine sisters and brothers, their aunts and uncles.

One afternoon Mary Flynn called Edward down from his room, into the living room of 587 5th Street. It was winter and she had on her trademark black Persian lamb coat and hat with the thick black curly texture that complimented her own white skin and stylish, newly-waved, dark brown hair.

"Edward, I have a surprise for you," she explained, stooping down in front of the boy.

"What is it, mother?" Edward asked. Her beautiful coat was cold from the snowy day outside.

"Why look what I have for you, Edward. There seems to be a puppy in here!," Mary said as she unfolded the black Persian coat to reveal a small black cocker spaniel puppy hidden in its folds.

"His name is Smoky. He is to be your dog," Mary said softly.

Mary loved both her sons, Edward and Frank, very much. Being the oldest of 10, she knew a lot about children. She had a kind firmness about her and while she knew how to discipline, it was very rarely that people could ever recall her saying, "No."

Mary and Frank Flynn, both born in the late 1895, upheld Victorian values in their household. They valued decorum, good manners, etiquette, charity and kindness toward others. They dressed well and wore their wealth tastefully, understated, but definitely there. The bright red siren geraniums in their concrete window boxes and shiny brass door plate announced to passersby that the people within were substantial, much as Michael Flynn's home on Baltic Street conveyed the same silent, but unmistakable message. The family may have begun as poor "lace curtain Irish", (meaning they might be starving but they had beautiful lace curtains in their windows!) but they certainly had come a long way.

Mary had lost her littlest sister, Jenny, to consumption and so was very careful with her sons, watching from the window as they played stickball or kick-the-can with the neighborhood boys in the street. All the row houses along 5th Street had high square concrete porches outside the front door with a small utility passage far below for the coal man to gain access to the cellar. It was terrifying to watch the neighborhood boys leap across these concrete porches from one house to another.

"Frank, get down from there right now!" she would call.

When they went on trips to The Breezy Point Surf Club out on Rockaway where they had a cabana for many years, Mary stood at the shoreline with her arms folded, watching the boys in the water like a sentinel. Never once did she allow her gaze to wander from them, calling, "Edward, not so far! Come in now!"

Brooklyn in the 1920's and 1930's was an amazing place for children to grow up, rich and colorful, from the fire hydrants that were turned on in summer to the water balloons that were hurled mysteriously from roofs at passersby, to the vendor wagons selling pots and pans, fresh vegetables and sharpening knives for free, from their wagons every morning. Baseball was the Olympics to the people of Brooklyn. You could actually hear the soft roar of crowds cheering the Dodgers and bats cracking at Ebbets Field if you listened softly on a summer night.

And then there was always the excitement of the ever-expanding Michael Flynn Manufacturing business. One day, the boys heard their father and grandfather talking at dinner of another factory that had gone bankrupt. They had decided to purchase the building, its machinery and its inventory, which happened to be chocolate. Frank and Edward had chocolate bars in the house for an entire year!

Brooklyn, New York, 1943

Joan Ellen Dillon

Joan Ellen Dillon was a serious, brown-eyed Irish beauty who lived in a modest home on Avenue M, beyond Prospect Park, off Flatbush Avenue. The house had a huge horse-chestnut tree in the backyard which almost covered the home, bringing wonderful shade in the summer.

While not wealthy, John and Eleanor Dillon raised their two children, Joan and her brother Jack, to be excellent students at St. Thomas Aquinas Catholic School. They never owned a car, but walked to Flatbush Avenue for shopping and took a vacation once a year to Boonton, New Jersey.

Joan's father, John, a quiet, gentle man, had served in France during WWI and retired after 30 years from New York Life in Manhattan where he was manager of the billing department. He had blondish hair and blue eyes and took Joan for walks to Flatbush Avenue for shopping. In those days the shop owners knew all their customers through the years and it was great fun. John Dillon was known to all for his kindness, to some, his saintliness.

For conversely, Joan's mother, Eleanor Dillon, was known for her "difficult" nature. A good-looking woman, she kept a meticulous Victorian home, wearing her housedress and a freshly-ironed apron. One of six children, she could be very funny and charming at times, but also very critical, vain and argumentative. She was often heard to be complaining about some imagined slight or insult from a friend or neighbor. She enjoyed a martini with a cherry at 5 pm with crackers and cheese as was the custom. Neither John nor Eleanor would ever speak much about their Irish ancestors. They were both born in Brooklyn and status, in the Victorian tradition, was important to Eleanor.

During the Great Depression, the Dillons were proud of the fact that John always had work, although his brother, Neal, came to live with them for a while. Joan recalled looking forward to Sunday night "dinner", which was often only biscuits and jelly, but great fun and eaten in the dining room on her mother's fancy Irish linen tablecloth.

Joan went on to St. Angela Hall, a prominent Catholic high school for girls where she won the English Medal from the New York Board of Regents and was editor of Veritas, her yearbook. She won a partial scholarship to The College of New Rochelle, a school for "daughters of the elite" in Westchester, but was not able to attend as there was only enough money to send her brother, Jack, also an excellent student, to Brooklyn Poly Technical Institute.

One day, Joan's friend, Grace De Stefano, arranged a blind date for Joan. In Prospect Park she was introduced to a tall, shy boy with copious braces on his teeth. Joan had magnificent thick, mahogany hair which curled thickly, laying softly about her shoulders.

They ended up taking a trolley up Flatbush Avenue to a soda shop. On the trolley the boy regaled Joan with his wealth of knowledge about such topics as his new brown suede shoes. Her serious brown eyes flashed as she discussed her opinions, how she would be attending St. Joseph's College in Brooklyn. The boy had just received a commission to attend Kings Point, the Maritime Institute. His name was Edward Flynn and the rest, as they say, is history.

Brooklyn, New York, 1945

Joan Dillon and Edward Flynn were married on Lincoln's Birthday, February12 of 1945. Edward had served as 2nd Lieutenant in the Merchant Marine, piloting a Liberty ship out of New York Harbor. The Liberty supply ships were a popular target for German submarines and due to the ever present stress, the officer in charge of the engine room went insane and Lieutenant Flynn assumed his duties.

His ship made it safely to Europe and the Mediterranean where the young man from Park Slope, Brooklyn got to see pyramids in Egypt and glass being made from hot desert sand. He brought back artifacts for his mother made of ivory and ancient local currency, coins with holes in the middle.

Edward's brother, Frank Jr., was a sergeant in the army, fought at The Battle of the Bulge and won a Silver Star for his bravery in jumping out of a foxhole and saving part of his regiment that was pinned down by the Germans.

When the war ended Edward and Frank returned to take their place in the ever-expanding Michael Flynn Manufacturing Company whose factory in Philadelphia had done very well with the war effort. Along with Reynolds Aluminum and Alcoa Steel, Michael Flynn was one of three companies allowed by the government to continue making residential windows during the War, the rest of the factories converted to military production exclusively.

The Company expanded after WWII as demand for affordable housing-and residential windows- for returning soldiers and their growing families, grew. As in WWI, The Michael Flynn Manufacturing Company skillfully found salvaging opportunities, only this time they salvaged WWII destroyers and submarines, using the metal to make windows, both for residential homes for veterans and commercial buildings. To this heady environment Edward and Frank returned.

Part 5: A Paler Shade of Green:
<u>My</u> Story
Philadelphia, PA, 1948

Joan Flynn Beesley

How far back can you remember? To the very beginning? I can. I was born in 1946. My beginning, at least my earliest recollection, was lying in my crib on Barnett Street, near Godfrey Avenue where my father worked at The Michael Flynn Mfg. Co.

The war was over. My father, de-commissioned as a First Lieutenant in the Merchant Marine, came home to marry his Brooklyn sweetheart. They settled in Philadelphia in Winchester Park so he could work his way up in the Philadelphia plant of his family's aluminum and steel window business. From my crib was always the soft cadence, the late night conversations of hope and excitement, as my father discussed the work of the day, the people he was introduced to, working his way up in his family's business.

Barnett Street was a community of brick row houses built after WWII for G.I.'s and their families. There were many other young post-war couples in the neighborhood that my mother greeted as she took me for walks in my large blue pram. It was very comfortable with a special pillow and a heavy navy blue blanket with my monogram "JEF" on it. I must have been about two years old. My white crib was near a window with beautiful sheer organza curtains that used to stir softly in the breeze.

I remember a small cream and blue ceramic figurine of a girl and boy on the window ledge. My mother found a woman artist who did murals and she painted a picture of a fairy with a magic wand and a rainbow on the inside end of my crib for me to look at, stimulating my imagination at a very early age. I've had a distant memory of all this, but found a picture of me in my crib which reinforces the memory. It was all exactly as I remember it.

I was the first of eight children and my parents were very much in love. I remember the sound of a hose thumping water up at my window as my father, in his early twenties, washed his car in the driveway below. Again, I couldn't move around much in my crib to see, but could always hear my mother laugh and call, "Ed, *stop* that! You'll wake her up!" I always knew I was loved.

My other memory of Barnett Street is a very vague sense of a small kitchen and my mother reaching up to a small wooden cupboard above me for Pablum.

Somewhere around the age of three, my parents bought their first home in the Philadelphia suburb of Winchester Park. I would live there until I was eight. Winchester Park was a very special place. It was a new subdivision being built around historic Pennypack Creek, named by local Indians meaning "deep and muddy."

Our home was a dark-brick two-story with red-brown trim and several large unusual stones set in the front which gave it character. I spent a lot of my time outdoors, I recall, playing with other children, but in my earliest years, I played alone, in the wonderful private kingdom of early childhood.

I had a best friend there, Bevy Banister. Bevy lived across the street. At age 8 my parents would design a new custom home in Rydal, Pennsylvania and we would move away from Winchester Park, but it was quite a magical place growing up.

In the summer, Bev and I played outside all day long. Behind her house was the dense, native Pennsylvania forest where we would hide treasures from the boys in the neighborhood. The deep Woods were somewhat mysterious. The area had pretty much remained undisturbed from the time of the Indians. You could find interesting old things in the Woods, especially some dirt formations that we knew were Indian mounds or gravesites. As we played in the woods, I often felt the presence of the Indians. Sometimes we would come upon a deer and once or twice I saw some very large tortoises. The woods with their glorious fall foliage were an enchanting place to me, a silent kingdom I loved to roam, the crisp leaves of autumn with their soft crunch below my feet as I trekked the paths below the wooded canopy as the Indians had done before me.

Behind the Woods, you would come across a strange area where the forest had been all cleared away - nothing but dirt - and then the forest would reappear. What was merely excavation for a new street in the subdivision was a constant source of mystery to the two little girls of five, as were the mysterious, deep excavations along the street, simply the basements of the new homes to be built. Later we had an endless supply of lumber, two-by-fours, all types of freshly sawed planks with which to make doll beds.

Bev's house was lovely and a lot of fun. It had a wonderful front green lawn we could roll down. There was a blue Ford always parked securely in the drive. In the garage you could eavesdrop on kitchen conversations by putting your ear next to the copper pipes. In the summer a beautiful pink flowering oriental cherry tree grew by the side of the house up by Bev's window. There were also two large, round shrubs in front of the tree that we could hide under and not be seen. Often we would run and hide from Bev's younger brother Scotty, playing an improvised game of "He's Coming!" much to Scotty's chagrin. We would run around the outside of her house, through the gate, across the backyard, climbing frantically over the fence on Teddy Klatt's side, lurching down through a massive shrub until the Klatt's asked us to be quiet, as Mr. Klatt was a policeman and had to sleep.

Bev's mother, Bunny, was a beautiful young woman with lovely skin and shoulder-length light brown hair which she wore pulled back. On summer afternoons she would let us pick her white, purple and blue chrysanthemums from the flower beds along the white wood horizontal fence enclosing their backyard. When we were older Mrs. Banister made cut-out paper dolls for us on her back patio. As we sat at her wooden picnic table on the small fieldstone patio with the green striped canvas awning cover, Mrs. Banister designed and cut out outfits with paper strips for us to fold onto paper dolls she made for us. "How did she do that so effortlessly?" my five-year old mind often wondered.

Bunny and Walt Banister, Bev's parents, became life-long friends of my parents. There was a woman's social group in the neighborhood to which several of the young mothers belonged. Mrs. Banister and another good friend, Connie Brennan, were members with my mother. It was called "The Winchester Park Twelve" and each member had a beautiful heart-shaped filigreed gold pin with the words "Winchester Park Twelve" engraved on the back. My mother had her initials "JEF", for "Joan Ellen Flynn", monogrammed on the front. My mother loved and treasured that gold pin and wore it throughout her life on her suits for special occasions. When she died at 79 years of age, the pin still had a special place in her jewelry box and is worn today by my youngest sister.

My father and Mr. Banister were also life-long friends. Walt Banister was in real estate and one day my father pointed out his office. On the window I recall seeing "Roland T. Banister and Son, Real Estate" in ornate black and gold letters on the window.

Mr. Banister was a very tall and handsome man with wonderful blue eyes and wavy brown hair. One summer afternoon there was a knock at our front door. I opened it. It was Bev.

"Joan Ellen, my dad's in a Minstrel Show at our church tonight. Would you like to go?" asked the older girl with blond hair and the same blue eyes as her father's.

"Oh, yes!" I replied, having no idea what a Minstrel Show was. But if I was doing something with my best friend, Bevy, it was going to be fun!

Later that evening, Bev, Mrs. Banister, Scotty, and Bev's younger sister Laurie and I took our seats in the small auditorium of their church. Two men in blackface and showboat clothing-green-striped shirts, vests and colorful armbands - sat on barrels on either side of the red velvet curtained stage, playing banjoes and telling jokes. Suddenly the heavy red curtain parted slightly. The show was about to begin. A tall, dignified man in a showboat outfit came out on stage through the curtain, slowly removing the black top hat he was wearing. Holding it in his hands in front of him, he began to sing an old Southern song.

"Ol'Man River, Dat Ol'Man River…He Don't Know Nothin…" he began slowly.

The audience was transfixed by his deep, velvety bass. I had never heard anyone sing like that. As he sung the sad, haunting melody, everyone sat perfectly still, riveted to their seats. I knew nothing, at age five, of the South, Minstrel Shows or slavery. Although I knew nothing about the context of the song, the sad, slow, plaintive melody made an indelible mark on me and throughout my whole life, I cannot hear "Ol'Man River" without recalling that magical moment.

"That's my Dad!!" Bevy breathed excitedly in my ear.

"No!!" I replied. That magnificent, powerful singer couldn't be Mr. Banister of Albion Street.

I watched the rest of Minstrel Show, with its dancing and antics, the thigh-slapping jokes of the minstrel men with their tambourines, in a type of trance, never to forget the riveting deep voice of Bevy's father.

Bev and I spend lazy summer days playing on the heavy cast iron swing set in their backyard. Right outside the white fence behind their property and the beginning of "The Woods", the Banisters had a wonderful wooden sandbox, about 10' by 10', filled with sand, placed under a shady tree. It had wooden seats, planks along the inside, where a child could sit, reach down and play with the sand without getting all sandy. It had a roof over it with black shingles. Mrs. Banister would make us lemonade and peanut butter and jelly sandwiches. We spent many an afternoon playing there, devising where to hide our next batch of treasures in The Woods, from the boys in the neighborhood. The boisterous pack was constantly on the prowl in The Woods, looking for the "Girls' Treasures": old bottles, mysterious rocks, mica and the like, which we hid in plain sight for them to discover.

Summer evenings we would all be out catching fireflies-the boys making glittering rings on their fingers from the unfortunate slower ones- in the damp, fragrant evening air, listening to the soft chant of night crickets.

It was a simpler time when kids played outdoors most of the time. The only real shows we watched were "Howdy Doody", and a show called "Winky-Dink" in which kids could draw on the television screen after receiving their own special magic plastic transparent TV cloth from Winky himself. We watched "Kukla, Fran and Ollie", a puppet show and a popular Saturday circus show called "Under the SealTest Big Top".

One of the best evenings I remember was a summer evening when we played "Puss-in–the-Corner" in the Banister's backyard, cunningly "stealing bases", running between the four green cast iron posts from which clothes lines were strung for Mrs. Banister to hang the billowing white sheets we loved to dash through on summer days!

It was an endless, wonderful childhood, each new day filled with new adventures. Some days we would all go up the block to an intersection within the subdivision with our metal skates and keys and skate on the newly asphalted intersection (incredibly smooth!) until the neighborhood bully, Georgie Miller, intimidated the smaller children, ruining our fun.

In late afternoons, Bevy and I would run home for money, hearing the distant bell of The Good Humor Man and his treasure truck of ice-cold chocolate cake or snowy coconut popsicles, ice-cream sandwiches and the like. I can still recall the thrill as "Bob", the handsome Good Humor man Bev and I liked one summer, opening the heavy levered door on the side of the truck, reaching into the ice-cold, frosty interior, to retrieve the treasured popsicle, the cold, moist foggy air escaping into the summer heat until Bob closed the door with a smart "thug," bolting the stainless steel lever securely.

There were many wonderful families on Albion Street. Next door were the Lamberts and their friendly dog, Chief. Between the two white wooden fences which ran along the side of the Lambert's property and ours was a shady grassy area where a five year-old could hide and look up at the climbing red and white rose hedges her father had planted, cascading over the fence above her. One day Mrs. Lambert invited the little girl into her house.

"Would you like to see my daughter's room?' she asked.

"All right," I said as she led me upstairs to a flowered bedroom, a four-poster bed with chenille bedspread.

On the dressing table were some small perfume bottles, white porcelain thimbles, pretty, feminine trinkets. She gathered up some of them and put them in a flowered handkerchief.

"These belonged to Esther," she explained somberly.

Did she get married and move away? Did she die? I was too shy to ask, but I kept Esther's things for a long time.

Between our house and the other neighbor, the Mann's, was a large mysterious dirt road which would later become a street. Much to my amazement I would watch the great orange caterpillars and construction vehicles carve out and grade the street, watching from the safety of an area that would soon become a sidewalk. My father had named the long dirt street "The Old Ox Trail" and would sing an old Roy Rogers song about it on summer nights when we took our black and white Springer Spaniel, named "JEF", my initials, out for a walk on it.

JEF was an extremely high-strung dog who knew how to do only two things: barking or jumping high into the air. I thought that was why he was called a Springer Spaniel. He was eventually given away to a farm.

Our backyard was enclosed by an ornamental bark fence, very decorative and good-looking. It had replaced the first, simple white-picket fence my parents originally put up. As you followed the winding concrete path along the side of the house, you were met by shade from the imposing height of our two story brick home above you. Tall evergreens and then the bark fence sheltered the house from the street, adding privacy. It was a good place to play. You could bounce rubber balls on the side of the house and if you didn't throw them too hard, they would land back on the concrete path.

I spent many lazy days as a child roaming around the outside of our house. I would often lay down on the grass and listen to the distant drone of an airplane somewhere in the distance. I would study the shapes of the clouds, watching them as they came and went. And always, in the background, was the calm, comforting sound of buzz saws, as construction men sawed their 2 by 4's, slowly building our subdivision.

One bright, beautiful day I was told that men were coming to put in a screened-in porch and they would also put up a wooden swing-set for me. I remember waiting in the back-yard for them to arrive and work their miracles. I watched them construct the beautiful screened-in back porch. They used two different colors of light pastel concrete, a mint green and rose pink. I watched in awe as the big concrete mixer slowly lifted skyward, pouring the mysterious heavy sludge, how the men labored quickly to smooth it before it set.

I would later spend many hours playing on the screened back porch. It was sprayed a dark reddish brown. You could rub your nose against the new screen, cold and metallic, its wires bending somewhat under the warm pressure from your nose. In winter, snow drifts would pile high against the screen porch, coming in somewhat through the screen, making the concrete cold and wet, not a place for playing in winter. You didn't want to stay out there for long.

My parents eventually put up bamboo-slatted blinds over the screens and these could be rolled up or down in the summer by cords, making a soft, reassuring plat-plat sound. My mother used to iron out on the enclosed porch in the summer. I remember having chicken-pox one summer and being confined to the porch while my mother ironed, which was actually very pleasant. There was a big glass black wrought-iron table on the porch with wrought-iron chairs, turquoise corduroy cushions and a smaller glass-top table with a magazine rack. As you walked out the screen door of the porch, there was a green metal below-the-ground garbage pail. If you stood on a lever it would open and close with a heavy clank.

Life was wonderful in those days, probably because I was an only child and my parents were very much in love. The days were long and timeless. We lived in the immediate now of the day. Life was enjoyable, things were fun, golden memories in the making. Truly, as my father was to say, far into the future, life was to be enjoyed. Lots of laughter, mystery and I was very much a part of their world, a sort of treasured guest.

My parents eventually planted a long divider of evergreens down the center of the backyard, dividing it two halves. Trees were also planted and under one was a small black wooden figure of a "Watermelon Boy". I would often bring a blanket out in the back to play or lie under a tree by The Watermelon Boy. I loved running around in my bare feet, amid the grass and clover. Bumble bees, however, were often hiding out in the white blooms of the clover and you had to be very careful not to step on them.

I can remember the first time I took off my shoes on that blanket and ran around the grass in my bare feet, much against my mother's protests. It was cold and soft and very refreshing on the soles of my feet. I kept running in circles, refusing to come back to the blanket until my mother grabbed me.

I was my parents' first child and very much loved, included and doted on. My earliest memories are linked to my mother. I remember lying in my white crib, probably at age 2. I had children's wallpaper with little bears and flowers. I remember waking up and pulling off the wallpaper in small little curling shreds. First I would stick my fingers through the slats and then scratch it a little. If I heard no one coming I would then pull off a small curled piece. I did it here and there. You could hardly notice it with the busy pattern.

I would lie there and wait until I would hear a beautiful tink-tinkle sound floating up reassuringly from the first floor of our home. Over time I knew the brisk melody was my mother dusting the black and ivory keys of our piano, starting with the low, sonorous dark notes and ending with the light, happy keys. She did this every day around lunch time. It always gave me a warm secure feeling that our home was well-taken care of.

Through the flat, white slats of my crib, I would lay there, listening to the lovely notes, slyly pulling small strips of flowered wallpaper off the wall with my tiny nails with a delicious vague sense that I was doing something I shouldn't. Eventually mother would come up and lift me in her arms and set me down on the bathinette by the window in my room with the white, graceful curtains.

My parent's bedroom was next to mine and sometimes at night I would climb out of my crib and sneak into my parents' bed. My father didn't like this and eventually put chicken wire across the top of the crib to keep me in it. I loved to sneak into bed on my mother's side. I would slip in next to her and she would always let me stay. She was an ocean of warmth in her cotton nightgown, comforting, protecting and loving and I was her much-loved child. My parents' bedroom, from my memory, was very beautiful with its soft, striped yellow floral wallpaper. It had two front windows, looking out onto Albion Street and I would pull myself up to the white wooden sills and look out.

My mother had a dressing table with a bench and mirror and sometimes she would put my hair up in pin curls by it. Their closet was dark and exciting, with a musty, forbidden scent! It had a shoe bag in it and a mirror on the inside door.

The Philadelphia summer nights were very hot. Sometimes my father would go play poker at the homes of other young fathers in the neighborhood in a poker club. One of his favorite shows was a very scary one called "Lights Out" by Motorola, sort of an early Twilight Zone. If my mother went out he would let me watch it with him in the living room.

I remember one night, balancing, then lurching my sweating self over the plastic rail of the crib once more. It was an unusually hot summer night. My parents were in their room, watching a small TV from bed rests. It was the wonderful age of early TV with Sid Caesar, Omnibus, Playhouse 90, and my favorite, "I Remember Mama" with TR and Dagmar, the children, a show I loved. It was sponsored by Maxwell House Coffee, "Good to the Last Drop".

Slowly I cautiously inched open the door and pushed my three-year old nose inside. As I opened the door I was hit by a chilling, refreshing blast of air, like stepping into the refrigerator. It was icily delicious. Above the loud hum coming from the window I heard my father yell, "Close that door!!" The icy chill was theirs alone it seemed and reluctantly I slunk back to the crib. I recall on another humid night making my journey again to their bedroom and again experiencing the same wonderful chilly hum. Coming from my hot bedroom it was quite a marvel as the cold air struck my sticky face. My parents had magic in their room and wanted to keep it all to themselves!

Not all my experiences were as wonderful. One Saturday afternoon my mother was out shopping and my father was outside doing the lawn. I was four and Bev and I were in the kitchen. We pulled up chairs to the sink and decided we would do the lunch dishes for my father. We filled the sink and were adding liquid soap. A loaf of Wonder Bread half opened in its colorful red, yellow and blue dotted paper wrapping was laying across the back burner of the gas stove.

Suddenly one of the pockets of our jackets caught on the knob that turned on the gas burner. I don't remember whose pocket it was, but I think it was mine. Whoosh! Suddenly the wax paper wrapping ignited in flames and then to our horror, it swiftly climbed up the white organza curtains my mother had around the kitchen window. In a panic we threw water at the monstrous sight, afraid of what my father would say. But it was out of our control and began to dance and lick the ceiling. In terror I ran to get my father who was working in the backyard.

"Daddy! Daddy! There's a fire in the kitchen!" Dad came running.

"Get out of the kitchen !" "Get out of the house !" he yelled.

Soon Dad had the fire out. The kitchen was damaged, black and smoky, but never once were we yelled at for what happened. We were very afraid and shaken. It was a good lesson learned. I realized if Dad had been out of reach we probably would have burnt the house down as fast as the fire moved. Perhaps things were less fire-resistant in those days.

Summer was a wonderful time. My mother would make summer meals, corn on the cob and salads that she would serve beautifully on her new glass-top table with straw placemats on the screened-in porch.

It was the early 50's and vaccines for many childhood diseases had not yet been invented. I remember spending many days in bed with chicken-pox, measles, pink-eye and the like. And always at the end of the day I could count on my father hurrying upstairs, animated from a day of work at his father's business, The Michael Flynn Manufacturing Company, to check on his little girl. Sometimes he would bring me a new toy or game board, Candy Land or Sorry.

My room had two windows. One looked out on the backyard. One winter night I was awakened by the sound of a persistent "tap! tap!" on the window. I looked out into the starry night to see my father throwing pebbles up at my window. Eventually my shredded baby wallpaper was replaced with a blue floral print and my crib was put away. I remember going with my mother to a furniture store where two beautiful maple twin beds, a dresser and nightstand were chosen for me. My room had pink lamps and pink throw rugs which could be shaken to make the pink yarn stand up straight and erect. They were gifts from my grandmother, Mary Flynn in Brooklyn, who told my mother to take me with her and "pick out the very best!"

I listened to stories on the radio a lot, Roy Rogers and Stella Dallas being some of my favorite dramas. I had a long red vinyl toy box between the two twin beds and a blond Madame Alexander doll, with shiny, wiry, blond curls. I also owned my own small Hop-along-Cassidy mirror in the bathroom with a red toothbrush holder and cup so you could check as you brushed your teeth.

One cold winter afternoon I was playing with my friends in our living room with a stand-up green chalk board. Bev was trying to teach me the alphabet, of which I hadn't a clue. I tried writing the strange symbols on the black board. Then I saw my mother, who was ironing, come running over. "A 'B' ! She made a 'B' !" I couldn't understand her excitement as I looked at the odd design I had made. And then I saw it. I had made a mark that looked like one of the symbols on the colored alphabet printed at the top of my chalk board. I remember the thrill I felt as I finally saw I had made a connection with what they were calling the letter 'B'. I had arrived. I was no longer a small child.

One evening I came home from playing with Bev across the street. My father pulled out a chair for me out of the garage and put it by his on the driveway. I remember the night as if it were yesterday, Dad and I just sitting out on the driveway on plastic folding chairs, listening to the evening sounds, watching the dusk falling in the new neighborhood carved out of the Pennsylvania forest. I sat there looking down at the oil spots that had leaked from our car onto the driveway. We didn't say much. Just sat there side by side, father and daughter, experiencing the fall of creeping night. Again, a feeling that he loved me and I was special and he wanted to be with me, enjoying my company. Crickets were beginning to chirp. In short, to use an expression from Grandma Flynn, it was grand. In those days it seemed time moved slower. We just watched the night fall. Soon it was pitch black outside there on the driveway: there was no moon. Eventually we folded up the plastic chairs and went into the house.

The building of new homes in Winchester Park provided an ever-changing playground for a five-year old and her friends. We loved to play in the foundations of the new homes as they were being built. First a big hole would be dug for the basement. You could look for arrowheads in the dirt. After the construction men went home at 5 o'clock we would slide down the dirt embankments. It usually felt somewhat damp. It was exciting to stand in the newly-dug hole that would be the basement and look up at the level ground above.

And then there were the sewers. There were long, wide trenches dug. These were dark and damp and the workmen repeatedly warned us to never jump down in them as they could collapse on us and so we never ventured down in them.

We had our favorites among the construction men. "Happy Jack", for instance, was probably not the brightest of the workers, but he used to save unusual things he would find during digging, old horseshoes, bottles and such. He especially, took great pains to warn us to never, under any circumstances, go down into the freshly-dug trenches, that they could collapse and we would suffocate.

But the sewers themselves were a lot of fun. These huge concrete structures were lifted by a large crane, then carefully lined up along the sides of the street. They were massive and imposing and a kid could walk right through them standing up. Or if you jumped really high you could manage to sit on top of them, shimmying up, your clothes clinging to the rough cement. Sitting on top you sensed the power of the huge cylinder below you, the feel of its graceful curving geometry beneath you. You had a sensation of grandness or royalty as you sat high up upon the sewers, just before dinner time, at dusk, surveying the neighborhood and the progress of the day: the many homes under construction; this one had siding going up where there was none yesterday, studs for the second floor had been completed on one, or most exciting, a new foundation had been dug.

Our home was on a corner lot and eventually a long street beside it was cleared from the forest. It was simply a massive dirt road that went through the forest. It would be a main thoroughfare of the subdivision in years to come. But for what seemed several years for me it was simply the wide dirt road my father called "The Old Ox Trail" after an old song. On the sides of the road were gullies that would fill up with water and freeze over in the wintertime.

This became my own private playground in winter. As dusk would settle in, I would walk along the gullies, my boots crunching the thin ice. I loved to hear the odd wrenching sound the ice made as it was deciding whether or not to give way and break below my feet. Sometimes it would just stand its ground, solid and firm, but if it was going to break and crack, it gave out a grinding sound of resistance, then finally defeat, as it struggled to keep its frozen form. Breaking the thin ice was fun. Fragile and weak, it broke right away, the splintered ice flying right and left, the water trickling below. Sometimes at dusk I would run down these gullies wrecking, it felt to me, havoc in every direction. I would run the length of two or three new houses, cracking the grinding ice where ever I went, my coat flying. It seemed to make a mournful sound. And then I would look over my shoulder as if I had just participated in an evil act. I had disturbed and broken what was there, violating nature with my actions. I would slowly walk back to our house on the corner for dinner, sly with the delicious weight, literally, of what I had done.

One day I arrived home from school to find large piles of gravel along the Old Ox Trail. And one winter night I made a circular fort out of the gravel I amassed from one of the nearby piles. It was a gravel fortress actually, with various buildings surrounded by a medieval moat-like gravel wall. There were turrets. When it was finished I fairly danced around it. When I looked up I was astonished to see that it was now dark. No architect could have been prouder than I was of that gravel fortress. I breathlessly ran up to the house to get my mother. I knew she would be amazed at the wonder I had built. As I pulled her down to the street in the darkness by her apron in the cold, I feared she wouldn't be able to fully appreciate what I had done due to the darkness which probably accounted for her subdued appreciation of my masterpiece.

In the winter we went sledding down at the entrance to Winchester Park where there was a box culvert and a small sloping hill that led down to Pennypack Creek. I recently returned to Winchester Park with my son after a 52 year absence and found the hills where we used to sled, pretty much as they were, yet so much smaller! I recall one late afternoon when we were all sledding down there. Night fell, supper time passed and there was a great deal of commotion because none of our parents knew where we were.

The snow was falling around us in the soft early night. We could see the stars and moonlight on the snow as we sat on our wooden sleds, trying to steer, pushing the stubborn metal steering apparatus on the front of our sleds in our rubber boots and cumbersome snow suits. Inevitably we were each thrown off as we swished over some mysterious man-made humps of snow at the bottom of the hill. We were soon discovered by Mrs. Weiker, the ever watchful grandmother of the neighborhood. I remember trudging home through the snowy streets in the cold night air, wet, exhausted, happy, anticipating my supper and listening to "The Tales of Roy Rogers and Dale Evans" on our radio, with their familiar trade mark closing song "Happy Trails to You Until We Meet Again!"

Mrs. Weiker was a grandmotherly German woman who always seemed to take care of us when we gathered. She had a very thick German accent. As I walked down our long street in the cold gray morning, there was always a certain exhilaration in being *alone*, in charge of my destiny, walking there in the frozen morning, to gather at the front of the subdivision to meet the school bus. This meeting place was near a stone wall in front of Mrs. Weiker's house and her granddaughter, Rita Jean, would be among our crowd.

Mrs. Weiker would be out there at 7am to wait with us until the school bus came rumbling up to the front of the subdivision, seemingly to protect or guard us, admonishing with her thick German accent. "Here it comes! Stay together. Line up, line up!" Years later I reflected about Mrs. Weiker and how she seemed to always wait with us, protecting us from something. And then I thought maybe it had something to do with her upbringing in Germany where there was plenty to protect and plenty to fear.

Pennypack Park with its wonderful Pennypack Creek surrounded the Winchester Park subdivision. One magical winter night, my father, Mr. Banister, Bev and I went ice-skating in sub-zero weather when the Creek had frozen. The two fathers, bundled in their jackets and scarves, skated up the creek, going around bends in front of us, as Bev and I tried our best to keep up.

"I can't see them," I said to Bev as they rounded a curve in the creek.

She was older. She would know what to do. It was like a scene out of "Hans Brinker and the Silver Skates" as we skated along. The black bare branches of the tall trees along Pennypack Creek loomed against the full winter moon as our fathers swayed back and forth together in unison as they skated effortlessly on their long legs up the creek, their scarves flying, metal blades scraping the ice. As they went around the bends in front of us, we would lose sight of them. As we caught up behind them, the two tall skaters would reassuringly come into sight once again, illuminated by the white winter moon above.

Holidays in Winchester Park were wonderful. On Thanksgiving, my father would take me and my younger brother Michael into Philadelphia to see the Thanksgiving Day Parade before the Army-Navy game. We would take the train from the station down on Frankfurt Avenue. Dad would hold Michael up for a time on his shoulders above the crowd to see the wonderful floats and the colorful Mummers strutting by, dipping and twirling in their satin capes. As we got older he would joke that next year he'd have to bring a ladder for us. Then we'd return home, the wonderful aroma of our Thanksgiving turkey permeating the house as we opened the front door. Mother would have everything ready in our dining room with all her very best china and sterling silver, which she kept in a special black lacquer box with a red rose painted on the cover with its secret drawer for special silver serving utensils.

Halloween was also a great time. We would go from house to house in a group of about 12 children in our costumes. It was fun to just go with the flow. No matter who rang the bell we were all sure to have our bags filled at each stop. The Tolands-I had a crush on their oldest boy, J.J.-would invite the group in to walk around their dining room table for cider and donuts. Their younger brother, Terry, had a terrific model train set in their basement, equipped with tunnels, mountains and bridges.

There were great neighbors and they were always especially kind to all of us. There were the Hoffmans, and the Trailias, who had a deaf son Michael who used to run wildly through the homes under construction with me. We'd play on the wooden first floor of homes, running between the wooden 2 by 4's, Michael trying to communicate to the wind in a garbled, passionate voice that no one could understand, one that he would never hear. When they brought the great concrete sewer pipes and laid them by the side of our street, Michael and I would hide in them or better yet, sit astride the tops of them, playing Fish or Hearts. Directly across the street lived the Parks and their child Carol, whose mother, sadly, had an advanced case of Parkinson's. In the afternoon, she would be brought out in her wheelchair where she would sit in the shade up on her lawn, watching the cars. From our house, peering through the blinds, I could see the tremendous, uncontrollable shaking she experienced.

I learned about the world through my parents as they worked together planting shrubs, putting in the plain white picket fence which they eventually replaced with an ornate birch bark one. On Saturdays I would watch my father, a handsome, muscular young man, hoist massive bags of peat moss on his strong shoulders, in his striped polo shirts, lugging them to the flower beds he had dug around the perimeter of the backyard. On the Lambert's side they planted climbing red and white rose bushes all along the fence line. They planted a long row of shrubs across the center of the backyard and six large fir trees along the side of the house. Everything thrived exquisitely under my parents' Irish green thumbs! Eventually they put in a concrete side walk along the side of the house from the driveway to the backyard with pink, yellow and blue snapdragons in a flower bed along the walkway.

Everyday around six my father would arrive home in his starched white shirt and tie, carrying his bulging, musky, brown leather briefcase with the gold "**ERF**" monogram, overflowing with mysterious rolled-up architectural blueprints. After kissing my mother hello and spending some time with her as she fixed dinner in the kitchen, he'd "walk the grounds" with me. He'd inspect his new seeded lawn, part of it covered with white gauze sheets. I'd stand by his side as he carefully "gave it a watering" each evening. We'd proudly admire the flowering pink crab trees they'd planted on the front lawn, our stroll ending up at the beanstalk at the side of the house.

My father had pointed out the beanstalk to me one day, growing down there in the window well, asking if I had noticed the magic beans. Standing there the next day all alone, looking for the magic beans, I leaned over, spilling a new box of crayolas I was holding. Upon telling my parents, they explained I would have to leave them in the well for rat poison had been placed in our window wells as a precaution and I couldn't retrieve the crayons.

Despite the rat poison, the infamous beanstalk mysteriously spiraled up from the ominous window well, a wild uninhibited being that grew along the side of the house. The spiraling curiosity eventually became a thick, knarled affair, reaching up to my parents' second story bedroom window. Birds lived in the vine and you could here them chirping happily in the morning when I played with my dolls on the floor of my parents bedroom.

While I loved to roam the neighborhood with my friends, I was also a rather solitary child and often played alone. When I was four, I loved to conduct imaginary tours of the property my parents were so proud of. During the weekends they would plant rose bushes and trees, put in large birch bark flower boxes under the front windows to match our new fence. I, in turn, would first pick up twigs and occasional branches, then meet imaginary groups of people, conducting grand tours of the property, explaining my parents latest shrub and flower additions to important and curious, imaginary visitors waiting impatiently at the end of our driveway.

❧

As the treasured first child in the family, I spent my early years in the company of my mother, Joan Ellen. Knowing she named me after her, giving me her exact and unusual name, was very special to me. My mother had lush, thick shiny brown hair which she worn shoulder length. I can remember as an infant, being held against her neck, secure in the soft brown warmth of her hair. My mother was a happy young housewife who loved her home, proud of her tall, successful husband who worked in the Philadelphia aluminum and steel window company started by his grandfather, Michael Flynn.

Listening to my father explain the exploits of the day to my mother over dinner, I certainly didn't understand the business details, but even at age three, I was very aware of my mother's pride in his accomplishments in the business, the fun and excitement they shared as they met and bonded with other young couples in Winchester Park.

I, the proud, early product of their union, absolutely basked in the fun and exploits of the handsome young couple from Brooklyn! True to their Irish roots, they loved gardening and landscaping their new home.

And being Irish, they loved music, my father often playing the piano and his clarinet while he waited for my mother to finish getting ready for a night out in the neighborhood with friends. And they loved the wonder of their small baby girl, taking turns reading me "Heidi" by Joanna Spieri, sitting by my crib as I fell asleep. My parents also bought me a wonderful set of children's classical small yellow records for my record player. I learned to love the powerful melody of "The Pier Guint Suite:In the Hall of the Mountain King" at age three.

One of my earliest, simplest, most beautiful memories was of Easter, again when I was about 3 years old. I awoke one lovely Spring Saturday morning to be told by my parents that we were going on an Easter Egg Hunt. I had no idea what that meant but my mother and father were clearly excited! After breakfast we put on our jackets and left the house.

"They're going to have it for all the neighborhood children down at the entrance to Winchester Park," my mother explained excitedly to my father as we piled into the car.

My mother and father were usually excited about everything. So many things in their life were wondrously new for them, including me!

As we drove down to the entrance, other families were also arriving with their children. Much of Winchester Park was still undeveloped, dense woods, much as the Indians left it. We were directed to a long, flat, elevated area, dense with beautiful old trees, not yet carved out with streets. Dad pulled mom up onto the long plateau from the street. I held onto his head from my perch on his shoulders.

"All right, families!"a man called from a bullhorn.

"Welcome to our first annual Winchester Park Easter Egg Hunt!"

We walked through the scented, wooded area, wet and lovely with brilliant pink azaleas, white and pink dogwoods and yellow forsythia, purple crocuses pushing their way up through bright green moss as we approached the yellow ribbon where other families stood waiting with their children.

"Waiting for what?" I wondered.

Effortlessly, my father lifted me down easily from his strong shoulders. My mother held a small bowl from the kitchen.

"Now when I blow the whistle, you can start!" came the loud, barking voice over the bullhorn.

"Start what?" I wondered.

Then my father lifted me back up onto his shoulders. The whistle blew and we all broke through the yellow ribbon. My father strode through the woods several yards in front of the other families before setting me gently down.

I didn't know what we were supposed to do as we walked slowly forward, holding hands, the damp, moist aroma of pines and the early morning light filtering, flickering through the light green leaves, illuminating patches of bright green moss. It was magical. There were small, light blue birds, an occasional red cardinal and wild, yellow, canary-like birds as well, up, up in the trees above us. I just stood there, looking up.

"Joan Ellen, pay attention and look carefully as we walk," my father instructed me, gently moving me along.

There was another show just as lovely, at my feet, I realized. As we walked, the colorful yellow and purple crocuses lay bursting from the earth at the base of the huge oak and maple trees that had been there forever. A timid child, I could see many excited families milling about behind us, soon to catch up, and I became afraid.

"Say, what's that over there?" my father asked dramatically, pointing to a tree trunk.

I saw a patch of something bright and wonderful. It was a brightly colored pink egg, lying secretly under the leaves of a small plant. How could it be? What was it doing there? To my three year old mind, it was beautiful, but a real puzzle. What was it doing out in the woods and why was it colored?

"Let's pick it up and put it in our bowl," my mother encouraged me gently.

I picked it up, holding it against the bib of my soft, light pink corduroy overalls. We continued walking on the soft forest floor.

"Oh, my goodness!" my mother exclaimed happily.

"Do you see what I see, Ed?" she said breathlessly, pointing out another perfectly symmetrical beautiful egg, lying under a yellow forsythia bush.

In wonder, I reached down and put it in our bowl again, holding the bright yellow oval against my overalls. I couldn't believe my luck. This one had a sticker of a duck on it. Then I looked over my shoulder.

The growing army of families and laughing, excited children would soon be upon us, also discovering the wonderful treasures. As we hurried through the forest, I looked up and incredibly, I saw a green egg carefully lodged up in the branch of a tree, far above my head. One more for our bowl! As we proceeded, I stopped by a log we had to step over.

"Look carefully, Joan Ellen!" my father instructed me.

And then I saw it, a beautiful blue egg with a rose on it, lying just inside the log. Carefully I reached down to retrieve it. How did these beautiful eggs come to be there? How did they get their color?

As we made our way, we came to a large rock.

"Never can tell what's lying on the other side," my father announced mysteriously.

"Ed, let her find them herself!" my mother scolded.

Then she laughed and I saw her kiss him above me, as I spied a beautiful yellow egg with small chickens pasted on it. As my mother lowered the bowl and I carefully placed our fourth egg in it, several screaming, gleeful children dashed ahead of us, hurrying to be the first to discover the treasures hidden in the forest ahead.

Our wondrous, private interlude had been broken, invaded by other families just like ours, with small, excited children, discovering for the very first time, the strange circumstance- a true miracle!- of real, beautifully colored eggs, carefully hidden throughout the lush forest. I don't remember the rest of that amazing Saturday morning and the proceedings of the First Annual Winchester Park Easter Egg Hunt, but I do know there was never a happier child, slowly discovering the eggs, placing them in the small glass mixing bowl brought by the radiant, chestnut haired, soft-spoken beauty who was her mother and the tall, handsome, funny and confident young father in trousers and zylon jacket.

Years later, I still feel the love and excitement of that day as a small child, treasured and care-for, basking in the fun, love and good times as the laughing, good-looking couple from Brooklyn introduced and shared the wonders of their world to the sometimes timid, adoring little girl who loved them so.

My parents were social people. I recall one October weekend when my father took me with him to The Hunt Club which I believe was a small country club or riding academy not far from Winchester Park. I was about four years old and proud to be with the tall, energetic, likeable man who took me about with him as he checked on things for the social event he was helping to plan that evening. It was a cool, crisp day with bright colored leaves swirling as we walked hand-in-hand through the facility.

"We're having a Square Dance here tonight, Joan Ellen", he explained to me.

"Oh," I said, not knowing what he meant, but definitely picking up on the excitement and anticipation in his warm, Brooklyn voice.

He spoke with someone about refreshments and then asked me if I'd like to see the barn where the dance would be held. We walked across the hardwood floors together, scuffing through small piles of straw and sawdust.

"And they have a horse here. Would you like to see it?" he asked.

We walked across the barn floor to an area of horse stalls. All were empty except for one. The stall was very dark, but through the blackness I could see a white horse, facing us, standing very rigid, there in the darkness. It was very large and somewhat frightening.

"Are there other horses here, Dad?"

"No, not any more."

As I looked back at the white horse, I notice he hadn't moved at all. Then I realized he must be just a statue or model of a horse. A member of the Hunt Club staff joined my father as we walked through the sawdust in the stall area.

"Just checking up on the horses!" my father said amiably and they both laughed congenially.

"Well, everything's ready for tonight, Mr. Flynn." My father became preoccupied with the man, asking some further questions.

As we walked away, I wanted to ask my father about that horse. It wasn't a real horse and I knew it. Why hadn't he shared the joke with *me*?

One of my earliest memories was of my mother taking me down to Pennypack Creek for picnics. We would walk down the street through Winchester Park beyond the entrance and from there descend into the thick, green, leafy forest, walking along Pennypack Creek to an area where it swelled like a river. My mother was knowledgeable and soft spoken, pointing out butterflies, Queen Anne's lace, and forsythia, "the Flower of Brooklyn!" along the forest trail. There were high rock ledges, one in particular where my mother and I would sit above the rushing water. From our vantage point on the high, flat rock we would look out on a rushing waterfall not far from us, a small Niagara Falls, pleasantly spraying the four-year-old little girl.

Surrounded by the cool, leafy trees hanging above us, my mother would take out a brown paper bag and carefully unwrap delicious peanut butter and jelly sandwiches from the wax paper. We would sit and watch boisterous neighborhood boys swing out on a rope high above the swirling water, whooping, then dropping dramatically into the water below, pretending to die. On the way home, we would stop and pick raspberries and blue berries that grew wild in the Pennsylvania forest. I enjoyed this time with my mother, knowing how special and important I was to her as she tried to impart to her small child all the wonderful things in the world around her.

There were two movie theatres I remember on Frankford Avenue that my father used to take me to, one called the Merben and the other, the Mayfield. The Mayfield was very unusual in that the front half of the building was actually a jewelry store in the form of an inverted horseshoe. While waiting in line to buy a ticket, theatre goers stood in long lines in the evening beside glowing windows full of beautiful engagement rings and necklaces as the ticket line slowly snaked past the marvelous windows. Even at a very young age, I recognized the cleverness of this marketing arrangement!

I recall the day my sister Marianne was born and brought home from the hospital to our home on Albion Street. Marianne was number four. There was nothing unusual as I recall. My proud mother did have quite a number of the neighborhood children in to see the brown-haired little girl with the lustrous, beautiful brown eyes, just like hers. But as the days went by, I heard my mother say that Marianne seemed very cranky, that she would cry painfully each time her little legs were raised to change her.

"I think there's something wrong, Ed..." I heard my mother say one night. "The doctor says it's nothing. Still, she's so cranky. I don't understand it...

I was playing at my friend Maureen Donzay's house about 4 o'clock on a Sunday afternoon.. Suddenly the phone rang. Mrs. Donzay answered it, hung up and anxiously told me I had to go home right away. When I arrived home, my father was hurriedly piling my two little brothers into the car. He drove us all quickly to the family doctor. I remember waiting in the office for Dr. Roscoe to arrive from his home and looking at his enormous collection of china dogs. His nurse arrived and each of us went into his office where he extended a long cotton swab down our throats.

"I'll call you in the morning, Ed, with the results," he informed my father solemnly.

The next morning there was a white piece of paper nailed on our front door. "**QUARANTINE**" it said in heavy black letters. No one could leave or enter. We were told that Marianne had spinal meningitis and was gravely ill in Nazareth Hospital where my mother was keeping watch.

That week was very difficult. I heard my mother crying one night.

"She's just sweating and tossing her little head back and forth..." she sobbed.

"If I could just trade places with her..." I heard my father say downstairs.

"They've started the antibiotics. We just have to wait..."

We came very close to losing Marianne. I came to understand there was more to life than my little world, my little house: serious things I didn't yet understand, that could scare even a parent. Like death.

A more pleasant early memory I have is that of visiting "Grandma Booth", Bevy's grandmother. Bevy's mother dropped us off several times that summer, out in the country, to play. We were both about 5 years old.

Grandma Booth's was an enchanting place. It was a simple two-story wooden frame house out in the magnificent Pennsylvania countryside. It was gray with a screened-in front porch that slanted as we ran excitedly across its planks. Bev and I often sat on the green straw summer rugs in the living room with lemonade and cookies, watching Buster Brown. I first saw Disney's "Alice in Wonderland" one afternoon at Grandma Booth's and it was spellbinding.

Grandma Booth's was a place where one could run. They had lots of property behind the house and we were constantly exploring. The bright summer morning heard the insistent crow of roosters. The endless summer days seemed to go on forever. Behind the house, right outside Grandma Booth's kitchen window, was an apple tree with a wooden swing.

I don't recall much of Grandma Booth, just a soft, maternal voice above me, grey hair pulled back in a bun with a net, house dresses made of soft prints, and aprons. Bevy's grandmother loved to have her granddaughter come for a visit and seemed to enjoy my company as well.

There was one special time I will always remember. It was a soft summer evening. The day had been hot. A bright red sun was setting over what I gradually learned with excitement was a farm! Behind the house was a barn with a few cows and perhaps a horse. We loved to run through the barn and out the other side where the Booths had planted a small field of corn which was now shooting up in the summer twilight. Up and down the rows of corn we would run, hearing the baleful hoot-hoot-of owls somewhere beyond the farm when we stopped to catch our breath.

That evening after supper we went back out to run around in the fragrant summer night. The air was dark, damp and alive. Here and there the night was lit by the spontaneous, elusive sparks of lightening bugs, those black winged creatures of the dusk who magically shone their small beacons just before spreading their two slender black wings momentarily and rising into the air from your finger, disappearing into the night, unless one was skillful enough to trap them temporarily in a mason jar with leaves and blades of green grass!

Beside the barn were two long rows of rose bushes which Grandma Booth had planted. These flower beds were somewhat elevated from the green grass on dirt beds and the rose bushes were spaced well enough so that we could run between them without getting scratched. There were several colors but mostly deep reds, their wonderful perfume delighting us as we ran by, immersed in a game of tag or hide and seek.

But suddenly we stopped short. We stood in front of a low, long wooden structure we had never seen in the daylight before. There was a strange whirring sound coming from the odd building and light bulbs were strung all along the inside. As we crept inside, our bare feet left the damp evening grass for gravel. The soft whirring sound continued. Where was it coming from?

Bev and I walked cautiously down the low structure. It was warm inside and then we could see them! There were rows and rows of cages with inquisitive beady eyes looking down at the two little girls. Turkeys! There must have been about 100 of them. The whirring sound grew louder as we walked down the aisle. We would hear them rearranging their feathers as we passed and a few feathers flew as some became frightened and tried to take flight unsuccessfully from their cages. I could clearly see their red chins shaking as they admonished us. The chorus seemed to be getting louder and now that we knew they were turkeys we could hear the unmistakable sound of "Gobble! Gobble!" as we explored their domain. Feathers flew and we squealed with both fright and delight as we ran out the other end. We had made an amazing discovering.

"Those are our turkeys. We raise them," the tall figure in brown informed us pointedly as we fled from the shed.

 It was Bevy's grandfather. He was rather quiet and seldom spoke to us.

A final memory of that summer is a simple one I have always remembered. Bevy was somewhere else in the house. It was probably about 4 o'clock in the afternoon and I wandered into the kitchen to find Grandma Booth rolling pie dough. It was very hot.

As I watched her there making the pie, the whistle of a train could be heard, hooting far away in the distance. I saw her pause from her work, look up in a vague sort of way and whether she said the words to me or to herself, I didn't know. I will always remember them, for even a child of five perceived how much they conveyed as she said softly, but with a certain quiet finality, a note of love in her voice:

"That will be his train."

169

Nazareth Academy
Philadelphia, PA, 1950

My world of endless summers and neighborhood adventures changed abruptly.

"I *said*: 'Fold your papers in half down the middle, open them, put your name at the top right, then number your paper from 1 to 25, skipping one line between every number."

Whew! So confusing. Too many instructions. What to do first. I could see the dreaded dark shadow now floating down my aisle from the corner of my eye, inspecting the format for our Friday Spelling Test. I didn't dare look up. It paused menacingly by my desk. "I said skip a line, young lady, *and I mean skip a line!*"

My hand shook. My six-year old mind struggled with the stern commands. My perfectly starched white Peter Pan blouse began to sweat. I couldn't understand Sister Agatha's impatience with me. My mind froze. Tears came to my eyes. My throat burned. It was so personal, so intimidating.

Now the shadow was hovering over me.

"Skip a line between each word!!" she threatened, thumping my paper.

 Horribly embarrassed, I finally understood, changing my offensive format as the class waited.

The year was 1952. I was a first-grader in my first week at Nazareth Academy in Philadelphia. The nuns were relentless on structure, order and discipline. Their order had survived persecution under Hitler in Poland. Their extreme strictness was certainly the result of harrowing ordeals. In fact, while left alone waiting for my interview for admission in the massive stone Motherhouse, I saw a huge oil painting I would always remember, of nuns kneeling and praying in the bottom of a huge dirt pit with Nazi soldiers standing above them with machine guns.

Perfectly uniformed, we all lined up for recess. The lovely grounds had lots of oak trees, ivy and low stone walls. My grade school was a two story stone building, originally a stable for an estate. The picturesque old building was very hot, especially when an impatient, frightening figure in a long black robe with beads was scrutinizing your work.

"Time's up. Pencils down. Exchange papers with the student next to you. Incorrect words will be circled in red. Put the total *correct* in the

right hand top of the page. Number one: House. H-O-U-S-E. House."
And so it went.

"Pass all papers forward and Row Leaders, you know who you
are, pass them across. Now, papers and pencils away. Close your
desks. Stand up. Row 1, Row 2. Row 3. No talking. Single file!"

Time for recess. I shuddered as huge 7th and 8th grade boys
pushed by us, playing their noisy games, almost crushing members of
my class.

"Did you see that?" a little girl asked incredulously, looking up at a
second story window.

"What?" I asked.

"The box. There was a large box sitting in the window. It moved
away," she whispered.

"Really?"

"That was spooky. I bet it has something to do with Halloween!"
she said breathlessly.

The event was repeated the next day for us, at recess, at exactly
the same time. One minute we were watching a large box sitting on the
window sill of a classroom. The next minute it moved away. The
happening was a constant source of anticipation and mystery for us.

Then one day a wonderful event happened. A lively group of
popular girls always huddled together importantly during recess, talking
excitedly and making plans. My days were pretty predictable: I was
always outside the circle, busy avoiding being crushed by the older
boys or watching with my friend, waiting for the mysterious box to move
or levitate.

"Hi. We would like you to join our club." I looked behind me. No
one there. She must be speaking to me. One of the most popular girls
took my hand, ignoring my friend and led me up one of the hills where
her group was excitedly moving piles of crisp red, orange and yellow
leaves, making paths for their "Village".

"Just start making piles like this!" she said happily, gathering up a
pile of swirling leaves in her arms. The thrill of belonging, actually being
asked to join a group, remains with me to this day.

The most welcome time of the day was lunch.

"All right. Pencils down. Pass your papers up. Close your
workbooks. Row A stand. *Elliot, if I see that again, you're staying in!*"

We would walk in formation from our building to the Dining Hall of the Academy's college. Sitting at assigned seats with our lunch partners, we were served the inevitable "hoagies", complete with lettuce, bologna and tomatoes, every day. The menu never varied. Hoagies and a wax carton of white milk, chips on a good day.

Over time, I relaxed somewhat, no longer freezing when instructions were given. I derived the greatest pleasure discovering I could actually associate and recognize the names "Dick", Jane" and "Spot" in the cloth readers. I had broken the code. *I was reading!!!*

And then it happened. One day we were walking single file, girls first, on the pleasant walk through the grounds to lunch. A fantastic fall day, one of Pennsylvania's best. There were red maples, oaks, old hickory trees and towering elms so tall that they must have come from colonial days, their huge knarled trunks rising from the bright green moss and lawns along the path.

It was getting chilly now. Everyone wore their navy blue cardigan sweaters with the Nazareth Academy monogram. The colorful leaves scratched and swirled their way across our path.

"Eyes ahead and no talking. Frankie, that means *you* !!"

Three first grade classes, approximately 60 six year olds, made the daily pilgrimage to the Dining Hall. Everyone really enjoyed the 10 minute walk, a welcome break from the relentless emphasis on spelling, math and reading.

Everyday during our odyssey, Sister Agatha stopped the group halfway, both to and from the Dining Hall and counted heads. The ritual always took place by a designated large hedge. "Class Number 1, stop. Class Number 2, stop. Class Number 3, stop!" We would have stopped anyway. Then we would count out by numbers and move on.

On the day in question, I had just called out "10", relieved I wasn't higher up in the spectrum.

Then I saw it. I couldn't believe my eyes. Where did come from? There on the edge of the concrete path over was the largest, reddish leaf in the world!

"It must be a giant Tobacco Leaf!" I told myself. It was about 2 feet long and a deep red, totally unlike any leaf I had ever seen.

"Eyes forward. No talking." Did she mean me? I watched The Tobacco Leaf shift with the wind from the corner of my eye. Did no one else see this marvel?

"Move ahead. Stay in line. *John, leave her alone! Donald, if I see that again, it's Detention!!*"

Reluctantly I moved along with my class, in total disbelief.

The next day I couldn't wait for lunch. When Sister Agatha stopped to take the count, I held my breath and looked to my right. I must have just imagined the amazing sight yesterday. But there it was, looking even bigger and redder today! It had shifted position slightly.

"45." "46." "47."

"If I hear anymore talking up there we're going to stand here and count all day *and I mean <u>all day</u>.*"
If I could just step carefully out of line, I could reach that leaf. I told my parents about it the night before. There were no other leaves like it. How could a Tobacco Leaf that size wind up on the grounds of Nazareth Academy?? This wasn't just an ordinary leaf. It was magical. I would take it home. The prize would be mine.

"Eyes ahead. Single file!" The line lurched forward toward the Dining Hall.

I sat at my table with my hoagie, dreaming of The Tobacco Leaf.

"You sure are quiet today, Joanie, What's wrong?" the little girl across the table asked.

"Nothing!"

Maybe one of the bad boys would distract Sister Agatha and she would not notice me dart across the path and retrieve The Tobacco Leaf which now held mystical properties for me.

"Time's up! Clean up your lunch, milk cartons in Bin #1, food in Bin #2, trays on the counter!"

As we approached the hedge I held my breath. Would it be there? Could I dare retrieve it? I closed my eyes.

There it was. It had blown away from the hedge and was now lying by the stone wall, about 5 feet from our line. If I could just dart out and scoop it up.....

"I said '*Move!*'" I turned forward to see a large space between me and the girl in front. I quickly caught up.

That night in bed I could think of nothing else. The Tobacco Leaf was obviously getting larger each day. It was such a lovely shade of red. It was mythical, a powerful talisman. Tomorrow would be the day. I could hardly wait for the bus to arrive.

11:45 a.m. "Homework papers to the front. No name means *no credit!* Line up!" Eagerly I rounded the turn in the path, trying to move casually so as not to call attention to myself.

"14." "15. "16". Perfect. Innocently, I inspected my black and white saddle shoes, still new and stiff from the box. Sr. Agatha was now at the back of the line.

"Edwin, that's it. *Spitballs are not an option!!!*"

She was really mad now, really distracted. Nonchalantly I reached down, picking lint off my white knee high socks. So far, so good. Time passed. But now I couldn't move. My feet were stuck in concrete. Everything was going in slow-motion. I felt like a goldfish in an aquarium. I began to sweat.

"57." "58." "59."

I had to act quickly. Yes, this was it. *I was going to step out of line!* Run and grab that leaf. I'd be the envy of the school. Other kids' parents would stare in disbelief. Their parents would be calling my parents that evening, wanting to see the leaf. How would I protect it on the bus?

Now or never. I envisioned myself being caught: "Who is that moving up there? Did I see someone *dare* step out of line? And what do you think *you're* doing? *Say, what is that you have there???*

I didn't care. The spoils of victory were mine. I inhaled deeply. Slowly I turned my body. I took the first step out of line. What? Where is it? I looked up and down the bottom of the hedge. Along the stone wall. At the base of the oak trees.

The Tobacco Leaf was gone.

Breezy Point
Brooklyn, New York, 1952

Joan Flynn Beesley

I was a guest at 587 5th Street in Brooklyn in 1952, ten years after Michael Flynn died there in 1942. The narrow flint stone row houses each possessed small, square front porches overlooking the sidewalks, each approximately 12 feet square, with a small iron drain in the center. These structures were topped by cement ledges from which, they told me, the neighborhood boys of Brooklyn would leap from porch to porch, under the huge leafy oaks that lined the sidewalks of 5th Street all the way up the block to the famous, historical Prospect Park, a mammoth park with luxuriant trees and wonderful sledding hills. When my father and uncle were growing up this activity was a constant source of worry to my grandmother, Mary Flynn.

Brooklyn, 1952 was indeed a very special time and a special place for a six-year old girl traveling from Philadelphia to Brooklyn with her distinguished grandfather. The day finally arrived when my parents drove me from their beautiful new home in Philadelphia to meet my grandfather at the Michael Flynn Manufacturing Co. where my father worked. As early as I could remember, I knew my grandfather was president of the company founded by Michael Flynn, his father born in Ireland. I had always heard how Michael Flynn started a scrap business by collecting hawsers on the docks from all the immigrant ships arriving daily in New York Harbor in the early 1900's.

They told me the company had evolved from the scrap metal business in 1930 to a highly successful aluminum window business when they purchased the massive 11 acre factory of the bankrupt David E. Lupton Sons Window Company. During World War II, the government gave special contracts only to Reynolds Aluminum, Alcoa and The Michael Flynn Mfg. Co., allowing them to continue producing residential and commercial extrusions and fabricating, during the war. For the war effort, the company built metal airplane hangers in the United States and as far away as Peru.

My father told stories of accompanying his father down to the original scrap metal yard in lower Brooklyn where he played with old diving helmets and airplane propellers in the lot next to the office. The company had salvaged whole destroyers for scrap metal after the war. My Uncle Frank had actually gone out to Telluride to investigate scrapping parts of the narrow gauge railroad. They had even investigated battleships half-sunken by the atomic blast off Bikini Island to salvage for scrap metal for the business. After WWII, the Michael Flynn Company produced windows for skyscrapers and office buildings in New York, Philadelphia and other cities in the east. My childhood ears would always listen for remnants of wonderful stories about "The Company" from the elders at 587. How proud I was of it all!

My parents parked the car in front of "The Michael Flynn Manufacturing Co.", and led me up the steps and into the building where we were to meet my grandfather, past the receptionist window with block glass where the telephone operator, Margaret, would answer the phone with her melodic and pleasant "Michael <u>FLYNN</u> !"

"Why hello, there! I'll bet you're here to meet your grandfather, aren't you? I heard you're traveling back with him today to spend a week in Brooklyn!"

"Yes, I am." I felt so special. I was the granddaughter of the president of the company.

"Would you like to see the drafting office while we're waiting?" my father asked. I had been there several times before on Saturday mornings with him while he worked on finishing up a proposal or quote for a job. I had gone from desk to desk, drawing little ghosts on the draftsmen's jobs while waiting for him to finish his work, certain I would frighten them when they came to work on Monday morning. I liked the orderliness of the desks with their lamps, sheets of paper and pens and pencils all lined up and sharpened, ready to go.

Finally, my grandfather appeared, jovial and grand, very dignified in his dark grey pinstripe suit, white shirt and tie. Grandpa Flynn stood about six feet tall, an impeccable dresser whose shoes were always polished. He had a large desk in an office suitable for the company president. He always had time to talk and sing "Take Me Out to the Ballgame" and "If You Knew Susie" to a six year old girl calling him on the phone from her house in suburban Philadelphia.

"We'll catch the train in about an hour. Margaret will take us to the train station," he explained to my parents. "Your Grandma can't wait to see you. She can't believe we have you for a whole week!" This was the first time in my life I had been away from my parents, with all the dread and excitement that it meant.

On our way out, my grandfather paused at a large door marked **"PLANT"**. "I'll bet you've never seen the factory", he said. "Would you like to see it now?"

I nodded and he opened a door to what looked like a scene from Dante's inferno. I had to hold my ears from the loud screeching of machinery. As we walked along railed platforms, sparks flashed and metal grinded and squealed as aluminum and steel windows and extrusions were hoisted high above the factory floor, suspended on cables, then dipped into a giant, orange pit of molten liquid. It looked like a volcano. A train was moving slowing through the factory, squealing loudly on tracks embedded in the factory floor. It would be forever cast in my childhood memory as "The Noisy Room". I held onto my grandfather's hand as he spoke to my father and mother, discussing business. I had a remote sense of pride that this huge enterprise was somehow connected to me.

And so I said goodbye to my parents and left for the train station to Brooklyn with the president of the company, my grandfather, dignified yet approachable, balding with glasses, with his briefcase and "The New York Times" - proud, also to be taking his granddaughter home to Brooklyn with him for the week.

I remember the excitement of the trip. I had a window seat in the gray corduroy upholstered compartment and watched the suburbs and then the city of Philadelphia flying by, out the window. So many sights. And then a man in black came around, calling "Ice Cream. Cold Ice Cream!" and my grandfather bought us vanilla ice cream in small wax Dixie cups with blue and red snowmen on the side and round, cardboard lids you had to carefully pull up by the by the small tab. As I sat there next to the tall man in the grey suit and polished shoes, eating my ice cream with a small wooden flat spoon, I reflected what a lucky girl I was as the small towns flashed and rattled by.

We changed trains for Brooklyn at the huge white marble and brass palace that was Grand Central Station. Such energy and movement. Excited people going everywhere. And then, after a while, we emerged in Brooklyn itself and walked up the stairs to the 7th Avenue Station.

Brooklyn in the summer? How can you even begin to describe it. A little like Dorothy waking up in the Land of Oz. It was about five in the afternoon with people from the City returning home from their jobs, a gentle ebb and flow of pedestrians emerging from the subways below.

The sunlight refracted down through the huge oaks and green-fingered, wispy maples lining the sidewalks, casting a magical late-afternoon golden light on the strange architecture, brownstone and lighter flint stone row houses, as we passed. Yellow forsythia, the flower of Brooklyn, was in bloom. I could hear the comforting, rhythmic, "honk-honk" of cars, softly muted, echoing up through row house canyons.

I had been to 587 5th street several times as a child. But this was different. I was six now. I was in the company of the tall, distinguished figure in grey suit and hat, beside me, who effortlessly carried my suitcase in one hand and held my hand with the other.

As we walked up from the stores on 7th Avenue - Ebinger's Bakery, a fish store, a butcher shop, Tarzanian's Hardware - we passed an organ grinder in front of a drugstore on the corner with a small monkey in a uniform and cap, a sight I had never seen. Then we started the accent up 5th Street. My grandfather explained that Prospect Park itself was at the end of their block. They lived in an area called Park Slope, several blocks from the magnificent Grand Army Plaza arch and the Brooklyn Library. There was a soft note of pride in his voice as he explained these things.

As we made our way up 5th Street with other pedestrians coming home from jobs in New York City, there was an air of festivity in the air, a happy expectation of dinner and reuniting of families.

"Hello, Mr. Flynn", was repeated by several neighbors, taking the air on their concrete stoops.

"Good afternoon, Mrs. Kelly. I'd like you to meet my little granddaughter from Philadelphia, Joan Ellen. She'll be staying with us for the week."

I looked up at Mrs. Kelly, sitting on the ledge of her brownstone near the door, in a casual cotton housedress or pinafore, worn by many women of the day.

"Tis hot today, Mr. Flynn."

"That it is, Mrs. Kelly."

"Take good care of that granddaughter of yours and remember me to Mrs. Flynn."

"That I will, Mrs. Kelly."

We continued up 5th street, crossed 6th Avenue, and then my grandfather announced,

"This is our block."

It was a shady street. Huge oak trees bordered the sidewalk and the street, making it nice and cool. A soft, late afternoon breeze was coming down from the Park. On our side of the street were all flint stone row houses, the lighter stone, with many darker brown stone homes across the street. Each flint stone home was connected, all having a large concrete porch which rose above the sidewalk with a row of concrete steps that lead up from the sidewalk to the front door.

"Do you remember which one it is, Joan Ellen?"

I couldn't tell. Each one looked massive and mysterious to me, all that stone, so different from our suburban ranch in Philadelphia.

"Well, it looks like Grandma is waiting for us."

I could hear the sound of pleasant anticipation in his businessman's voice. I strained to see what he saw from my position at his side. There, about five houses down, I saw a woman sitting on the ledge by the front door, brown chestnut hair done up in a thick braid around her head, wearing an apron, looking expectantly down the street as we made our way up the block.

As we climbed the concrete steps, my eyes took in the magnificently polished brass doorplate and elaborate in-laid brass handle on the door. Siren-red geraniums with velvety-green leaves sat proudly in their cement flower boxes as if to inform the caller that this was a residence of importance in the long row of Brooklyn flint stones. My grandmother set aside the bowl of string beans she had been snapping for dinner as my grandfather kissed her on the cheek and handed over his charge.

"We are just delighted to have you here with us, young lady," she said as she gave me a hug and kiss. Her warm brown Irish eyes sparkled. She was a handsome looking, stylish woman, slightly tan, wearing a soft pink lipstick. "We are going to have a wonderful week."

The entry to 587 5th Street was like none I have experienced since. The doorbell, when pressed, chimed a beautiful one-line greeting, a musical who-goes-there, a dignified, mellifluous statement acknowledging the presence of a caller. With its magnificent brass doorplate and doorknob, the front door was an extremely heavy, glass and mahogany affair which responded slowly to the push of a six-year-old girl. The perfect slowness and precision as it opened, made me think it rested on great ball-bearings, a stately machine, as it swung smoothly, slowly and grandly open.

The elegant exterior was equally matched by the interior of the home. I followed my grandparents past the china umbrella stand holding a large black umbrella with wooden handle, down the black and white tiled entry hall with the green border tiles. These were small tiles, not the kind you might think of today. The hall walls were made of highly polished brown mahogany. There was a huge grandfather clock with its heavy brass pendulum, ticking its soft heartbeat and marking the hour with its distinguished Big Ben refrain.

At the end of the hall one was greeted by a lovely dark red Victorian lamp, a deep rose silk affair with long fringe, casting a soft light in the dark entry hall. It had many long silken tassels which could be touched when no one was looking.

We came to the small living room with its mahogany walls and paintings by Jasper Cropsey and Charles Jacque, misty Hudson River landscapes and French countryside paintings, heavy dark green oil paintings with shiny patina and lots of sheep. That night my grandparents told me the story of how my great grandfather Michael Flynn had made his fortune, then crossed the Atlantic where he made friends with Cropsey and bought several of these paintings as well as beautiful diamonds in England to have made into earrings and later rings for the women of the Flynn family.

The living room had a fireplace on one wall with a fender that kept logs from rolling out and small folk away. Adults could rest their feet there while warming up. It had belonged to Michael Flynn as well. A green onyx clock ticked complacently on the mantle.

One end of the living room led back to a parlor room with exquisitely soft pink floral and lime green oriental rugs with white fringe that caressed the hardwood floor. Heavy brocade loveseats in mint green and dark pink lined the room under an elaborate crystal teardrop chandelier. The parlor was seldom used. I have a memory of what had to be a funeral in that room. Among many large bouquets of fragrant flowers, I recall making my way among the legs of dark suits, shiny black shoes that kept walking over to a long box above me that must have been a coffin. Years later I would read that Michael Flynn was waked "at home", four years before I was born, and I would imagine this parlor room receiving many visitors to bid him farewell.

As my grandfather set my suitcase down, my curious eyes traveled along another wall of the living room, below the massive dark staircase. There was a small mahogany enclosure with a red brocade curtain that half hid a red velvet cushioned built-in love seat. It had an Oriental or Turkish feeling and I know today that many well-to-do

Victorians built this type of mysterious Turkish alcove for rest or reading. New York travelers visiting the Mediterranean tried to replicate this popular exotic design in their homes, finishing the space with ferns and potted plants. It was very much the fashion in the early 1900's and can be seen in many photographs of the time. As I followed my grandparents through the living room I definitely knew I wanted to spend time in that special place!

Next we entered the dining room with its huge dining room table under an elaborate canopy lamp suspended above the table, almost its total length, giving the table and its embroidered Madeira beige tablecloth a feeling of intimacy and importance. I paused to look at an oil portrait of a horse's profile in an elaborate gilt frame of acorns and leaves.

"Do you know who that is?" my grandfather asked. "That is Rat-a-Plan. He was my father's race horse. He was very fond of him and one day had his portrait done. He called him "Rat-A-Plan" because of the sound he made when he ran."

I felt very important. A small emissary from my parents back in Philadelphia, my grandparents taking the time to confide and explain family lore and secrets. As we walked through the dining room, my eager eyes took in the small alleyway, separating my grandparent's home from the brownstone next door, through the soft white curtains gently shifting with the summer afternoon breeze from the park. An aqua and cream colored picket fence separated the two properties.

I followed my grandmother from the dining room through a narrow pantry which contained a small "Frigidaire" on one side and a counter and high glass cabinets on the other side. Her small pumps click-clacked amiably over the linoleum floor as I followed her into the heart of her home, the kitchen.

The black and white linoleum floor had a large red star in the center. There was an enormous white enamel stove named "Roper" and a large white-curtained window at the end of the room, above the radiator, and next to it a built-in cabinet with glass shelves and counter which held a huge scotch-tape dispenser.

Looking through the curtains at the rear of the kitchen, I gazed down into the square backyard with high flowerbeds around the perimeter. It had a formal, narrow concrete path around a center square area of flower-beds, a kind of English garden in a small shady Brooklyn backyard.

The kitchen table, with its red vinyl chairs, was placed by a window looking out above the cream and aqua picket fence, providing a glimpse of the gardened backyard of the house next door. Soft white nylon curtains moved in the breeze. Pert bamboo placemats on the colorful embroidered table cloth told me all was well in this kitchen. A soft pastel mosaic looked down from the kitchen wall above the table, a festive scene of a Mexican village coming to life in the morning.

Suspended in a golden cage by the window, a small yellow canary chirped happily as my grandmother ran the tip of her summer-pink, well-manicured fingernail across the metal rungs.

"Petey's glad you're here, too," my grandmother explained. "We'll be eating in an hour. Let's go up and get you settled."

My grandmother led me back through the dining room with its dark paneling, dark brown ceilings and ornate gold crown molding into the living room with its mysterious Turkish nook and up the stairs to the second floor of the brown stone.

587 was actually a very deep, narrow dwelling of 3 floors joined by a spine of plush, red velvet carpet staircase on each floor, very still and dark, flanked by deep brown walls and modernized gas lights now lit by small electric bulbs. There was a carved banister with an ornate, heavy square lid you passed at the landing as you ascended the stairway. I later learned it could be lifted off by its knob, and many a marble and other toys had been nonchalantly dropped down into the bowels of the banister by my father and his brother, my Uncle Frank when growing up.

At the top of the red velvet stairs was a long dark hall connecting the back with the front of the house. At the back of the house where we stood was my grandfather's study with his easy chair, beige leather hassock, two paintings by Gainsborough, a bookcase with books and a radio, and a TV. At the rear of the study were 3 small steps leading up and then back down to a very small room, the back-study, where my grandfather, Michael Flynn, had spent the last of his years confined to his bed with terminal arthritis. There was a wooden pedestal with a ceremonial brass plate, "The Michael Flynn Manufacturing Company" it read.

Leaving the rear of the house we proceeded down the dark and luxurious hallway towards the front of the home and my grandparents' bedroom. It was an elegant room with chintz rose floral cushions all along a window seat that ran the entire wall. Later in life I would learn they were replicas of FDR's upholstery in Hyde Park. Beyond were white-curtained tall windows which looked out over 5th street below.

"You and I will be sleeping here and Grandpa will take the guestroom while you're here," my grandmother explained as she lay my suitcase on one of two twin beds.

The beds were somewhat high with ornate white satin and chenille spreads and intricately-carved mahogany headboards rising in a semicircle over the beds. Between the two beds was a night-table with a lace cloth and beautiful china lamp in the shape of a woman dressed as a French aristocrat.

Mary Flynn was about 5 feet, 2 inches tall, the oldest of 10 children. She told me her parents came from Ireland and her father had managed horses for an emporium in Brooklyn. As she unpacked and laid my carefully selected summer outfits on the bed, she showed me a little stool to climb up into bed that night. Over her bed was a circular painting or "tondo" as they were called, of *Madonna della Sedia* by Raphael. *The Madonna of the Chair*, I would learn much later in life, was a copy of the original done by one of Raphael's followers.

My six-year old eyes traveled the room as she unpacked, taking in her beautiful mahogany dresser with beige lace dresser scarf, silver hairbrush and hand mirror and silver tortoise-shell comb. There were several fancy bottles of perfume with glass stoppers displayed on a mirrored tray. But what really caught my eye was a dark passageway at the rear of their bedroom.

The passageway began with intricate dark rosewood lattice work in the shape of birds and flowers. Right inside was an upright round white porcelain sink with men's shaving equipment and toiletries laid out. Further down the passage were many dark wooden cabinets and drawers. It had a musty, exotic, camphor scent, full of mysteries.

"That passageway leads all the way back to Grandpa's study. It is where he shaves each morning. You may hear him tomorrow. Grandpa always wakes up early, shaves and then goes down to squeeze the orange juice," she explained.

Looking back, it was a different time, when life was to be enjoyed. It had a certain rhythm or cadence, with long-established customs and traditions, courtesies and sensibilities.

"You may visit with Grandpa in his study if you wish. I'll be calling you both for dinner in about an hour," she said as led me into the study where Grandpa was reading The New York Times in his easy chair. He folded his paper, laying it down on the leather hassock in front of his chair.

"I bet you think those are books over there in my bookcase, don't you?" he asked, smiling. They certainly looked like books to me. Grandpa walked over to the bookcase and opened the leather "books" to reveal a radio inside. He showed me around the room, explaining many interesting objects including a gold barometer which told the weather, a secretary which opened, holding important papers, and lastly, a ticker-tape machine which spewed out odd-looking tape with holes.

"If you know how to read this, you can keep track of your investments," he explained matter-of-factly to me, showing me an example of a company stock symbol and what it was worth that very minute. He was very deferential to me, talking to me as an adult. Having only sons, my father and my Uncle Frank, I sensed having a granddaughter to talk to was very special to him. He took great pains to explain things to me.

Finally it was time for dinner. My grandfather took his seat at the head of the table, the canopy chandelier glowing above the beautifully set table, my grandmother's Desert Rose Franciscanware accompanied by her heavy, monogrammed silver. My grandmother hurried back and forth through the pantry way into the kitchen, her low-heeled pumps happily marking time on the linoleum floor, serving the family favorite, baked potatoes, green peas fresh from the pod that afternoon, and meat cakes. No one in the world could make meat cakes like my grandmother.

"The Irish made these with bread so as to make the meat go further," she explained to me. They were made with hamburger meat, onions, egg, salt and pepper, cooked in butter and were absolutely delicious. Her baked potatoes were always wonderful as well. When I became a teenager I would one day hear the family joke about "saving the tin foil from your baked potato," presumably for the scrap metal business, when out at a restaurant!

We had strawberry shortcake for desert with whipped cream made from real cream. While the three of us talked at dinner about my life in Philadelphia and plans for my week in Brooklyn, I learned that once the large dining room table held many other people, including my father, his brother, my Uncle Frank, and my great grandfather, and that there had once been Irish boarders and servants in the house.

After dinner, my grandfather retired to his study upstairs to watch the Brooklyn Dodgers play at Ebbetts Field on TV. I worked at my grandmother's side by the sink. She tied one of her aprons around me and together we did the dishes, she washing the beautiful pink Franciscanware in the warm sudsy water, then laying the pieces on a dishcloth for me to dry and stack, to put away with the sparkling silver.

I struggled to keep up with her efficiency, to properly dry each piece. "When I was a young girl of twelve, I delivered hats. I was called to deliver a hat one day to your Grandfather's mother. I rang the bell and they were eating dinner.

'Which one of my sons would you like?' she said. I picked your grandfather because he was wearing a fancy uniform from his school," she informed me. Thinking back, I realize now they were choosing to share with me some of the most intimate events of their lives, although they were private people, not prone to discussing their emotions. They reported these things in a formal way, as I recollect now, so touching to remember, sharing information, informing me of matters they felt I was entitled to know.

During the week, I was to learn more from my grandmother, about the pony-cart that pulled my grandfather and his brother Charlie through Prospect Park when they were growing up at the turn of the century, which now I realized, must have been owned by Michael Flynn. I treasured every bit of information she shared with me.

The dishes done, we took off our aprons and Grandma put the cover over Petey's cage so he would go to sleep. We watched the ballgame with Grandpa in his study until it was time for bed. That evening I watched Grandma take down her beautiful chestnut hair and braid it into a long, thick braid as she sat on the edge of her bed. After she made sure I said my prayers, she said her rosary silently by her bed with a beautiful rosary made of gold. Using the stool, I climbed up into the twin mahogany bed with the satin sheets next to hers and dreamed of the week to come, believing I was the luckiest little girl in the world.

The next morning I awakened to the soft hum of an electric razor and remembered my grandfather would be doing his morning toiletry in the passageway behind the mysterious rosewood screen. I fell asleep, to be wakened again, this time by the sound of a man calling "Veg-tables! Fresh Veg-tables!"

Going to the window seat with the rose-printed chintz cushions and soft white curtains, I looked down on 5th Street to see a man with a mustache beside a large brown horse pulling a wooden wagon with "Fresh Vegetables" in gold letters on the side of a wagon, piled high with corn, watermelons, lettuce, tomatoes and other vegetables. I climbed back into bed, listening to the Fresh Vegetable Man and the ebb and flow of his melodic announcement as he made his way up to Prospect Park, one of my earliest memories of the rhythms of Brooklyn.

Somewhat later I was awakened by my grandmother. Putting on one of my new summer outfits, I came down to my place at her kitchen table near the window, a glass of my grandfather's wonderful fresh-squeezed orange juice near my placemat. My grandfather explained he would be going into the New York office today, which was a Friday.

"And tomorrow, we will be going to the beach!"

Later that morning, I accompanied my grandmother on the subway to Abraham & Strauss's or "A&S's" and to Best & Co. in New York where Grandma tried on hats for a wedding. She loved hats and had many beautiful flowered ones which she stored in fancy striped hat boxes in her closet. Women in the department stores knew her by name as did the hostess at Shrafft's in New York where we had lunch. I was her granddaughter from Philadelphia and she seemed to love introducing me to everyone she knew. Years later I would reflect that Mary Flynn was blessed with two boys but never a daughter.

We took a bus from the subway to Seventh Avenue.

"Just wait 'til we get home. I can slip off my heels and put on flats and make us something nice," she confided to me.

"But first I want to stop on Seventh Avenue and pick up some things I need."

I knew 5th Street sloped grandly down from Prospect Park to 8th Avenue, then another beautiful residential block, then to 7th Avenue with its plethora of small shops. Beyond this, 5th Street kept going forever, it seemed, beyond 7th Avenue and eventually down the whole length of Brooklyn towards the East River and New York. I had never been beyond 7th Avenue where my grandmother did all her grocery shopping.

She always went on foot. During my week there, I would accompany her to specific stores where individual merchants knew her name and what she liked to buy. They seemed sincerely delighted to meet her small granddaughter from Philadelphia.

There was the butcher, John, pork loins and sausages hanging in the air from a blue wire over his white enamel cases of meat.

"John, give me your best cut of veal. I want it lean, John. By the way, I want you to meet my granddaughter, Joan Ellen, from Philadelphia. She'll be staying with us for the week. And give me four chicken breasts as well."

John asked me all about Philadelphia and my school while he wrapped my grandmother's purchases in stiff white paper from a huge roll.

"Shall I put it on your account, Mrs. Flynn?"

"Please, John, and thank you very much."

All the merchants were very differential to my grandmother. She was very courteous, but also had a dignified, non-nonsense manner when it came to her purchases.

Next we visited Ebinger's Bakery, where the long line moved slowly, allowing customers to view loaves of bread displayed in the white enamel and glass cases next to them, enjoying the warm aromas of bread, cookies and pastries rising from ovens in the back of the store. Young women in white uniforms and hair nets waited on customers, wrapping blueberry muffins in white waxed paper for my grandmother and crisply tying the package using blue string from a huge ball with sharp hook for cutting, suspended above the marble counter.

"Anna, this is my little granddaughter from Philadelphia who will be staying with us this week," my grandmother explained to the young Irish woman at the counter.

"And pleased I am to make your acquaintance, young lady, and I would be even more pleased if you would try one of me oatmeal cookies just out of the oven!"

Returning to Philadelphia was going to be hard at the end of the week.

We stopped at the liquor store where my grandmother introduced me to "Frank" and had some things "sent around." Frank had just come back from a Florida vacation and presented me with a small pink purse decorated with seashells. I recall looking up at all the mysterious bottles along the walls of the store.

Finally we turned into the pungent "Fish Store" as my six year old mind thought of it, a long narrow entrance, thick with mounds of sawdust, spread along its wooden floors. As we entered a little bell over the door rang amiably, signaling a customer had arrived. As we waited,

I was at eye level, literally, with all types of salmon, perch, flounder, shrimp, packed on ice in long white display cases, staring back unblinking and hopelessly at me with their cold silvery scales and motionless gills.

"Mrs. Flynn, so nice to see you."

A man and his son in blood-stained aprons emerged from the curtained rear of the store to their place behind the long display case. Again, the merchants seemed to treat Mary Flynn with great respect when she did her shopping. They all took meticulous care to see that she was well-satisfied with her purchases. Her requests were always very courteous yet precise and exacting, explicit in her quiet way.

"Hello John. How are your crab cakes today?"

When my grandmother was assured the crab cakes were good, she ordered a dozen and several filets of sole.

"John, I think I'll also have some of your herring and two pounds of shrimp for the beach tomorrow." Then the man would select what my grandmother requested, showing it up close to her for her inspection.

"Those will be fine, John."

Then he deftly wrapped her purchases in white wax paper from a big roll and reach up over his head to a big ball of white string, tying the package with a flourish. She would pay the man from her red leather wallet. Then my grandmother would present me, her business concluded.

"By the way, I'd like you to meet my little granddaughter, Joan Ellen. She's visiting me from Philadelphia."

"Well, we're having good beach weather this week, Mrs. Flynn. And I hope you have a great time with your grandmother, little miss." Then we would leave, the little bell announcing our business there was over and we were on our way with the purchase.

I enjoyed meeting each and every one of the 7th Avenue merchants, listening to my grandmother's requests and how they strove to please her. I experienced the environs of wonderful small Brooklyn neighborhood establishments and how they worked.

Later I accompanied my grandmother to the drugstore on the corner, a small old-fashioned store with a wooden floor and ancient smells. The store had a white shingle out front with black letters and you entered it oddly, from an angle as if the door had been forgotten and then placed at the front corner of the building.

There was quite a display of large, exotically-shaped, ornate glass containers in the window filled with authoritative deep azure, jade green, potent red, and honey-yellow elixirs. There were all kinds of interesting items and scents in the drug store, but the purpose of our trip, I was told, was to buy sunscreen for me and a plastic pail and shovel, metal sand strainer and "forms" to make molds in the sand.

I liked the store because it also had a small toy section. It was here that I discovered Trading Cards. I remember the first time I saw them. Trading Cards were quite a phenomenon in my youth. To my six year old mind they were real treasures. You could buy them in packs of twenty for about a dime.

You never knew what you'd get. Interesting packs included landscapes, animals, cottages, cars, trains, movie stars and even calendar girls, sitting on traveling trunks, swinging their long, nylon legs. We divided our trading cards, which were the size of playing cards, into categories, Houses or Cottages, Glamour Girls, Animals, Nature Scenes, Transportation, etc. Where these cards came from, I'll never know and why someone hasn't remembered how little girls loved them back then and made a fortune today, I'll also never know. Many women are by nature, good analyzers. We love to sort and categorize things, and I think much of my skill in doing this activity came from Trading Cards. Perhaps it was the satisfaction of imposing order and control.

We would always trade in a category, asking to see someone's collection of Cottages, for example. Usually there was a cottage in every pack you would buy, an English or American variety, probably printed from early American or English landscapes.

I remember one such cottage. It was my favorite and every time I looked at it, it seemed prettier and more perfect than the last time I pulled it out. It was a card I would never trade or part with. It was a colorful picture of an ivy-colored cottage. The lights in the cottage glowed within. There was a brick path leading from the front door and a stone fence bordering it with lots of flowers and trees.

In the Glamour Girls part of my collection, there were pin-up girls, probably influenced by the Betty Grable era of WWII. My parents were married in 1945 and so the war, or their memories of it, were part of my childhood. Usually the Glamour Girl was sitting on a trunk or piece of furniture with platform shoes, fishnet stockings with a short dress, her hair in a chignon, and a big smile. Or she would have her hands on her hips and be smiling at you from over her shoulder.

Sometimes we would trade for a prettier Glamour Girl or trade a Cottage for a Glamour Girl, depending on what we needed. In our way, we slowly learned what was important to our partner and to use this information to get the best deal or card for our collection.

The really fun part of all of this was trading up or working to have the best collection in the neighborhood in one of the categories. Then there was the fun of buying new cards because you never knew what would be in the pack. There always seemed to be fresh cards. It was very rare that you ever had two of a kind. I often wondered where all these cards came from and how they kept a constant flow of fresh cards in the store.

When you bought a new pack of trading cards it was exciting. You took off the cellophane wrapper and then looked at each of the cards to see how they would enhance the categories in your collection. Some of the cottages were very beautiful. Occasionally you had a pair of cards. One of my favorite pairs was a mosaic of birds in a tree. They had come into my collection from different purchased packs. They were two distinct pictures, colored differently, but each had the same unique style, the mosaic, and were considered a pair, a rare occurrence and highly prized.

I remember losing, at one point, one of the mosaics, and was hopeful, upon opening every new pack, that a new mosaic, by the same artist, would someday be staring me in the face. But it never did. And, over time, I eventually also misplaced the card with the little cottage with the lighted lantern by the brick path that invited you into the picture. It was so lovely. I never found anything to quite match that trading card, but you never knew what you would find when you opened a new pack.

That summer I accumulated quite a collection, ultimately trading with my friends back in Philadelphia, building up our collections. We would sit in a circle on the grass with lemonade and trade back and forth, increasing the size of certain sets that we favored. My favorites were mosaic cards (if you looked closely you could see animals in the designs) and thatched cottages, very similar to Thomas Kinkade cottages of today. I used to fantasize about living in them. And nothing felt better than knowing my collection of three hundred cards was all organized into sets, each with its own rubber band.

My grandmother would take my hand as we walked home from 7th Avenue, under the leafy canopy that was 5th Street, the sidewalks lined with enormous oak trees. Neighborhood children I didn't know by name played games I didn't know in the streets. The continuous brownstones that lined either side of 5th Street created a sort of echoing tunnel that magnified the delighted cries of children at play as they darted noisily around the cars parked on both sides of the street. The tunnel effect also amplified the sounds of the night, sirens and conversations that would waft their way up to a sleepy granddaughter from Philadelphia secure in the twin bed of her grandmother's beautiful bedroom.

During the week I learned the secrets of 587 5th street. Following my grandmother down a linoleum circular stairway, I watched her do laundry in her spotless laundry room with Ivory flakes, a wash tub and an old-fashioned wringer apparatus with a red handle through which she rung clean wet clothes before hanging them on a single white clothes line to dry, there in the basement. She had an ironing board and an oversized, heavy iron.

I also had the opportunity to see a coal bin and actually met The Coal Man, who pulled up in front of 587 one morning in a big truck full of coal. Each of the row houses had a small walkway between each house, leading to a side door in the basement and it was here The Coal Man delivered his wheel barrow of coal. He asked me to stand back as I watched him shovel pieces of black coal from a pile next to his truck into the wheel barrow for the delivery.

"Stand back now, Miss! This here is *dirty* work!!" he told me with a big smile. This was something I had never seen and I had great curiosity about the entire project.

Looking back on this time and in that household, I recall that everything was done well, with a certain grace and finesse. A properness. It was a stately house, with an Irish cleaning lady who wore a white uniform and cleaned, polished Grandma's silver, dusting the furniture, changing the bed linens.

There was a small picture on a table near the fireplace. A somewhat heavy, serious-looking woman whom I was told was "Grandma Flynn" in a high white collared blouse and a broach, thick dark hair piled on top of her head, wearing a large black-rimmed hat. A black and white picture, but you could tell she had great coloring. Thinking back, she must have been Mary Anne Flynn, wife of Michael Flynn, my great-grandfather, both of whom were in their forties with three children that included my grandfather, at the time of the 1900 Brooklyn census.

One afternoon Grandma opened a closet in the dining room and pulling on the metal chain above, exposed all kinds of treasures. My favorite was a heavy, round mahogany chip-holder which turned smoothly on ball-bearings and had about a dozen vertical slots for holding chips. The chips were red, white and navy blue round tiles with imprints of race horses and four-leaf clovers on them. Playing with it on the floor, I could spin the chip holder very fast so that it hummed, making a pleasant low whirring sound. I could imagine the spirited card games played at the large dining room table between my grandmother's ten brothers and sisters. Through the years, I held onto several of the chips which I kept in my jewelry box.

Sometimes I would go into the parlor, or "front room", as my Grandmother called it, the ornate sitting room with its pink and pale green tasseled Oriental rug that seemed to embrace the hardwood floor. From the red satin brocade Victorian couch below the window, I sometimes peeked through the white sheers out onto the street. Over time I would see a group of neighborhood children-loud, dirty and noisy-having the time of their lives, playing endless games in the street below or hiding from one another in the dark recesses and secret places of the brownstones across the street.

And on one especially hot afternoon, I watched as they opened a fire hydrant, rejoicing in the huge, glorious plume of water that filled the street. Eventually I came to know the leaders, ones the younger children would follow, loud, lusty kids of the neighborhood, who never saw the little girl peeking behind the white curtains, eagerly watching their antics and exploits in the street.

That night I lay in the safety of the high twin bed with the ornate circular mahogany headboard while my grandmother again undid her long chestnut hair which she wore in a braid held by several tortoise-shell combs. She brushed her hair with a heavy silver hairbrush and then deftly braided it into a long thick braid down her back. Having said her evening prayers with the beautiful rosary made of gold, she turned out the lamp on the bed stand between our beds.

I lay there taking in the sounds of the 1950's Brooklyn night. So very different from the crickets and owls I heard at night in the wooded suburbs of Philadelphia. I heard the sound of rough voices down on the street, laughing and talking. They seemed to get closer and then drift away.

"What is that, Grandma?" I asked.

"Don't worry, dear, just the sound of boys coming down from the Park. Go to sleep now. Tomorrow will be a Beach Day."

"Joan Ellen, time to get up!" my grandmother said cheerfully, standing in the doorway of her bedroom at 587 5th Street.

I looked out the window. In the cool Brooklyn morning of 1952, people were going about their business on the quiet street below. Welcoming scents of toast and bacon came from the kitchen as I showered, dressed and made my way downstairs through the ornate, Victorian, turn-of-the-century home.

"Tucker will be bringing the car around in about an hour," she explained, bringing me eggs and bacon as I sat at her cheerful kitchen table.

The white nylon curtains shifted themselves softly in the cool morning breeze. The canary, Petey, a small, nervous soft-yellow creature, scampered endlessly, jumping from post to post in his brass cage above the table.

Grandma explained that instead of parking in the crowded street, they stored their car in a garage around the corner and had it brought around when they were going out.

"I have a few things to pack for the beach. When you're finished, why don't you go to the front room and watch for Tucker," she said, untying her apron and folding it over a chair.

Soon I sat on her red Victorian couch, my beach bag and bathing suit ready to go. Looking out the front window, I admired my grandmother's siren red geraniums gracing her two front windows, blooming contentedly in their ornate cement window boxes. No sign of Tucker. I did see a beautiful teal blue Lincoln Continental come gliding to a stop in front of 587, announcing its arrival with a soft honk-honk.

"That will be Tucker. Frank, are you ready to go?" my grandmother called and in another minute we were locking up the front door and heading down the cool stoop and into the car.

"Good morning, Mr. Flynn."

"Good morning, Tucker."

"You watch those Dodgers lose again last night, sir?"

"That I did, Tucker. There's absolutely no hope for them."

Tucker lifted himself from the driver's seat and put our beach bags and ice chest into the trunk. He was an enormous Afro-American man, very quiet and deferential to my grandparents.

He sat in the front of the car beside my grandfather with my grandmother and I in the back. This was the most beautiful car my six-year old eyes had ever seen, with its light velvet blue and silver interior with an arm rest between the seats in the back. We drove Tucker around to the big old-fashioned working garage where luxury cars were serviced and maintained and stored safely from the street.

"Frank, there are a few things I need to pick up," my grandmother announced and soon she and I were in the 7th Street Deli.

It was a beautiful Brooklyn morning. A cat crouched lazily in the corner of the tiled floor as sun streamed in through the deli windows.

"Al, give me two pounds of shaved turkey - I want it thin, Al - sweet pickles, a half pound of liverwurst, six Kaiser rolls and a pound of your German potato salad and, Joan Ellen, do you like tapioca? Yes, so do I. And a pound of your tapioca, Al. Also, give me a bit of your pound cake there. And we should be good with that, Al. We're going to the beach today."

"Should be a fine day, Mrs. Flynn. Here's your order. Do you need help out to the car?"

"No. Joan Ellen and I can manage, thank you."

And out to the car we went. Soon we drove a few blocks from my grandmother's neighborhood to pick up my Aunt Frances, one of her sisters. Aunt Frances lived in a large stucco ground floor apartment with a big green awning with brass poles out front. The cold lobby was all green marble with a gold chandelier and a large table with a formal floral arrangement. It always seemed somewhat lonely to me. My grandmother rang Aunt Francis's door which was right up some steps from the lobby. An attractive, lively woman with blue eyes, short blond hair and freckles opened the door, first unhooking a clanking brass chain.

"All set, Mary!" she said cheerfully.

Our voices echoed as we set off across the lobby and into the waiting car. Later during the week, Aunt Francis told me the story of how her husband had run away with the secretary in his office.

"But my seams were always straighter than hers!" she explained to her grand-niece ruefully.

Aunt Francis sat next to me in the back with my grandparents in the front. We left the Prospect Park area and drove up Flatbush Ave. to another part of Brooklyn to pick up my Aunt Helen, another one of Grandma's sisters.

Helen was also a diminutive woman, with short, graying brown hair and heavy, silver rimmed glasses on a chain. She was also very lively and quite a bit of fun. She lived with her husband, Greg, on the second floor of a home in an old, but well-kept neighborhood. Later that week we would drive back around in the evening where Grandma, Aunt Helen and I went to a corner restaurant to try something an Italian restaurant was introducing.

"How do you like it? It's something new called "pizza."" my aunt informed me as I ate my first slice of cheese and tomato pizza.

"It's good," I told her.

"Well, I don't think it will ever make it, it's too hard to eat!" my aunt had complained.

❧

Soon, my grandmother collected her sisters and Helen's husband, Greg, and we all headed out Flatbush Avenue, past Ebbet's Field, out towards Jamaica Bay. By the time we reached Floyd Bennett Field we were singing old Broadway show tunes at the top of our lungs. Floyd Bennett Field always intrigued me with its huge hangers, windsocks and aircraft. The older people had a special regard for Floyd Bennett.

We sped past the landfill and stopped to pay our toll at the base of the huge Marine Bridge that spanned Jamaica Bay, separating Brooklyn from the Rockaway peninsula. It is a distinctive bridge with its two huge cylinders that can be seen for miles away. As we waited in line to pay our toll, red lights started to flash and there was a loud sound of grinding, squeaking metal. I watched in horror as a metal guard gate swung, clanging down in front of the cars before us. The road in front of them actually started to move vertically upward, making a groaning sound. Was it an earthquake?

"Don't be afraid," my Uncle Greg said. "This is a draw-bridge. See that large ship waiting over there? The draw-bridge opens all the time to allow tall ships to go through Jamaica Bay and out to sea."

To me it was a Colossus, an Eighth Wonder of the World. When the draw bridge was raised high enough to allow the ship to pass through, it appeared almost vertical to the mesmerized child of six.

Slowly the ship glided though, just like my uncle said. Then at a given signal, the motorized bridge clanked and jerked in motion, magically beginning its slow decent, returning to its horizontal position below, locking into place with a thud.

"Will it open up when we're crossing it?" I asked nervously.

"No, don't worry. That will never happen."

Still, when crossing Jamaica Bay, speeding high over the magnificent blue water, I would look out between its steel cables at the white seagulls boisterously announcing our arrival, praying the bridge would not start going up with us on it. Finally, we crossed the bridge and headed west from Jones Beach, out the Rockaway Peninsula.

Driving along the two lane road were beach houses, clapboard summer homes with awnings, boats parked alongside, front screened-porches, wooden boarded slats for sidewalks. A Catholic church, some small Irish social clubs, a few restaurants, a grocery store. And everywhere, white sand with small broken clam shells. Everything was aged, seasoned with timeless summer salt and sea breeze. It was simply the ultimate place to be in the summer: with Jamaica Bay on one side and glimpses of the massive Atlantic Ocean on the other. Seagulls dove in complicated formations, crying out in the air above us.

We were singing Irish classics as we turned into the Breezy Point Surf Club parking lot. We stopped at small white hut where an attendant in white uniform carefully punched a yellow membership card my grandfather took from his wallet.

"Your grandmother and I are the oldest living members this year," he confided to me softly.

Breezy Point Surf Club is the last structure on the long peninsula that extends out where Jamaica Bay and New York Harbor meet the Atlantic Ocean. We parked the car and entered the "original" cabin area through a large, white domed wooden building that served as a reception area. My grandfather carried the heavy ice-chest with ease. He wore a light grey, conservative summer business suit.

The cabins were all built on a board-walk arrangement high above the sand. I could smell the salt water in the wild ocean breeze and it was very exciting. My grandparents, Aunt Helen, Uncle Greg, Aunt Francis and I made our way along the grey wooden decks of Breezy Point Surf Club, awash with a quarter century of paint, sea-gulls crying out, circling in the windy blue sky above us as we walked. The place had an energy all its own.

Finally we reached the area where my grandmother, her sisters and their friends had their cabins, all in a row, side-by-side, opening to a big deck facing Jamaica Bay. We took turns changing in the small, closet-shaped cabins which had a double door, the top half of which swung open. It had a half moon in it. The door latched with a little hook.

"Don't worry, dear. It's safe to change. No one will walk in on you!" my grandmother reassured me as she latched the hook from the outside.

It was musty and somewhat dark in there. Gradually my eyes adjusted to see women's stylish skirted bathing suits and rubber bathing caps with colorful flowers hanging from wooden pegs along the walls.

There was a little seat in the rear of the cabin to sit while changing. There was a small ledge, covered in flowered contact paper, for holding cokes, ham, Swiss cheese, onion roles, German potato salad, pickles, potato chips and paper plates for sandwiches. There was a high shelf with bottles labeled "Tonic Water", "Gin" and "Vodka", some with colorful, whimsical bottle stoppers. There were playing cards for canasta, wooden playing chips, suntan lotion, a large canvas beach umbrella in the corner, a banjo and an accordion. The locker had a wonderful old musty smell of canvas, suntan oil, good times with good friends.

For countless years, my grandparents had come to this place, socializing on the weekends: Saturday night barbecues with baked potatoes and corn-on-the-cob, wrapped in tin foil and buried in the sand when done to keep them warm. I was lucky enough to experience a Saturday night at Breezy when the men would grill steaks on small grills and everyone would sit around on canvas chairs and wooden benches, enjoying the cool of the evening. The drinks would flow. Before long Uncle Greg had his ukulele out and everyone would sing Irish and early New York show tunes as if they were members of the cast.

One rainy Saturday night, my cousin Eddie Reece, who was Aunt Francis's son, played the accordion as we ate deliciously buttered corn-on-the-cob and potato salad on paper plates, in and between the cabins. Singing along to such wonderful old songs, no one really cared about the downpour.

That summer, the brilliant summer sun, fresh salt air, and the noisy Breezy Point sea gulls, specially-trained to spot a good sandwich left behind, all worked their magic against the cobalt sky, delighting the six year-old grandchild from Philadelphia. After we all changed into our bathing suits and put on sun-tan oil, Grandpa would put up their table and secure the big beach umbrella in its hole in the deck. Grandma would make our sandwiches, and their frosty gin and tonics. She and her sisters would play canasta at their table under the big canvas umbrella.

I would watch the college boys from Fordham come down our way from the Ice House, toting large blocks of ice for drinks, which they carried with giant tongs. How handsome they were with their tanned, hairy legs, kaki Bermuda shorts and cute navy blue Fordham tee shirts with white lettering!

My grandfather would soon settle into his striped canvas lounge chair, listening to the Brooklyn Dodgers lose yet another one on his small red transistor radio, a fairly new innovation. "The bums just lost another one!" he would call to my Uncle Greg, feigning disgust at the team he loved.

Years later, my grandparents would take me to the window of a luxurious apartment they had moved to while I was in college, 35 Prospect Park West, right across from Prospect Park. They opened the window, the white curtains stirring in the summer breeze. "Listen," they told me. I could hear the crack of a bat and the roar of a crowd in the distance. "That's Ebbett's Field you're hearing. There, on the other side of the Park," they explained simply, their voices filled with a tone of reverence and respect.

I simply loved this place and I hadn't even been down to the ocean yet! I strolled around the deck, listening to the click-click of the deeply-tanned elderly Italian men playing bocce on the long, dark-sanded courts near my grandparents' cabin.

I was standing along the wooden rail, looking at the beautiful blue water of Jamaica Bay and the draw bridge, proudly arching itself in the distance. I had a superior sense of now knowing its secrets.

"If you look really hard across the Bay, you can see the Empire State Building," a soft, older voice said behind me.

It was my uncle Greg, in his swim trunks and sandals. His skin was old and tanned from many summers at Breezy, his white-haired chest glistening with coconut oil. He wore thick glasses and was fairly quiet, but was the life of the party when he brought out his banjo on Saturday nights.

There, very faintly in the distance, I saw what I now know is the

Manhattan skyline as seen from the furthest point of Brooklyn. And there, the tallest building by far, stood the Empire State Building in its stately majesty. It was a very clear day, clear enough to see New York City across all of Brooklyn.

"See those parachutes?" Uncle Greg asked, as he pointed to an area at the end of the land, west across Jamaica Bay.

"That's Coney Island." he explained with a proud finality to his voice.

"I believe your grandmother has plans to take you there during your visit," he said secretively.

I felt like royalty. A visiting princess.

I spent some time alone on the deck, trying to figure out what was below, looking through the knot holes in the wood, at the broken sea shells and myriad of bottle caps. I roamed the adjacent deck areas to the Ladies Room, with its soap dishes, sinks, complicated, ancient liquid metal soap dispensers. The weathered restroom had been freshly painted this season, the most recent of many decades of heavy white paint. There was an industrial antiseptic odor coming from the stalls whose creaking doors were kept closed by a simple latched hook.

"Hello, Miss," a white uniformed janitress said.

"Hello" I said quietly as I washed my hands, feeling privileged, guilty and yet delightfully lucky.

Going out the swinging door of the Ladies Room, I investigated the other cabin decks, looking for someone my own age in this world of older people. I noticed a man sitting alone on a set of wooden steps, leading down to the large sand lots that separated the cabin "neighborhoods."

"Hi. How are you today?" I ventured, cheerfully trying out my new social skills by meeting people.

He seemed to be in his forties, with curly black hair, flip-flops and colorful bathing trunks. He had a great tan, dark eyes and was smoking Camel cigarettes. The word "Playboy" came to mind.

He talked to me as if I were an adult. I perceived that he was very lonely. We talked about the weather. He told me in a quiet, flat tone that he had just returned from a Caribbean cruise. I could hear in his voice that he had hoped it would fill a void in his life and it hadn't. In the course of our talking he told me he was divorced. That little talk made a great impression on me. I made a mental note that people who have money aren't always happy.

Next I wandered down to the handball court where I saw a pretty girl with blond, curly hair, a little older than me, playing handball by herself. I recognized the girl as the leader in a group of kids who were playing handball as we drove up. I ventured near her.

"Hello," I said confidently. "My name's Joan Ellen and I'm here from Philadelphia.

"Mind your own business!" she said tersely, turning away.

Whoops. Time to go back to my grandmother's deck!

"Would you like it if I took you down to see the ocean now, Joan Ellen?"

My grandmother stood there in a black, skirted bathing suit with a floral pattern. She and my grandfather spoke with a certain formality. As their first grandchild, they seemed to approach me with a certain deference I was unaccustomed to.

The ocean was quite a distance away from the "back" cabins where my grandparents were, facing Jamaica Bay. I grabbed my metal pail, shovel and plastic forms and walked with my grandmother away from her section, past a large open informal restaurant where you could smell hamburgers and fries sizzling. We walked past children with their pails and mothers with their towels in line, past the screened-in clubroom where men and women played bridge and canasta in their shorts, halters and bathing suits, with waiters bringing ice tea and drinks from the bar. A piano was playing.

Soon we walked down some wooden steps away from this back area of cabins and over a long boardwalk beside shallow waters, grasses and fascinating tiny black tadpoles. I would stop and stare in fascination at the marine life in the shallow, grassy marsh waters.

"Someday they will be frogs," my grandmother explained.

We walked for what seemed like forever. On the narrow wooden slats, people walked single file in two rows: on the right, people like us going down to the ocean, on the left, people trudging back, sandy, wet, happily exhausted, carrying towels and umbrellas.

Then we came to the larger, newer, front "cabanas", more spacious than the original "cabins" of my grandparents and their friends. They were built in horseshoe fashion around large, open, common areas of sand, about the size of a small baseball field bordered on three sides by the colorful, open cabanas with striped awnings, the end of the horseshoe open to the ocean. The cabanas all looked down on the sandy common area set up with barbeque grills. Handsome, tanned older women with floral bathing suits and platform shoes were busy preparing lunch for their husbands or proudly sweeping their decks, many with upswept "beehive" blond hair and loop earrings, popular at that time. Many of the cabanas had refrigerators, eating areas and were colorfully decorated with American flags, sea shells, large mounted marlin and swordfish. Radios were playing. The Dodgers could be heard intermittently evoking cheers or jeers as we made our way. We passed another large clubhouse area where "Mr. Sandman" by the Andrew Sisters was playing on the jukebox. Sandy kids in wet bathing suits happily ate fries and burgers.

We passed a large outdoor swimming pool, writhing with children, tanned and serious college lifeguards with white zinc cream noses, calling to those disregarding the rules, for a timeout.

"Would you like to go in for a dip?" my grandmother asked.

"No," was all I said.

She knew what I was waiting for. We continued down wide wooden steps, following the narrow wood boardwalk over hills of blinding, blistering white sand, almost like a desert. The clam shells were less broken now, larger, and I began to see black muscle shells and an occasional broken conch. Still no ocean.

"Each year the ocean moves further and further out to sea," my grandmother explained.

A few more sandy knolls and then I saw it, the great Atlantic, an expanse so flat, blue and magnificent, I caught my breath and just stood there. And geographically, I was in a wondrous spot to see the ocean for the first time: facing due east from the tip of the Rockaway peninsula which separated the Atlantic and New York Harbor.

I gazed out at the Atlantic Ocean, massive and powerful, its windy spray pounding the flat beaches with violent surf, to the right and left as far as I could see. Looking up, I watched as a small airplane, carrying a streamer boasting "Nathan's Famous," flew proudly out over the ocean, horizontal with the beach.

We walked closer to the crowded bathers and pastel umbrellas. Elevated white wooden life guard stations blew shrill whistles, red flapping pennants indicating an under-toe. My senses were assaulted with the wild energy of it all, the circling, screaming gulls above me, the pounding, galloping, wild surf, frothing at the shoreline of seaweed, clam shells and a giant brown-black kingfisher with a prehistoric tail that horrified me.

Everything was in constant motion from the lucky children riding high on the surf with their yellow and navy canvas floats, to the bright, bobbing red and green barrels enclosing the swimming area with thick rope, gnarled with green brine and seaweed. We stood watching as lifeguards suddenly jumped down from their station and quickly pushed a white rescue catamaran to the water's edge, running dramatically at top speed out through the surf to rescue an older man who had ventured out beyond the ropes to do some long distance swimming.

"Do you want to go in?" my grandmother asked me as we stood together at the shoreline, surveying the noisy crowd of bathers, children with their mothers, older women in bathing caps, teens bodysurfing, most everyone struggling to get out beyond the pounding surf where the bottle green sea rolled and then crested into breaking waves, foam flying in the wind.

"Oh, yes," I replied.

I couldn't wait to get my new bathing suit wet in the ocean, heavy with salt.

"Then you must promise to keep your eyes on me always. If I motion you in, you must come in. You're in my charge, you know."

I ventured slowly out, knowing my grandmother was watching my every move. I watched her standing formally on the shoreline, her arms folded across her chest, like a sentry. I struggled to hold onto the bobbing red and green barrels, and slimy, silken ropes thick with briny green seaweed. When I was waist high I saw her gesture for me to come in a little. Then a large wave broke over me un-announced, knocking the wind out of me as it rolled me back into shallow water. I couldn't help laughing out loud. I had sand in my bathing suit, salt water up my nose, salty sea air in my hair. I loved it. Nathan's plane droned on above me.

Now closer to shore I watched as tiny, colorful sea cowries scurried to quickly re-bury themselves in the wet sand before the next receding wave exposed them again. Becoming more comfortable with my swimming skills, I strove to inch my way carefully out beyond my waist-high position, but as soon as I did I saw the inevitable imperial wave from my grandmother beckoning me to come in closer.

Mary Flynn had remarkable eyesight. As soon as I put one toe back in the direction of the more open, rolling sea, hoping to slowly position myself up to my neck, there she would be, beckoning me back. Years later it dawned on me that my grandmother, Mary Margaret Cummings Flynn, had been the oldest of the ten children that had lost their littlest sister, Jennie, early in life.

It was a wonderful day, my first introduction to the Atlantic Ocean!

As we began the long walk back on the narrow board walk, my grandmother let me stop and fill my metal pail with heavy, bone-white clam shells.

"Now, your grandfather will want you to walk with him down here over to the jetty. Don't ever let me hear, Joan Ellen, that he has taken you out on it. I know you would never do it."

I was at once forewarned and very curious about the jetty, which I could see very far down the beach in the distance, at the very end of Rockaway peninsula where the ocean met Jamaica Bay. Its massive black rocks were piled high and it extended far out into the sea.

We stopped at the first clubhouse where we ordered vanilla fudge ice cream cones which became a ritual every time I came down with one of my grandparents to swim in the ocean.

The next day my grandfather walked me down to the ocean, he in his bathing trunks and white sneakers. After a dip in the ocean, he asked me if I'd like to go with him on his "customary" walk, which I found out was to the very end of the peninsula, to the infamous black boulders of the great jetty.

As we walked, sometimes we would talk, sometimes we'd say nothing at all. The surf pounded the broad white beach and the wind blew wildly as we passed many other bronzed, older walkers, nodding amiably at the stately grandfather. The hair on his chest was white and his skin bronzed from many summers walking his route out to the jetty.

We walked side by side on the solid wet sand below the shoreline, the cold surf rushing in over our feet, the small colored cowry shells scurrying to conceal themselves. Several very large seagulls dive-bombed around us.

"Don't worry, they won't hurt you," he assured me.

Little by little, he talked to me about the family business, but only in very general terms, recollecting, without passion.

Later in life I would learn how his father came over from Ireland at the age of three, eventually starting the Michael Flynn Manufacturing business along the docks. At first he collected hawsers, the huge ropes used to tie up the many immigrant ships arriving each day at the piers of Brooklyn. He had a warehouse at Congress Street right on New York Harbor. He began to collect scrap metal, old diving helmets, airplane propellers and the like, in a vacant lot next to his office. Grandfather never mentioned any of this.

With the end of WWI, he converted discarded bronze bombing "sites", used in planes to manually drop bombs on the enemy, into small banks, giving them out to neighboring businesses. He developed the scrap metal business into an aluminum window business with offices in New York, Philadelphia and California which made airplane hangers, windows for New York skyscrapers, Florida office buildings and hotels, and did jobs as far away as Peru. After WWI, the company bought many destroyers and submarines to salvage for scrap metal and after WWII, even sent his son, my father, to check out the radiation levels on ships remaining after the atomic bomb was set off on Bikini Island, for salvage.

Much of all this I only learned later in life, from my father. Looking back, what my grandfather told me then, were only very general, high-level details of the business: that he had an office in New York as well as the plant in Philadelphia, that the company had originated as a scrap-metal business and now made windows for office buildings and sky-scrapers.

He was a kind and stately man, very easy to be with, inquiring about my school, my friends and my life in Philadelphia. Later in life I would also learn that he was very charitable. He dressed as the president of a large company would. He was a gentleman. It was implied to me at a later time in my life, that my grandfather, as president, was the figurehead of the company, lacking perhaps the intimate knowledge and exceptional entrepreneurial talent of his father before him.

But today, I could feel his love of the beach and the ocean and the regard he had for me, his granddaughter. He explained carefully the things that perhaps, in this later stage of his life, meant more to him, like the ocean and the beach. I sensed how much he really enjoyed his solitary walk along the beach every day. And, looking back, I knew he had the same solitary side that my father and I inherited from him. The Flynn's are people that often just enjoy being alone, resonating within themselves.

He was also very much into the moment. He explained that he tried to get down to the actual beach and walk the mile or so to the jetty, which marked the end of the peninsula, every day. As we walked together he talked about the seagulls that flew above, squawking, and circling dangerously close to us. Older walkers, bronzed and white-haired, just like him, would nod amiably as we walked by. He walked without a shirt, just his trunks and his white sneakers.

"I always wear my sneakers when I go in for a swim, just to be safe!" he explained. Sometimes we walked on the soft, dry sand above the waterline which was difficult. He would explain many things to me, side-stepping a horrific black kingfisher, dying, laying on its back. Mostly we would walk on the hard, wet sand, the frothy surf languidly swirling, gently, sparkling around our ankles. I was very proud to walk with him. He confided many things he knew about the beach, pointing out small sand sharks that had swum too far in and washed up with the tide. He pointed out jelly fish called "Men 'O War", instructing me to walk round their long, colorful-and poisonous-tentacles.

"See those parachute jumps in the distance," he said, stopping to show me tiny people floating to earth from a parachute tower way in the distance.

"That's Coney Island," he said with finality, a note of pride in his voice. As we walked on, I saw a huge black line before me on the horizon. As the mist lifted, I could see these were the forbidden rocks, looming larger and larger as we approached.

"And this is the jetty," he announced to me.

"Don't tell your grandmother I brought you this far."

We jumped up onto the massive rocks, extending far out into the ocean. We were at the very end of Rockaway peninsula, Jamaica Bay behind us, the vast Atlantic in front of us. We could now clearly see the parachute jumps across the Bay at Coney Island.

"Look, Joan Ellen. That's the Queen Mary, leaving New York Harbor for Europe," my grandfather explained to me proudly, as I gazed out at one of several cruise ships on the horizon, long and majestic with stately slanted, black smokestacks. I wanted so much to make our way out to the end of the jetty.

"Grandpa, have you ever walked out to the very end?" I asked, looking at the fishermen casting out from the rocks.

"Not in quite a while," he told me.

Looking down the top of the granite rocks, I could see you almost had to jump from top to top as the waves swirled and crashed, leaving their foam as they retreated, sand crabs struggling between the black rocks. Yet the crashing and swirling of the ocean was very exciting to me. I longed to venture out to the very end of the jetty where I imagined it must be thrilling and frightening at the same time.

"Don't tell Grandma I let you climb up on the jetty. She'll be very concerned," he cautioned me.

We jumped down to the hard sand and began the long walk back to the Surf Club beach, then back up the long wooden boardwalk, stopping for ice cream cones and then back to the cabin area. Sometimes we just walked in silence, the water swirling up around our tennis shoes, the crash of the surf, the groups of loud seagulls diving around us along the shoreline, the small crabs washed ashore, trying to avoid the seagulls, scurrying down under the protection of wet sand. We enjoyed the amiable companionship of the other walkers. Along with the magnificent blue sky, surf and wind, the older man beside me was very much a part of the beach with his weathered white tennis shoes, swim trunks, bronzed chest with white curly hair.

We talked easily about this and that. He was born in 1895 had been in the army at Fort Slocum in the 1920's. He stopped to point out Fort Slocum which I could just barely make out on the Jersey Shore. As a boy he had gone to St. Francis Military School of which he was very proud. He seemed interested in my school work and my life in Philadelphia. I so enjoyed the easy exchange as we walked, his telling me about himself and his life. Again, my grandparents never had a daughter and I had the feeling it was a real treat having me stay with them.

In 1955 I received a wonderful letter from him on navy blue monogrammed stationery in response to a thank you note I had sent when I returned one summer to Philadelphia. The letter began formally, answering some questions I had, but then changed in tone, telling me how very much he had enjoyed our companionship, our long walks to the jetty, almost as if he were writing to a daughter.

"And by the way," he wrote, "your Uncle Greg and Uncle Bob and I made our way out to the end of the jetty. It was quite challenging, but we made it. Don't tell your Grandmother!"

I spent a week each summer with my grandparents for several years as I was growing up. When I was ten years old I finally got to know a group of friends at Breezy Point. That summer our favorite pastime was roaming under the boards of the cabins, collecting bottle tops from every type of bottle imaginable, Coke, Seven-up, Pepsi, Hires and Barks root beer, even fancy bottle tops from whiskey, gin bottles, tonic water, all of which would fall between the grey planks of the cabin areas, all destined to become part of our immense and varied collection. Eavesdropping on conversations above us was great fun. I proudly amassed large shopping bags of these bottle tops which my grandmother kindly allowed me to store in the back of her cabin, under the skirted changing seat, no questions asked. She also let me store brown paper sacks of heavy, white clam shells I collected, never throwing them out between summers, ignoring the pungent, fishy smell they brought to the tiny cabin.

We continued to watch the old, bronzed and oiled men, playing bocce in their swimming trunks, the soft click-click of the wooden bocce balls under the blue sky, as they pitched them, rolling across the long beds of hard golden sand, thumping against the wooden frames, accompanied by exclamations of joy or otherwise. They were a part of our summer landscape.

We ran as a small group, playing Pat Boone's new hit, "O Bernadine" endlessly that summer on the juke-box in the sandwich shop, eating hamburgers and fries. While I was allowed some latitude, the jetty was always off limits to me. When it rained, the adults would congregate in a screened club house where they would all play cards. Down the steps from the clubhouse and along the half-mile narrow set of planks that led out to the ocean, were my favorite "lagoons", which I continued to study. The stagnant bodies of standing water still fascinated me with their small black tadpoles swimming buslly, along with other tide life, and colorful, swift dragonflies darting about in the standing water.

As foretold, one night in the summer, my grandmother decided to take Aunt Helen, Aunt Francis, Uncle Greg, my grandfather and I to Coney Island. We walked along the boardwalk overlooking the moonlit surf as it crashed, swirling madly in against the pillars below. We watched the parachute jumps float to earth, eating pizza, going on several of the more tame rides. We piled into small bumper cars, called the "Whip" and tried, hilariously, to catch brass rings from a pole as it went around.

My grandmother and her sisters had a great time, even at their age. What fun this group must have had when they were young! Later we ate at an Italian restaurant set in a small villa-like environment with pillars and grape vines, very authentic to a young girl from Philadelphia.

My grandmother would take me back to Coney Island once more when I was ten years old, just she and myself, during the day. We rode the Ferris Wheel in a large rectangular metal cage that rocked and slid precariously from different angles as the gigantic wheel stopped and started. Eventually we arrived joltingly at the very top, enjoying the breathtaking view of Jamaica Bay, across to Breezy Point and out over Brooklyn itself.

My grandmother stood guard as I launched myself down long wooden slides and later on a frightening ride called The Rotor whose floor suddenly disappeared, leaving the occupants plastered by centrifugal force against the sides of the spinning cylinder.

I rode a magnificent merry-go-round with its wonderful painted horses, festooned with jeweled saddles and garlands, enjoying the calliope music, mirrors and ornate landscapes painted within the carousel itself, hoping I could lean out far enough to pluck a brass ring suspended from a chute. I waved to my grandmother, watching vigilantly in her black dress, hat and purse. I often thought that she, the eldest of ten, never forgot the responsibility she had, to insure the safety of those left in her care, a duty she took very seriously with almost grave concern. Whether I was riding the ocean's surf or galloping on a magical steed, she never let me out of her sight, not for an instant.

As we walked together, we paused to look out on an arena of sorts, that people would hurry across, pursued by a clown who playfully gave them small shocks with an electric wand as they ran by him. They all were laughing, but it was a cause of concern for me.

"It's all right," my grandmother explained, taking my hand.

"Those people are leaving The Steeple Chase!"

She showed me how the colorful mechanical horses transported riders, several abreast, in fox-hunt fashion, high above many of the other rides. I ended the day maneuvering through giant rotating wooden barrels, happy couples falling and rolling around together, disheveled and laughing breathlessly as they made their way to the end of the barrel.

It was a very special time.

Later, as a young adult starting college in New York, my grandparents would proudly take me on the Circle Line Tour, pointing out landmark buildings, as we sat on wooden seats in the cold air, eating hot pretzels with mustard, circling Manhattan. My grandmother even took me to the 1964 World's Fair where we marveled at the huge silver Hemisphere and rode the futuristic People-Mover.

The summer I turned thirteen I accompanied my grandmother to a preview of a new play where the actors presented the first act at a Breezy Point women's luncheon. I didn't know what to make of the teacher who violently struggled with her blind and deaf student. After it was over, the teacher autographed my program. "Anne Bancroft" she wrote. The strange new play was called "The Miracle Worker."

Those final summers at Breezy Point were ones of change for me.

One day my grandmother announced there was going to be a "Teenage Dance" that weekend at the main clubhouse. My mother had known about it in advance and sent with me a beautiful dress, a green and blue floral print with a large skirt, to be worn with a stiff horsehair petticoat. The neckline was lower than I was used to, and worn somewhat off my shoulders, like Scarlett O'Hara in "Gone with the Wind." I was awkward at that age, with my short hair, but was very tan and the green dress matched my green eyes, according to my grandmother and her sisters.

The evening of the dance, my grandparents, aunts and uncles were cooking steaks and baked potatoes. It was Saturday night and I knew they would soon bring out the accordion, banjo and ukulele, and there would be singing and a wonderful time. Then I heard distant music coming from the clubhouse, live music, wafting across the cool summer evening. I hoped they wouldn't hear it.

"Sounds like the dance is starting!" my Aunt Francis exclaimed excitedly.

"You look beautiful!" Aunt Helen informed me.

I felt like an awkward giraffe in that dress. How could I possibly go! What would the dance be like? I didn't know anyone. Would they laugh at me?

"Would you like me to walk you over to the dance?" Uncle Tom asked me.

"Oh, no," I said, "I'll just walk over in a bit."

I waved as they all cheered me on, telling me to have a good time. I disappeared around the corner of the cabins, terrified. What if someone asked me to dance? I couldn't dance. And yet, I had a suspicion that I looked very nice. I wanted to show off my new dress. I wasn't used to looking the way I looked.

Slowly I drifted in the direction of the clubhouse. The music became louder. I could hear people laughing and having a good time. I supposed they all knew each other. I recalled the popular girl from the handball court. I remember returning back to my grandparents' deck about an hour later.

"Did you have a good time?" they all asked.

"It was all right," I told them.

And it probably was. I had spent the hour walking around various decks with their groups of cabins and cabanas, like small neighborhoods, all having weekend cookouts. I never went near the clubhouse.

The last summer I went to Breezy Point was the summer of my sixteenth birthday. I remember the day I walked to the jetty alone. My grandfather made the walk less frequently now. He often decided to stay back at the cabins, listening in his lounge chair to the Dodgers play on his transistor. I walked the long mile or so to the jetty and jumped up on the large black boulders.

I felt an exhilarating freedom. It was delicious, the wind blowing in my hair. But at the same time I missed the company of my grandfather. Sitting alone on the rocks, I enjoyed the rhythm of the busy surf splashing up against the massive rocks, then hurrying out to sea after each attack! I sat down to watch the cruise ships move slowly out to sea from New York Harbor. Was that big one the Queen Mary? I couldn't tell. My grandfather would recognize her right away. It occurred to me I now had the opportunity to climb my way out to the end of the forbidden jetty if I wanted to. But I knew I would never betray their confidence.

"Hi, there."

I shielded my eyes from the bright sun, looking up to see a college student in khaki shorts and navy blue Fordham tee shirt standing above me. He was tall, tan and he was *talking* to me. He was very handsome with dark brown curly hair. I was acutely aware of the dark hair on his muscular legs next to me. He sat down. I was terrified.

"Did you ever think about why you're *here*?" he asked me earnestly.

His brown eyes were very serious. I couldn't believe this college student from Fordham was actually *speaking* to me.

"Not really. I'm on vacation from Philadelphia, visiting my grandparents," I stammered.

"Oh, no," he said, smiling gently. "I meant why you're *here*. What is the purpose of you're *being* here, your *existence*, why we were put on this earth?"

No one had ever talked to me like that, not my parents, not my grandparents or friends. It was unsettling.

"Oh, I've never really thought about it much," I murmured.

"Well, I think about it all the time. There must be a plan. God must have a reason for putting us all here on this earth. I think about it a lot and I'm trying to find the answer."

"Do you have the time?" I asked. "I'm afraid I've stayed away too long and my grandparents will be worried."

I wasn't prepared to have an existential conversation about the meaning of the universe with this stranger even if he was handsome and went to Fordham.

"Well, goodbye," he said as I jumped down from the rocks.

"And don't forget to think about my question. Maybe I'll see you again some time."

I felt uncomfortable with this handsome stranger and his difficult question. It was very unsettling. I thought he might want to walk by my side the whole way back to the club so I decided to take a different way back, not along the beach, but "bayside" as they called it, back around Jamaica Bay which hopefully would bring me to the entrance of the Club and my grandparent's group of familiar "original" cabins in the front.

I noticed the back perimeter of the peninsula was constructed with the same large black jetty rocks. I walked across them for a time, for the area around them was unimproved, with broken bottles and trash that had washed up from Jamaica Bay, lying in the sand and between the rocks. As I hurried back, I was nervous because I had now been gone for quite awhile and was not really sure of the way back. I assumed would lead me back to the clubhouse and the main entrance.

As I walked, I noticed unmaintained expanses of sand dunes, as far as I could see, littered with large white clam shells, broken bottles and long green grass blowing in the wind. The sun went in and it became cloudy. Somehow I was afraid. All the familiar markers of the beach, the people, the lifeguard stations, were gone. It grew cold and began to rain gently. It became very dismal. I knew my grandparents would be worried. Where *was* she?

Finally, with great relief, I made out the familiar large domed entryway leading to the club from the asphalt parking lot. How strange it was to come back this way. I passed the old refrigerated hut where I used to observe, from my grandmother's deck, the Fordham boys carrying large blocks of ice with pincers for the guests and their drinks.

Now I had actually *met* one of these boys. As I passed the hut I could hear an old refrigerator motor humming. I climbed some wooden stairs up to a deck around the corner from my grandmother's and walked casually over to her old familiar area where everyone was sitting down to sandwiches.

"Joan Ellen, where *were* you? I was just starting to wonder where you *were*," my grandmother asked gently. She was making chicken salad sandwiches on Kaiser buns. I could hear the subtlest hint of sternness in her voice.

"Oh, it just took me longer than usual," I replied. Something warned me not to share with her that I had taken a different route, probably one that was not part of the club. They would not approve.

When you step outside the borders and observe from a different viewpoint, things are never quite the same. Breezy had always been its own wonderful universe to me. It still was, but that day I learned it was part of a much larger world. I had stepped outside the perimeter, the boundaries, of my life.

Washington Lane
Rydal, Pa.
1952

Joan Flynn Beesley

Joan Flynn Beesley

When I was eight, the day came when my parents told me that while I was in school that day, 3rd grade at Nazareth Academy, a moving truck would come. I was somewhat older and wiser, progressing in experience beyond the incident of The Tobacco Leaf and The Levitating Box in the first grade.

That afternoon I would be going home to their newly-built custom home in Rydal, a beautiful up-scale neighborhood in another area. As I sat waiting in the car that morning for my father, who had gone back into the house to retrieve his briefcase, I recall looking up at the dark red brick home with the birch wood window boxes. How I would miss my house!

Lately I developed a talent of staring at objects until they looked new and special to me. It was a habit I discovered by staring at a black flowered mantle clock in the Banister's living room. It was an ordinary clock but the longer you stared at it, the more unusual and beautiful it became until it seemed like the world's most extraordinary clock!

As I sat, sadly waiting for my father, my eyes fell on a long brown feathery weed blowing in the wind, all alone, on my father's beautifully-mowed green lawn. I often also played another game with myself, focusing on an object, so that that particular moment in time would be preserved, like a leaf in a book, always remembered.

"Little weed," I thought, "I'll never see you again, or my wonderful house, but I'll concentrate really hard on you right now, the way you look gently blowing over there, so I'll always remember- no punctuate- this moment."

I've often thought of that morning I preserved, in my memory, throughout my entire lifetime. I knew it was a turning point in my life, leaving my beloved Winchester Park, our home and the Banisters. And it was.

My parents had been looking to move from their first home in Winchester Park for some time. One weekend I accompanied them to a new home with a large barn, out in the glorious Philadelphia countryside.

"What would we do with this barn, Dad?" I remember asking my father as we strode across the straw floor behind the realtor.

"We would hold square dances here," my dad explained to the inquisitive eight year old girl at his side. My parents loved to have fun and entertain and I knew this was well within the realm of possibility.

They searched for a new home for several weekends when suddenly there was a new plan. I understood they, with some help from my father's parents, were going to build a new custom home with an architect!

Several weekends later, I was riding in the back seat, always happily privy to their excited plans and secrets.

"The builder says we're not too old to build a home, Ed! We're only 32!" My mother exclaimed. For some reason that remark has stayed with me forever, as I silently watched them grow old together, to 79 and 83 respectively.

Then one weekend-I remember it well-Dad drove the car to a beautiful green, forested area with magnificent homes high on hills on either side of the road.

"This is Rydal," my father explained to me proudly.

Then he pulled alongside a huge lot going up a long slope, the surface actually above the roof of our car along the road. He stopped the car beside a big, rooted tree growing out of the edge of the lot, above our car.

"That will have to go!!" he laughed.

"Ed, it's simply beautiful!" my mother cried, as we all looked up at the rolling green elevated acre of land, rising up from the leafy street as far as we could see, then disappearing into the thick Philadelphia forest beyond.

My parents planned to have lots of children. They worked closely with the architect to put in a mud room, French double doors leading from the formal dining room to the backyard, custom cupboards in the kitchen for brooms and mops. My father was especially proud of the handsome redwood built-in bookcase he had designed around his piano, with vertical cupboards for card tables. He would keep his white models of the Titanic or USS United States and airplane models he built in places of honor, above his piano in the bookcases. Further along that wall was a beautiful grey stone fireplace, the focal point of the living room.

They put in a large picture window to capture the beauty of the magnificent backyard and forest. The year was 1954. They had the latest in a new countertop material called "Formica" and a linoleum floor that looked like real brick. Their roomy bedroom on the first floor was connected to another bedroom through a bathroom, with a large linen closet between the two rooms. I understood this bedroom was going to be "for the children." I had two small brothers, Michael and Kevin, and my little sister, Marianne, all born at Winchester Park.

My mother decorated the home beautifully. All the bedrooms, especially theirs, had beautiful white flowered organza curtains that shifted in the breeze. She brought home huge books of stiff wallpaper patterns from which I helped select the wallpaper for my room on the second floor. My room had built-in sliding closet doors-new at the time-all along one wall. I even had my own bathroom with a beautifully colored grey sink and bathtub. How novel, I thought, as all the bathtubs I had ever seen were white! She insisted that one of the walls be a different pattern with scalloped edging around the ceiling. I went with the program, thinking how very stylish and modern we had suddenly become! As the oldest child of eventually eight children, I was always given my own room, perhaps in deference to the help I was always happy to provide.

All the details of the home were carefully and lovingly planned. There was a playroom with special louvered windows set high up, custom-made from my father's window business, with the trademark rotating handles, co-designed by David Lupton and Michael Flynn. He loved to find closets where he could set up a television on a table inside the closet and then cut out a hole in the wall, creating an early built-in effect. He would also do this in our next home in Cleveland Heights!

One very interesting idea they had was to install a mammoth 9' x 9' industrial-size fan next to a window in the attic, designed to blow through three bedrooms adjacent to each other, connected to the fan in a fourth unfinished room. The huge fan pushed cool air throughout the house. I was always somewhat afraid of it!

If the interior was my mother's domain, then the wonderful 1 acre lot was my father's! He bought a small tractor to mow the enormous, rolling expanse of seeded front lawn atop which the beautiful 2 story fieldstone raised-ranch rested. True to their Irish roots, my parents loved to plant and work outside the house, in every home they were to own. When the home was complete, it rested like a crown atop the hill high above Washington Lane. Dad planted some pink crab apple trees and tall Lombardy poplars along the steep ribbon of asphalt that was our driveway, by the property bordering on the mysterious old Kelly mansion.

The Lombardy poplars separated our home from the massive Kelly estate next store, a wonderful stone grey affair occupied by nine brothers and sisters from Ireland who had purchased it together. The Kelly's home was very old and also perched on the hill high above Washington Lane. The Kellys all kept to themselves. Now and then we would get a glimpse of them, the women with their red hair piled high upon their heads, with high-neck white blouses and long dark billowing green or brown skirts. The Kelly men also dressed in outfits that seemed from long ago, dark, formal suits with vests and white shirts. Gradually we got to meet them. Our last name being Flynn helped immensely.

The Kellys' stone mansion was wonderfully decorated for the holidays, especially Christmas when all of them would be in the kitchen cooking turkey and many special dishes. They were a very merry group, but also very private. I became friends with a niece of the Kellys and we would wander through the immense kitchen with hanging copper pots. The home held fine old heavy furniture, breakfronts and the like, heavily-tapestried brocade curtains which I'm sure came from Ireland. A wonderful, ornate balustrade and curved banister leading upstairs. How I would have loved the opportunity to peak in the Kelly's attic to see all the Irish treasures they had brought with them!

We lived on Washington Lane for approximately 3 years. The day we moved in was especially memorable. My father picked me up from Nazareth Academy. How excited I was to be going home at last to our new home, after accompanying my parents on weekends to watch first, the land being cleared of trees, then the foundation being poured, then running across the wooden first floor which was only a gigantic deck. That next weekend we returned to see the studs going up to mark the different rooms on the first floor.

"This must be our room, Ed!" my mother had said excitedly to my father as we strolled through the first floor which had just been completed.

Their bedroom connected through their bath to another room for my sister Marianne who would be moved upstairs with me and my two little brothers when that room would happily become the nursery for the next child they planned to have. A week later a stairway was added. The second floor could be reached above the first! Carefully we made our way up, just a long wooden tabletop on the cleared lot. But the next weekend the tabletop had been again separated into rooms, marked by the wooden 2 by 4's.

"This is your room, Joan Ellen, and this is your own bathroom!" they told me.

How excited I was, and how special I felt. They had worked very closely with the architect to create a home customized for the large family they were planning.

"There's a guest room up here and two other bedrooms, Joan Ellen, close to yours, for "the boys and the others." They looked at each other and smiled.

Moving day was in January and a blizzard had set in. We drove slowly from Nazareth Academy to the new house.

"Grandma Flynn is coming to help your mother with the unpacking," my father announced. As we pulled into Washington Lane the snow was accumulating fast. As we approached the long, steep driveway, we saw the big moving truck struggling to maneuver the drive. Its wheels were spinning frantically and some of the movers were shouting out directions to the driver from the snow. The huge truck seemed to gain traction, lurching forward, then sliding hopelessly backwards towards the street.

"It's tipping! It's tipping! It's going over on its side!" the men yelled excitedly to the driver.

My father and I watched in horror as the van did a jack knife, sliding sideways down the driveway. We could hear the piano keys tinkle inside as the furniture heaved.

We made our way past the van and up the driveway into the house where my mother, impervious to the drama out on the long driveway, had just iced a chocolate cake for two of the neighbor children who had come over to meet us.

"Joan Ellen, this is Stevie and Buzzy Bond. They are brothers and sisters who live two houses away."

"Hi", I said shyly as I looked at the two red-headed, freckled youngsters, who would become some of our best friends, exploring the "Indian Woods", the vast forest directly behind our home, complete with its own Indian or "burial" mound.

The Bond family lived in a ranch house two houses away and their grandmother lived in an identical house next door. In the wooded area behind his grandmother's home, Buzzy Bond's father had put up a ladder held by ropes between two trees and also a tire swing which my brothers would soon be investigating! Each of the lots rose high above each other like a set of steps along Washington Lane, way back from the street with huge lawns in front, rising up from the street. Our house towered above Mrs. Bond's, on a steep cliff, down which my younger brother Michael would one day roll a tire, bouncing high onto the asphalt below.

Above Mrs. Bond's property, at the corner of our lot, was a wonderful, immense shade tree and below it the infamous Glass Top Table. My parents loved black wrought-iron furniture and they had brought their set from the back porch on Albion Street. Now with several more siblings, the glass on the long table was frequently broken by things or little people leaning, landing or throwing their toys on it. After replacing the glass about five times, my father finally cut a piece of plywood and inserted it across the top.

"There". He said doggedly one day.

"Try and break that!"

He painted it a light blue and it stayed that way for many years. My parents painted a lot of things blue.

One time I'll always remember was working with my father to build a rabbit cage. Many of my friends had rabbits and we looked forward to building a great cage on our property line near the Kellys' house. It was a hot summer Saturday afternoon. Dad and I had gone to the lumber store in nearby Jenkintown for the wood and chicken wire. We had also handpicked eight beautiful little rabbits, black and white. We were nearing the end of the cage construction. It had two stories, a rolling wheel for them to play in, a separate area for eating. Dad placed soft carpet in the bottom and hammered the final nail to hold the mesh chicken wire. Then came the moment of truth when we reached in the tiny door, inserting the little creatures into their new home. I remember sitting on our haunches admiring the rabbit cage and the new inhabitants when I heard a rustling behind me. What was that? A little rabbit!

"Dad, we forgot one!" My father reached back and we installed the last little one in place, admiring the brilliant design of the cage.

"Well, all done! All we need to get now is a bowl of water and the pellets!" My dad announced proudly.

Suddenly, behind him, I spied another little rabbit making a run for it behind my father.

"Dad, look, a rabbit!" I yelled and he reached back to scoop up another and put it back.

Quite soon the Master Builders realized they had bought the wrong size of chicken wire, as the little rabbits could escape quite easily right through the holes!

I worked hand in hand with my parents one Saturday, helping my Dad with the weed wacker as he cut down the remains of the forest in the backyard, removing large rocks that had been there forever, leveling the terrain to put in flagstone steps, eventually flinging handfuls of grass seed everywhere, carefully watering it down. Clearing the land was especially exciting to me. My father explained it had been virtually untouched since the time when the Indians roamed and hunted on it. He sometimes picked up arrowheads to show me. Whether a true Irish trait or not, we simply loved working with the land outdoors.

We had great times on Washington Lane with my brothers Michael and Kevin, born a year apart, with my sister Marianne, all born on Albion Street. My sister Elizabeth Grace, was born in 1957, nine months before we moved to Cleveland from this wonderful custom home. I remember arriving home from school one afternoon. I was now eleven years old. There was an aura of excitement in the house. My father was home which was unusual at that time of the day. My grandmother Dillon was there also. Mother was sitting in a chair in the living room, looking radiant.

"Joan Ellen, go into our bedroom. We have a surprise for you." I walked to their bedroom and slowly opened the door. The air was filled with that wonderful fragrance called "New Baby". On my mother's dresser was an enormous fruit display on a black metal enamel tole tray painted with flowers, wrapped in yellow cellophane with every kind of fruit imaginable, a gift from my grandfather, Frank Flynn.

There was a new canvas four wheeled affair on wheels which was zipped securely on all sides. As I crept forward, I saw the most beautiful baby I had ever seen, lying on her chest, secure in a beautiful blanket and baby outfit. My two brothers and sister Marianne all had been born with thick dark brown hair, just like my mother's. This baby was different, with delicate fair blond hair, translucent pink skin and blue eyes that were peaking open. The baby was absolutely beautiful! She looked like an angel. I turned to see my father and mother standing at the door smiling.

"Say hello to your new little sister, Elizabeth Grace," my father said warmly, his voice glowing with pride.

My mother was often pregnant but she always kept the fact very private. She never really mentioned it, but I always knew by the unusual colorful tops and black pedal pushers she wore! It was up to me, and our Irish mother's helper, Gwen, to babysit and entertain the children, letting her rest in the afternoons. It was like an Irish "Cheaper by the Dozen"! We used to turn on show tunes such as "Carousel", dress the little ones up and run them through the living room, helping them do flips over the couch or run around on the soft new grass in the backyard in our bare feet, dancing to all the wonderful music from "My Fair Lady" and "Brigadoon". Once in Atwood, a summer home my parents bought in Ohio, my father paused with me by the Atwood Dam, looking down into a beautiful green valley. "Just like Brigadoon," he said softly, "appearing every 100 years."

We had lots of visitors. My grandmother, Mary Flynn would drive in from New York with her sisters, pulling up in her big, black Cadillac for a fancy luncheon my mother would prepare: shrimp, Swedish meatballs, fancy egg, crab or tuna salad on small cocktail whole wheat or rye bread tea sandwiches. My mother's mother Eleanor Dillon would also come on occasion, stay for a few days, become offended and direct my mother to "order the taxi, Joan!", a rhythm we soon became accustomed to. Her older sister, Aunt Katherine, with her thick Brooklyn accent came several times for a visit, lovable and funny like her sister could be, but being the oldest of her family, very bossy.

"Joan Ellen, listen to yer motha. Come and fold the diapas!" I remember them both in their housedresses and aprons. I often think much of my childhood was spent sitting on the floor, folding endless piles of soft warm cloth diapers from the dryer, "right, left, top, done!" for my four younger siblings!

I have many wonderful memories of Rydal and Washington Lane. Once my father picked me up early from school in the fourth grade and took me ice-skating one winter afternoon on an estate called "Sharpless Stables," a small, but popular ice skating pond owned by the Sharpless Estate but open to the public. Every now and then the butler from the estate would walk down to the skaters in a big, black buttoned coat and top hat and offer the skaters small cups of hot chocolate from a silver try and then silently return to the estate on the hill. I felt so honored that my father, always busy with his father's window business at "The Plant" in Philadelphia, would take time off from work to pick me up from school to go ice skating before dinner!

My father and I would go to double-features at the Willow Grove movie theatre, once seeing "The High and The Mighty" and "Raintree County" on the same billing. As we breathlessly left the theatre, we both knew we had seen two of the movie greats.

My father also loved amusement parks. Once he and I went to the huge Willow Grove Amusement Park. My mother, being pregnant, could not go. He asked me if I would go on the Alps with him, the large roller coaster. He was clearly excited and I could see him as he must have been as an adolescent. I was afraid, but went with him, burying my face in his jacket, knowing I would be safe. It was such fun going places with him, father and daughter.

My father also loved ice cream sodas. We frequented a soda shop called "The Peter Pan Snack Shoppe" on Old York Road where we would sit in a booth, listening to the Everley Brothers and Elvis Presley, and order amazing hot fudge sundaes and "black and white" sodas.

My parents and I went to church every Sunday and often went for a ride afterwards. I recall sitting in the back of the car, with such a feeling of security as they happily enjoyed their new home and plans for their growing family.

For a miracle of sorts happened to my parents. Back in Winchester Park, my mother was told she would not be able to bear any other children after I was born. Not willing to accept it, my father and I spent many winter evenings, waiting in the car while he made up stories about "Jeffrey the Dog", as my mother sought the advice of specialist after specialist in downtown Philadelphia. Finally, she found a physician who agreed to try a radical type of radiation treatment, an x-ray, that is not allowed to be performed today. Somehow, my mother became fertile again and my brother Michael was conceived, the second of seven additional children! My parents were blessed. Their dream for a large family came true.

Rydal was a beautiful, very affluent suburb of Abington Township in Jenkintown. I had ballet lessons there, rode my bike to the lovely campus of Penn State to the beautiful duck pond with its ancient biology building. I loved my school, Our Lady Help of Christians. We all went to Mass once a week, played dodge ball and basketball. There was a large barn on the property and for lunch we would file in for hotdogs made by the students' mothers who volunteered there. I remember how we celebrated the May Crowning by all standing and practicing Catholic hymns to the Virgin Mary around a statue in the garden in the springtime. It was lovely. The nuns' rectory was by the school and I had Sister Paulita, Sister Cornelius and finally Miss Constance Kinslow for the first semester of 6th grade.

My teachers were all very strict but excellent teachers. Since we lived in Philadelphia, there was a real emphasis on Colonial Days, Paul Revere, The Boston Tea Party, The Constitution and the like, and I loved every exciting minute of it! When he turned five, my parents scoured Rydal, trying to locate the very best school for Michael, their oldest son. Michael started kindergarten at Melrose Academy, a very excellent and expensive private school with an old stone fence around the property, in a beautiful wooded setting not far from the Penn State campus in Abington.

I attended Our Lady Help of Christians from third to sixth grade. I was popular with the girls there and had several boyfriends! Our girls' club met on Saturdays. We would meet at each other's houses on a rotating basis and had a lot of fun.

As they had done in Winchester Park, our family continued to take a week's vacation every summer in Ocean City, New Jersey. My mother had a knack for finding great cottages to stay in. We would drive to Ocean City via the old Route 1. My mother would have my dad pull up to Carey's Realty, a pink stucco office right by the boardwalk over the beach. She would soon emerge triumphant, smiling, with papers and keys in hand.

"Ed, I found the most wonderful place!" and the places she found truly *were* wonderful.

One of them was right on the ocean and I worked hard to help my mother keep track of my two little brothers and two sisters. My brothers couldn't get enough of the ocean. They lived in their bathing suits, running down to the water, collecting shells, probably ages five and six. Marianne had to wear a brace on her leg due to the ravages of her fight with the deadly meningitis she had somehow contracted in Winchester Park. My father had made a circular, galvanized pen at the factory for her so she could play safely in the sand on the beach under an umbrella. One night there was a storm and the water actually came right up to the tarred wooden pilings around the back of the cottage where we were staying.

I used to love playing on the black rocks of the jetty with its old creosote wooden poles set side by side in the sand. I'd go quite a distance along the top of the rocks. You could wait for the tide to come swirling in, put your elbows up on the poles, suspending yourself just in time, as the sea rushed in around your feet. I've always loved the rhythm of the ocean, its pounding surf, always changing its personality, from the reliable, predictable and playful morning waves, to the lazy, gently-swirling late afternoon eddies and tide pools, to the relentless, pounding, storm-waves of cold, grey late summer.

The best part of playing at the jetty, before my brothers and sisters were born, was seeing my mother and father strolling down the beach in their bathing suits. I saw my *parents*, but I could also see, as anyone else could, that they were deeply in love, as they held hands, their young legs sometimes kicking up the incoming serf, splashing each other and laughing. They literally had the world at their feet, my mother laughing at my father's jokes, with her thick, shoulder-length Irish chestnut hair blowing in the wind, my father in his trunks and striped tee shirts, agile and tan, wind-blown dark blondish brown hair and green hazel eyes, just like mine.

Since he had been a Navy lieutenant, he knew every ship that appeared on the horizon out at sea, telling us to watch for the "demarcation line" indicating if a ship was carrying cargo or not, whether she was headed out to sea or back to New York harbor. I was the only child on my block who could discuss the demarcation lines of ships.

"Be careful on the jetty, Joan Ellen, we'll be right back. Stay where we can see you!", they'd call happily as they strolled along the waterline at sunset, leaving me to the mysteries of the jetties, tidal pools, sand crabs and kingfishers, fantasizing about the fate of unfortunate girls who wandered out to the far end of the jetty, reading Nancy Drew books, unobservant of the tide coming in, swishing silently, deadly, over the middle of the jetty, until they turned around, to face their peril, never to be seen again…

How completely happy I was as they turned and left me playing on the jetty. I was happy for them, for even as a small child I could see they were so much in love with each other. I also was very happy for myself as I instinctively knew they each loved me very much. As their first born, I knew I was part of their private circle of love and it felt wonderful. Somehow I knew I made them very happy.

Throughout my whole life, until they died peacefully at ages 79 and 83 in their home, their happiness was very important to me, even as I grew older myself with my own children. I never stopped sending birthday and Christmas presents to my beloved parents, forever young to me, because I knew it would make them happy. I've always felt a part of their joy, from my earliest years.

My parents loved and cherished gifts. They really appreciated that kindness from others. They loved holidays, the ocean, especially Ocean City, and Atlantic City where they honeymooned at the Clarendon Hotel. They loved the theatre, show tunes, Artie Shaw and the Big Bands, their many friends, their Irish Catholic religion, their proud Brooklyn upbringing, their businesses, family stories, their children, musical instruments such as the piano, clarinet and bagpipes, good books, boats, walks in the outdoors (we'd go for long walks in parks and arboretums when I was a child), cooking, my father's wonderful, -what I've come to understand only after he left us-unique, ever-present Irish wit.

This was a gift he gave everyone he met. People didn't always understand his wit, the sometimes unusual things he'd say, but he always made them laugh, taking them by surprise, off-guard. He always had a story or joke. I began to realize late in life he really had an infinite supply of very funny, usually Irish jokes. I've never met anyone with a sense of humor like my father, except perhaps for *his* father, who also loved telling stories and jokes, as do the people you meet in Ireland.

We had great times at the Jersey Shore. My Uncle Frank, his powerful boxer "Tiloilenspeigel," and Aunt Gerry came down and stayed with us once and we all had a wonderful time. Aunt Jerry did my nails for the first time, making "moons" with the polish. She took me to see "Daddy Long Legs" with Leslie Caron at the Village Theatre on the boardwalk. We had an ice cream sundae afterwards. I felt very grown-up!

I would take my little sister Marianne in her stroller for long walks, feeling very independent, a new teenager of thirteen. We'd walk past the fabled Grace Kelly mansion with its sophisticated, beige/brown Mediterranean stucco walls, imaging the beautiful actress within, who I was told I resembled, making her that much more intriguing and mysterious! Then we'd walk to The Chatterbox, also an Ocean City legend, a classic ice cream soda and hamburger hang-out, jukebox blaring with the latest hits, always overflowing with excited teenagers on vacation. As I made my way into the crowded, noisy Chatterbox with Marianne and her stroller, past the tall, tan adolescents with their friends and dates, scraping their red vinyl chairs noisily out of the way to let me pass, I indeed felt like The Ugly Duckling.

But that summer, my world began to change. Every now and then, strange boys out of nowhere, would come over to me as Marianne finished her ice cream and I, my soda, as we were leaving. They would say odd things to me:

"Are you from around here?"

"Pretty noisy in here, isn't it?"

"I really dig that hit by Pat Boone, want me to put a quarter in for you?" they'd ask, Marianne eyeing them suspiciously from her stroller with her big brown, all-knowing, four-year-old eyes.

I had been a solitary child and did not understand their attention. None of the pretty, blond, tanned girls paid me the slightest glance, annoyed as they flipped their page boys and impatiently scooted in their chairs to let us pass. But something deep inside me was trying to wake my sleeping child self: it told me softly, silently, the comfortable world as I knew it was beginning to change.

Then in the sixth grade, something else began to change. Completely unbeknown to me, my father's world of business began falling apart, prompting my mother's sad announcement one day.

With four siblings under the age of seven and a mother expecting once again, you had to move fast or things would get out of hand. The beautiful house in Rydal could be a wreck in a matter of minutes! On one of those days my mother was resting in her room, the music was on and my two younger brothers were doing their favorite activity, chasing each other across and around the sofas. They had just built another pile of the cushions I'd put back in place for the hundredth time. The living room was a complete mess, but my mother wasn't upset.

"Joan Ellen, we are going to move to Cleveland," she announced, standing by the entrance to the living room, pushing her beautiful thick chestnut hair back from her brow.

She looked very tired. I was thunderstruck. All the planning and wonderful things they had done to the house! I wouldn't know much for some time. They never spoke about what was going on. My father, my Uncle Frank, and my grandfather, Frank Flynn, son of the founder from

Ireland, Michael Flynn, were being sold out of their own company, The Michael Flynn Manufacturing Company, by the Star family, specifically Rubin Star and his son Seth.

Before anyone knew what was happening, my grandfather sold the company for $1 million. My father and my Uncle Frank had been raised in the business, assuming they would be the third generation to own and run it someday. It was a total shock. My grandfather Frank may have been taken advantage of, the true entrepreneur talent belonging to its founder, his father Michael Flynn. My grandfather accepted the offer-his son Frank insisted later it had been worth much, much more- without consulting his sons. It is said the Stars sold the company for many millions years later.

The bottom line is that the two Flynn sons took very different paths. My Uncle Frank, brilliant and aggressive like Seth Star, went into hiding in Great Neck, New York from the family. His extreme rage and disappointment at losing the family business, dominated his life. He hated his parents for a lifetime. My father also was hurt terribly and late in life my mother told me that in our final weeks in their Washington Lane dream home, she could hear my father crying at night before he fell asleep.

Years later I can truly appreciate the character of my father. I was only told that we were "moving to Cleveland." That was all I knew, my parents didn't say much, but positioned it like a great adventure. My father had actually made the decision to take the Company's Cleveland accounts and set up his own company in Cleveland. My 4th sibling, Elizabeth Grace, was born months before the move to Cleveland. What a chaotic time of change and uncertainty for my parents, moving from 1358 Washington Lane and the elite suburb of Rydal, leaving behind all the custom touches they had personally built into their new home with the architect. It must have been heart breaking for them.

Yet characteristically, they managed the difficult transition, as they always did throughout their lives, taught to handle crisis well.

"I'm going to show you all Valley Forge on our trip out! Those soldiers almost froze to death!" my father informed us heartily.

The day the moving truck pulled up to our home was in the dead of winter, January, and school had been cancelled since Wednesday. I planned to tell my classmates we were moving to Cleveland on Friday as I was shy and didn't want a lot of attention. However, due to the storm, we were off all week. Anxiously I waited Thursday and then

Friday, to go to school and tell them, but I never got the chance. We were to move Saturday morning and they would all come to school on Monday and find me gone. I had a lot of girlfriends and several boyfriends. They would always wonder why I never said goodbye. It bothered me for a long time.

"Softly, as I leave you softly, long before you wake and beg me stay for one more hour, for one more day. So I leave you softly, long before you miss me," as the song goes.

And so I left Philadelphia, the Jersey Shore, Willow Grove Amusement Park, Our Lady Help of Christians School, the rolling green lawns, the huge maple trees, the Indian Woods. But these things lived loyally in my memory for many, many years. When I returned 50 years later, there were many changes, but the things I loved most about Rydal were still intact and magnificent.

Brooklyn and Philadelphia, 1952

Just who were the Stars? In 1930 when Michael Flynn purchased the venerable but bankrupt David E. Lupton Window Company, he made the acquaintance of Rubin Star. A decision was made to purchase not just the factory for salvage as intended, but to reopen it and retain the entire workforce. Jobs would be saved by putting the men to work making not just residential, but commercial windows as well. Rubin Star, an equally adroit man of business, had seen this opportunity and now, working with Michael Flynn, was gaining influence in the company. And he had a son, Seth Star.

Rubin had fought in the Israeli army where he had noticed a young Israeli woman soldier driving a truck. Her name was Sophie, a no-nonsense dark-skinned beauty with thick brown hair and a mind of her own.

"Did anyone ever tell you, you drive like a man?" he yelled up to her one day as she maneuvered her supply truck recklessly by him down a wet, muddy road. Rubin was handsome with dark hair, a well-built, wiry man with dark brown eyes, a quick smile and a cigar in his mouth.

"Out of my way, Cookie, or I'll run you down!" yelled Sophie, hair wild and curly, her tan arms shapely in her brown Israeli blouse.

"I'd rather be killed by you, honey, than the Palestinians any day!" the handsome Freedom Fighter shot back.

"I can make that happen for you!" she fired back, jouncing down the muddy road.

Seth and Sophie were married after the war, like my parents, building a stunning new home in Elkins Park, Philadelphia so Seth could be near the factory and his father, Rubin. Seth was a talented and wily businessman like his father. "Smarter than Jesus Christ himself!" his family used to joke proudly about him.

And so Edward and Frank Flynn, their father, Frank, president of the Company, his father Michael Flynn, the aging founder, his longtime associate Rubin Star and *his* son Seth, expanded The Michael Flynn Company in ever-prosperous business ventures, dismantling destroyers and submarines through the 1940's.

Their pursuit of new and original sources of scrap metal was relentless. These were high times indeed. When dining out at restaurants, the brothers would joke, "Save the aluminum foil!" on their baked potatoes.

Frank came up with the idea of looking for scrap metal salvaging opportunities out West. The family had all traveled back to Brooklyn for Christmas at 587 5th Street. That evening around the old family table in the dining room with the large canopy chandelier overhead, Frank leaned back in his chair and lit his black pipe dramatically with its pungent Nunn's tobacco. Frank had fiery black eyes and thinning black hair, a broad forehead just like his father Frank and his grandfather, Michael Flynn.

"I've decided to take a run out to Denver," he announced dramatically. Geraldine, his wife and Brooklyn sweetheart, looked up at him, her blue eyes surprised by the announcement. Gerry was an attractive young woman with long dark blond hair wrapped in braids wound around her head. She wore a simple, tailored suit.

"Frank, why in the world *Denver*?" she asked. Gerry had gone to Bishop MacDonald High School in Brooklyn and then gone into retail at Sterns. She was a Brooklyn girl with "moxy", actually quite sophisticated for someone who had only been to Manhattan and New Jersey, but *Denver*?

"The idea," Frank explained, puffing on his pipe and pausing importantly for emphasis, "will be to travel to Telluride and buy old rails from the narrow gauge railroad down there for salvage."

"I believe it may have some merit," said Frank Sr., peering at his son with thick glasses from his place at the head of the table.

"Just be sure they pay us to have them removed and see if you can negotiate the trip back to Philly on their railroad!" Ed Flynn added, a comment that would have surely been made by Michael Flynn himself had he been alive.

Although the patriarch passed away in 1942, the family recalled his immense interest in any new business discussed at the dinner table, always intensely focused on how they could make the most profit on a deal. He would have surely appreciated and endorsed Frank Jr.'s Telluride proposal.

When he could no longer make it to the table, Michael Flynn took his meals in his room. It was thought losing his access to the evening discussions on the business of the day, hastened his crankiness and irritability, culminating in his death.

Perhaps the terrible cough that accompanied the infant down from County Leitrim, to the commotion of Cork Harbor and the intense cold in the crowded steerage of his ship crossing the frigid Atlantic, revisited his weakened lungs that August morning at 11am in 1942.

Maybe it was his boyhood, growing up 2 blocks from the East River, along the Brooklyn waterfront on Amity Street. Maybe it was working his entire life at the Michael Flynn Inc. office and scrap yard at Congress and Columbia, 50 feet from the docks. Maybe it was all of these.

Whatever it was, arthritis set in with a vengeance. It racked his knarled body until the old Irishman from County Leitrim was confined to his bed in the tiny back room of 587 5th Street, impatiently teaching his young grandson Edward how to count pennies in a can. And so he died one August morning at age 88 of bronchial pneumonia "actively involved in the business of The Michael Flynn Manufacturing Company until his death."

Being confined to bed for 13 years with "generalized arthritis", an unwanted souvenir of the cold trip across the Atlantic, itself may have hastened the proud Irishman's death. But born in 1852, he had outlived his years, years he had enjoyed and thrived in, shrewdly making his success from junkman to industrialist, "friend of politicians", in his beloved Brooklyn.

❦

"And, of course, I'll need to have Gerry go with me," Frank continued grandly, turning to his wife. "I won't want to be staying at The Brown Palace in Denver all by myself!"

"Oh, Frank, won't it be fun!" Gerry turned and gave the handsome man with the heavy black mustache and pipe a kiss on the cheek.

"Here's to Denver!!" said Ed Flynn with his new wife Joan at his side, and the family all raised their glasses high under the massive canopy of lights that hung above the dining room table at 587 5th street, the snow falling softly outside.

It was a wonderful evening as Gerry and Joan cleared the table and helped Mary Flynn in her kitchen with the dishes. The three men, spanning two generations - but probably with an invisible third listening intently nearby to the plans - retired to the living room to smoke and discuss the objectives of the trip. Frank had his ever-present boxer, Tiloilinspiegel, at his side.

"Say, there's a new movie coming out, called "The Apartment" with Jack Lemmon, my father announced to his brother and father.

"Did you hear? They're making it with Flynn windows!"

They all laughed heartily at his joke, one of many they often made, conscious and proud, of the success of the business. Later that evening, they all retired to their rooms upstairs in the brownstone. Mary Flynn kept Frank Jr.'s and Gerry's room on the street side of the 3rd floor with Edward and Joan's in the back. These were glory days indeed.

Then there was the time Edward was called into his father's office at the Philadelphia factory, from his work in the drafting room. Rubin Star and his son Seth were there as well.

"Edward, I think we may have another opportunity given us by the war's ending." This time it was Seth Star speaking.

"I've been reading about the atomic bomb that was tested on Bikini Island. There are many warships and destroyers that were at the scene but not sunk that we might want to salvage. Would you be willing to go out there and take a look? There are other companies that may be interested so we want to get there first. Only problem may be the radiation from the blast and we should be getting a report soon."

And so the world was their oyster. As it turned out, the radiation did make the ships unfit for immediate salvage for quite a while, but it was a heck of an idea.

Frank, Edward and Seth, being aggressive and quite ambitious, brought their ideas to their fathers regarding the company. Did Rubin Star promote Seth's ideas stronger than did Frank Flynn of his sons? Most probably. Frank, by nature, was the President of the company, excellent figurehead, but lacking the passion, shrewdness and business savy, that Michael Flynn had learned from necessity and want. Much to Edward's frustration, he did not champion or promote his sons' ideas, only passively agreeing at times.

So often had the quieter younger son, Edward, brought his well thought-out proposals for acquiring scrap metal to his father, only to have him go to Seth Star or someone else in the company for a critique or endorsement. It hurt Edward terribly. It was also a very big mistake.

One day a very odd thing happened to Joan Flynn. Seth and Sophie had invited Joan and Ed to their home in Elkins Park. Joan and Ed had just finished moving from their modest home in Winchester Park to the beautiful new home they had just designed with an architect in Rydal. Joan had just learned she was pregnant with a fifth child and Sophie had just given birth to their first son, a little boy named Danny.

The Star's home in Elkins Park was stylishly dark and contemporary for the 1950's with stone floors, dark tile and a steep backyard, terraced by railroad tracks. Seth Star, Sophie's sister Esther, and her children were also there and several other couples.

The children were running back and forth from the study to the family room, watching "A Christmas Carol". Television had just been invented and the Stars had one in each room. In amazement the children ran from one room to another. "How can the story be told on both TV's?" they wanted to know. "Look," they told all the parents in astonishment, sitting around the table after dinner, "we can watch the story in one room and catch what will happen next in another!" They were absolutely thunderstruck.

"Keep it down, Cookie!," yelled the still attractive Sophie from the kitchen, elegant with her long curly brunette hair held fashionably in tortoise shell barrettes over her deep burgundy satin dinner jacket. Everyone was "Cookie" to her. She was pouring juice for the children in brightly colored aluminum tumblers, ice cold to the touch, one of many new technical must-haves coming on the market along with nylon and zylon jackets.

A little later, a nanny put the children to bed and the dinner party was winding down. Seth, Edward, Rubin Star and a few of the guests retired to Seth's study for drinks.

Back in the dining room, the women were talking about their children when suddenly Sophie took Joan Flynn by the wrist, her charm bracelet jangling. "Come with me," she whispered urgently.

Sophie guided Joan into their newly-decorated bedroom and closed the door. "Always such drama!" Joan thought.

"They're plotting to take over the Company!" Sophie was looking at her with eyes wide with both fear and sympathy.

"What? What did you say?" Joan asked. What was she talking about?

"I heard them talking! They would kill me if I told you, but there, Cookie, I've told you!"

Sophie didn't elaborate, Joan didn't know what to say, so they simply emerged from the room in silence and went back to the party. It was like a dream. But change was indeed coming. The happy, heady days were coming to an end.

And change did come. Late one summer day.

Ed Flynn came home earlier than usual, pulling up the long steep driveway past their newly planted Lombardy trees and pink crabapples to the beautiful grey fieldstone home in Rydal, high on a one acre lot with other well-to-do homes, over the leafy and beautiful Washington Lane.

Ed parked in the garage and walked into the kitchen where Joan was preparing dinner and feeding Michael and Kevin. Their sister, Marianne, was in the high chair. The little girl had magnificent shiny brown mahogany hair just like her mother. Her metal brace with the yellow flannel support rested by the highchair, a token of the little girl's battle with the insidious spinal meningitis.

"You're home early!" said Joan cheerfully. Joan Dillon was radiant. Earlier that month she had learned she was pregnant with their fifth child, a blond baby girl they would call Elizabeth Grace, after Elizabeth Taylor and Grace Kelly.

"I've made a wonderful roast for tonight. I'm feeding the boys early so we can have a quiet candlelight dinner together."

Joan had set up places for two in their beautiful dining room with the French doors that looked out on the green backyard, reaching back to the native Philadelphia forest beyond, to the "Woods" as Michael and Kevin called it. Occasionally when they were dining there, two black and white Great Danes from the Kelly's mansion next door would come up to the French doors, peer in at the diners and then prance off, Ed and Joan joking that it was so hard to find good help.

Usually he kissed her when he came home from work and played with Michael and Kevin, a demolition team of fun and energy. Ed always looked impeccable in his white starched shirts, as the son of the president of the company should. Like his father, his shoes were always shined.

But today he walked silently by Joan into the breakfast room, dropped his leather briefcase, always bulging with architectural plans and drawings, with a thud on the floor, sat down and put his head in his hands.

Joan put down the roast, told Michael and Kevin to go play somewhere else, and put her hands on Edward's shoulders.

"Ed, what is it," she asked, her wonderful brown eyes full of concern.

"The Company. It's sold," Ed whispered.

"What?" said Joan incredulously.

"Dad sold the Company to Rubin Star and Seth. For a million dollars," he said flatly, in the hollow voice of someone in shock.

"Frank and I are out."

245

Cleveland Heights, Ohio, 1957

Joan Flynn Beesley

And so, just as my parents had proudly moved us in during a blizzard to their newly-built home on 1358 Washington Lane in Philadelphia, we also left in snow, early one morning, my parents and I and my younger brothers, Michael and Kevin, plus Marianne and new baby sister, Elizabeth Grace. I was eleven years old, in the middle of the 6th grade. It was January, 1957.

We piled into two cars with our suitcases, my father driving one car, my mother following in the car behind. We hadn't been told much about the move. We were moving to Cleveland, Ohio, was all we knew. My parents disguised their tremendous loss, of leaving the beautiful home they had designed, high up on the snow-covered hill. They instilled in us a sense of embarking on a great adventure.

Only years later did I fully understand that my father was leaving the family business behind. Now the legacy was gone. Those heady days of prosperity had been suddenly replaced by uncertainty. Dad's privileged days of financial security, hi-spirited investing and business expansion suddenly evaporated. Dad took the Cleveland accounts with him when he left the business and would start his own window business in Cleveland, The Edward R. Flynn Company, buying the windows from the factory in Philadelphia.

Yet Dad made the transition a great adventure. As he maneuvered down the steep snowy driveway, past the tall Lombardy poplars and crab trees he had planted by hand, we could hardly see three feet in front of us.

"Boys, we're going to stop at Valley Forge when we get to the Pennsylvania Turnpike. You think it's cold now. You should have been there with George Washington and the troops! We're going to see the actual huts where they almost froze to death that winter while they were waiting to fight the British in the spring."

Years later I recall there was never a "For Sale" sign on the property as we pulled away. All we knew was that we were moving to Ohio, that it was going to be a great adventure and a lot of fun, brand new friends, new school, new house that Dad had found for us. He had made several mysterious trips to Ohio, staying at a YMCA, working with a realtor, looking for a location to start his window business.

An hour later, we pulled slowly through the blowing snow into the well-known Gateway Exit along the turnpike where we let the kids run around and had some lunch. As we walked out of the rest stop, I looked at the big Mac trunks all pulled over, the drivers putting on or adjusting chains. I remember standing in the doorway of the restaurant and it dawned upon me we weren't heading back to Philadelphia. We weren't just out for a Sunday drive, after which we'd return to Sunday evening dinner and my homework for school in the morning. This was different. We weren't going back.

At Valley Forge, we piled out and went to the gift store where Mother and Dad bought a set of portraits of George Washington and his troops which would hang for many years in the living room of the Cleveland house he had picked out for us. Then Dad drove us to the small log huts where George Washington and the troops nearly froze to death in 1774. While Michael and Kevin ran excitedly in and out of the huts, Dad discussed whether these could *really* be the actual huts where the troops stayed, or replicas. My parents always had an appreciation for history and it was typical they would question and ponder the authenticity of the huts.

"You can almost see the soldiers coming over that hill," Dad said to me in a quiet moment.   He was like that. I was a lot like him and I could picture the ragged, exhausted men in blue, almost dropping from cold and hunger, stopping to make camp and build the log huts where they would stay for the winter, hiding from the British, who were now all over Manhattan. Years later I wondered if that stop at Valley Forge had been an inspiration to him, fleeing his life in New York and Philadelphia, starting out for Ohio, where he didn't know a soul, with his ever-growing family.

We pulled back onto the Ohio turnpike late that afternoon and made our way west to Cleveland. We moved slowly, crunching over the icy streets, following my father in the car ahead with Michael and Kevin. I, with my mother, Marianne and the new baby Elizabeth, followed behind as he turned off Lee Rd. and proceeded slowly west along Berkshire Rd. It was a tree-lined street with large houses back from the street with large front lawns.

My mother was clearly excited.

"Oh, look," Joan Ellen," she said. "The house is on Berkshire!"

We knew we were probably getting close to our new home but we didn't know which one it was. Apparently my father didn't either. He repeatedly turned into the driveways of several homes and then turned out.

"He's such a tease!" my mother said.

"Just look at him!" she laughed, as we realized he probably *did* know the house and was just fooling us. My mother, now pregnant with my sister Maureen, had not made the trip to Cleveland to pick out the new house. Dad had worked with a realtor to pick it out himself with her approval.

Finally we crossed Washington Blvd. another tree-lined street with large older homes and continued down Berkshire Rd. Then Dad made a left turn into another driveway.

"Here we go again!" I said. But he continued up the snowy drive and we followed him, stopping by the side of a dark brown brick English Tudor house with beige stucco and dark brown traditional Tudor markings. Excitedly, we piled out of the car. This was it!

"Oh, Ed. I love it!"

Dad had his arm around mother. I knew then that everything was going to be fine. The house had huge oak and maple trees on the property. Opening the heavy side door, Dad went in first and turned on the lights for us. I remember us running through the house, the thick, pretty floral carpet in the living room, the kitchen pantry with white wood and glass cabinets. We ran up the stairs to explore the bedrooms and who would be sleeping where. Dad explained that a moving truck would be arriving soon so we would have beds to sleep in that night. Since the wallpaper was in the process of being removed, my parents said we could write on the walls which we did with crayons from the car. It was great fun. We always had a good time, what with my father's great sense of humor and unique appreciation for the details and adventures of life!

Several days later, my mother informed me I would have to walk to St. Ann's School and
register myself alone as she was too pregnant and would not be able to go with me. I was to go to the Principal's office and ask for Sister Saint John.

Apprehensively, I walked up the school steps. It was a Monday morning and lessons were being taught behind the pulled-down shades of the many classrooms. I approached the smoked glass door which said "Principal's Office" in large, ominous black letters. I knocked on the door and was met by Sister St. John herself, dressed from head to toe in her black habit. She was very stern and somewhat annoyed as she had not received my grades yet.

"Very well," she said. "You will be in Sister Mary Margaret's class."

She led me to the 2nd floor of the school and knocked on the closed door of the classroom. My new teacher opened the door, took me to the center of the class, introduced me and finally assigned me to a desk. After class as we were filing out, a girl came over to meet the "new girl."

"Hi!" she said, "My friends and I would like you to be in our club!" How wonderful I felt. They wanted me to be in their club!

2862 Berkshire was a wonderful place to grow up, a very special home. I lived there from the middle of 6th grade until I went away to college in New York. My father once said that after choosing affluent Cleveland Heights as his choice of location, the realtor had shown him the English Tudor on Berkshire listed at $95,000.

"What do you think I should offer?" my father had asked.

"$92,000," said the realtor, which my father promptly did and the home was his.

He told us the story of sitting alone on the bottom step of the stairs in the center hall and looking out through the double glass doors into the living room with a fire place, once he knew the offer had been accepted and he had the keys to the house.

"This is a home where Joan and I will throw many wonderful parties!" he said to himself. And they did.

Some homes make noises. The dark brick English Tudor at 2862 Berkshire Rd. creaked at night, a series of five to seven long, painful creakings.

"Don't worry," Ed Flynn would assure his oldest daughter.

"It's just the house settling." Or sometimes he would say, "It's just the furnace."

Whatever it was, it gave the home character and a certain reassurance, a certain dignity that it was "settling".

If our home was special, Cleveland Heights was also. We lived about 3 blocks from St. Ann's Church and school in a large, very active Catholic parish with many growing families just like ours. We could walk to school along with many classmates and friends who lived nearby. It seemed everyone knew everyone else. We moved into Berkshire with my brothers Michael, Kevin and my sisters Marianne and Elizabeth, all born in Philadelphia except for myself, born in Brooklyn like my parents.

But there was more to come! Soon my sister Maureen was born, a beautiful chestnut-haired, twelve pound baby girl. My mother had to stay in the hospital a little longer than usual as it had been a difficult Caesarian delivery. A few years later my brother Eddie was born and finally John, when I was a freshman in high school. My mother delivered John at age 42.

Since I was the oldest, I still had my own room, which made me feel very special. Due to the English Tudor architecture, my room, in the front of the house, had many special alcoves and indentations. My mother chose a blue and white wallpaper with one wall in a different pattern.

I loved that room. I could close the door and find quiet and peace in a home of constant noise and commotion. Sometimes during the winter months, I would lie in bed at night, listening to the reassuring hissing of the radiator in my room by the window. I still had my bedroom set with the twin beds, bought in Philadelphia, the gift from my grandmother Flynn in Brooklyn.

The trees on our front lawn were very old and very tall. I could catch a glimpse of them at night, the clack-clacking of their bare branches, shaken by the strong winter winds from Lake Erie. My father would be in the TV room across the hall watching Ed Sullivan, The Twilight Zone or a variety show from the early days of TV, with a favorite evening bowl of ice cream, a habit he enjoyed his entire life.

Summer mornings were magical. I would lie in bed before the house awakened, listening to the soft "clink-clink" of the milkman in his navy blue "Hillside Dairy" truck, delivering milk to the front porches. My white nylon curtains would flutter with the summer breeze of the early morning. Sometimes I would hear alarm clocks going off in the neighborhood, awakening paperboys who would soon be delivering The Cleveland Plain Dealer with a soft thump to the driveway or front doorway.

Due to her numerous pregnancies, my mother always had an African-American maid in the house for as long as I can remember. Even when I returned from college, I would lie in my bed, only to be told "Eurie" or "Florence" would soon be reaching my room to change the sheets and that it was time to get up.

My mother always had breakfast, lunch and dinner ready for us. She loved to make pancakes of all types, apple, applesauce or blueberry, whatever she had on hand. Dinners were often fish sticks on Fridays, with baked potatoes, meat cakes and vegetables on other nights. She was a very good cook, always serving basic, healthy meals. I recall so many days walking home from St. Ann's for lunch. There would always be soup, often tomato with cottage cheese, and a sandwich, tuna fish or grilled cheese, waiting for me. Mother always made lunch for the maid working in our home.

The daily rhythm of life was so comfortable and secure in those days, going to school during the week, homework, Mass with the family at St. Ann's on Sunday morning (we never missed!). School was very important and I made sure I was a good student. With seven brothers and sisters there was always a lot of household work to be done.

My parents were very social, had many friends and entertained a lot. How I loved those Saturday evenings when my mother would be getting dressed in their bedroom for a party they were hosting for "The Couples Club" of St. Ann's. Many of these couples became their lifelong friends, sharing the triumphs and achievements of their many children with each other. Saturday morning my father would often go to the hardware store, the cleaners and then pick up some liquor for friends they had invited over.

Invariably my father would be finished before my mother and come downstairs with his slight scent of Old Spice. He would put on Frank Sinatra or play some of his favorite songs on the piano. I loved listening to him play, often standing there beside with him at the upright, his huge but nimble fingers playing Boogey-Woogey or Begin the Beguine.

Mother would have cleaned the house that afternoon with Swedish meatballs now simmering in her special black and white porcelain pan in the kitchen while dad checked the liquor for his guests' highballs. Always about an hour before the guests came, the last thing she would do before running upstairs to take her shower was wiping the guest bath floor on her hands and knees. Guest towels out and the clock ticking, she would rush upstairs to get ready. After her shower I would sometimes go in and quickly roll up her now short but still gorgeous, thick chestnut hair. She would apply her make-up, some light perfume, pick out a beautiful dress and some jewelry just as the front door began to ring.

She and Dad were wonderful hosts. I could frequently hear my mother and their guests laughing at my father's stories and jokes, listening intently to his theories about space, glasses tinkling all evening. My job was to see that my brothers and sisters went to bed after watching TV or reading to them, a very easy job. I loved my life in those days. I was happy to help, and enjoyed knowing my parents were doing what they loved to do, making life-long friends, telling and listening to the stories of their respective lives, especially the several couples in the parish from Brooklyn.

I loved my brothers and sisters. Curious and unique little people. I enjoyed teaching them things, reading and playing games with them, taking them for walks to give my mother a break. It seemed I was constantly folding warm, clean cloth diapers from the dryer for them on the floor.

West Islip, New York, 1970

Joan Flynn Beesley

It was many years before I fully understood the Hiroshima that had imploded the lives of Joan and Edward Flynn. And many years after that to appreciate how gracefully they managed the crisis.

The ominous warning Sarah Star told Joan at the dinner party proved to be true. The Stars had made an offer to the aging Frank Flynn, far less than the company was worth, and he, perhaps not realizing the true worth and potential of the company, had accepted it without consulting his sons.

Both Ed and Frank Jr. had enjoyed a privileged –and exciting – upbringing. They were each groomed to take over the company one day, brought up listening to business deals and opportunities being planned each night around the dinner table by Michael Flynn with his son Frank, their father. Needless to say, the sudden announcement that the company had been sold, shook them each to their very core.

From that day forward Frank Flynn Jr. viciously hated both his parents. He had a nervous breakdown, locking himself in his apartment, disappearing for eight years until found in West Islip, Long Island, by his niece, me, while I attended college in New Rochelle, New York. It is said he never spoke to his parents again.

Yet that evening when I and my future husband, Ed, were invited out to Frank's home in West Islip, how happy I was to see him, and he, me. Handsome and charming as ever with his black mustache and pipe, he treated us to a fabulous lobster dinner at a local restaurant with his new German wife, Inga.

Later that evening, he poured us chilled white Lancer's, holding the green clay bottle with a white cloth, serving the young couple with great ceremony in his cozy, wood paneled den. He was the perfect host, hilarious and delightful. He and Inga would invite us several years later when we were married and living in Brooklyn, out to their home each weekend for Sunday dinner. Once, when I gingerly brought up a vague reference to my grandparents, the strained and furious look I saw on his face told me never to do it again.

After I broke the ice with Frank and Inga, my father and his family of seven drove from Cleveland for a much-anticipated reunion. They all enjoyed a wonderful meal prepared by Inga, until Frank, enraged when Dad brought up their parents, ran upstairs in his home in West Islip, and shot off a shotgun, terrifying my parents and the children. Dad quickly herded the frightened children and my mother to the safety of their car, went back to check on Uncle Frank, then headed sadly, and angrily, back to Cleveland.

When my grandfather died, he left the larger portion of his estate to my father, due to his large family and life-long devotion to his parents, despite the shocking decision to sell the company. Uncle Frank contested the will, losing an ugly battle at the Supreme Court in Brooklyn, in which he tried to prove his father, my grandfather, incompetent. In the court proceedings, nonetheless, my father was a gentleman, deferential to his troubled older brother, never taking advantage of his brother's obvious rantings and distortions concerning his perceived unfair treatment at the hands of his father.

Although Dad advised me not to attend the trial, that it would make Uncle Frank even angrier to see me sitting there with the family, I did attend one of the days. How strange it was to hear some of the wild accusations against the grandfather I loved. As my Uncle Frank strode down the aisle the morning the suit was settled, I dared to look up at him and barely recognized the intellectual-looking, mustached man with consuming anger blazing in his black eyes.

Uncle Frank's fury at his parents, and losing what he surely considered his birthright, knew no bounds. Once, when my grandmother, Mary Flynn, then up in years, sent a small gold charm bracelet to his young daughter, her granddaughter, Uncle Frank chopped it up and mailed it back, shocking and hurting her terribly. It is said he never again spoke to his parents after his father sold the company.

Sadly when Mary Flynn was dying in 1976 at the age of 81, my father came in the middle of the night from Cleveland, arriving moments before her death. With her last breath, she took Dad's hand and whispered, "Frank, is it you?"

Cleveland Heights, Ohio, 1964

Joan Flynn Beesley

The leafy ambiance of oak-lined slate sidewalks nurtured me as a child growing up in Cleveland Heights. Later in high school, I rode the 32B bus, up Cedar Rd. to Green, safe in my uniform and armload of books, along with many other girls just like me, serene in the security and predictability of the rumbling, lurching bus and its route, with its many familiar stops from my home to the school and back.

The large marble church we attended every Sunday with my seven brothers and sisters inspired me with sermons and incense and made me look introspectively on how I could do better, as a person, each week. And I did. Cleveland Heights had high expectations of the eldest of eight as you were the example and the first ambassador of the family to the world. If you did well, it was likely the others would follow your legacy. If you did poorly, Cleveland Heights was unforgiving as news of your shortcomings quickly made the rounds at the dinner tables of the many-childrened families in the parish of St. Ann's.

I knew I wanted to be a writer at a very early age. But it was one summer at age 16 when reading "South by Java Head" by Jack London, that I knew for certain. I was intrigued by the main character, a young lieutenant. Years later at a book signing in Telluride, I asked Clive Custler if he had ever read the book, as his famous protagonist, Dirk Pitt, reminded me strongly of Jack London's lieutenant. To my astonishment, Clive told me that, indeed, he had fashioned his lead character after Jack London's lieutenant.

That summer afternoon I spent lounging on the side porch of Berkshire, the tall oaks, shrubs, forsythia and wild flowers, swaying pungently in the light breeze. I was fifteen and rakishly independent in my bare feet and shorts, not yet introduced to the working life. With my whole summer ahead of me, I sat at the frequently replaced glass-top table with the wrought iron chairs-I can still hear their grating sound when moved on the concrete patio-knowing I too had a talent at writing.

I could hear the woods move, the trees gently sway, outside the screened porch my father had built with Edward R. Flynn Company windows. I would drink lemonade there, finish a book and then walk down to The Cleveland Heights Public Library to pick out yet another novel, the next being Maureen Sullivan's "Seventeen" to read, marveling how I could select and then check out any great book I wanted from the shelves in the "Young Adult" Room.

It was at this library I would have my first real job working for the meticulous "Miss Cap" the next summer as a Carder. Miss Capp taught me well about the work ethic, punctuality and quality work. I recall her icy blue eyes flashing with disapproval when a certain brown-haired, freckled-faced newspaper boy brought his friends into the library one hot summer evening to see his girl friend up there at the front desk carding books. They circled the library reading room like young lions, pretending not to know me, and then left. But Miss Cap, in her high white blouse, silver hair, and all-knowing blue eyes, somehow knew immediately who they were...

I met that boy, who would be the man of my dreams, while still in grade school at St. Ann's. Lining up in single file in the parking lot, each child was being assigned to one of three eighth grades. From the back of my line I heard a commotion. The dreaded Sr. Benigna was dragging a grinning, freckled-faced boy with black, wavy hair in a brown suit by the ear up to the front of the line.

"When I say no talking, eyes straight ahead, that's exactly what I mean, Mister!" Sister Benigna's stern voice told the boy, looking back at her with amusement in his handsome brown eyes.

Looking down calmly at my perfect new black and white saddle shoes and knee-high's, I recall telling myself: "Now there's a boy I could never like!"

When I was fourteen I began to take my younger sister Marianne, still wearing the brace to straighten the leg whose nerves had been damaged by meningitis, down to the playground of Coventry Elementary School. Every day at 4:45 on the dot, the boy who had unleashed the wrath of Sr. Benigna at the back of the line, would cross the playground with his newspaper carrier's white sack on his shoulder, headed for his home on Edgehill Rd.

At first we just said hello. Then he would occasionally stop to talk and visit for a while. I found myself wondering, "Would he stop today?" I began to look forward to our talks and noticed how really good-looking he was. Ed was the second oldest of nine children and I being the oldest of eight, talked about the daily struggles of life in a large family in

St. Ann's Parish.

I soon found myself gathering up Marianne every day at 4:15 pm, whether she wanted to go for a walk or not, to be sure I was at the playground on time so as not to miss Ed. How excited I was everyday now to see the black-haired boy with the empty newspaper sack appear on the ridge over the playground and coming my way. He was very personable, funny, with a special streak of independence, a way of looking at the world that I loved. He often helped me position the dark-haired Marianne in her little sundresses on the swings and push her gently through the air as we talked.

I married this boy, the love of my life, Edward Beesley, on August 30, 1969 at a large, magnificent wedding at St. Ann's. The reception was held at the beautiful College Club with its rolling green lawn in Cleveland Heights. My parents' many friends attended, Frank and Mary Flynn and even Leonard and Sarah Star with whom my parents stayed in touch. My grandparents paid for my college education and also my wedding dress. It was implied by my parents that their generosity had something to do with the selling of the Company.

Cleveland Heights, Ohio, 1968

Joan Flynn Beesley

Addison Jr. High School was a bad school, underscore *bad*. The year was 1969 and the Cleveland Riots had taken place a year earlier, starting at The Lancer Steak House, not far from the school.

Those days seem like a much simpler time now. The only major concern was the Vietnam War and in the United States, how to help the "disadvantaged", code name for poor black urban students. No Iraq, no 9/11, no terrorists. No preoccupation with being politically correct. There was simply a very large, growing black population in Cleveland's ghetto dropping out of school, many becoming criminals. There was a growing awareness that something had to be done.

I had just graduated with a degree in English from a private four year women's college in New York, The College of New Rochelle. I had been awarded a grant towards my M.A.T. degree (Master of the Art of Teaching/English) to Disadvantaged Adolescents from a private Catholic University in Cleveland Heights. Part of the degree required us to teach for one semester in the inner city and I had been assigned to Addison. President Kennedy had just established Title I money to help the inner city schools. My masters program had, in fact, been funded with grant money from Title I.

The program was to select teachers who were very good in their majors, such as English, history, science, etc. and equip them with the skills to go into the ghetto schools, reinforcing the dedicated black teachers already there. I was to teach several classes of 7th graders and 10th graders, the junior high system going from 7th through the 10th grade.

For six months we were taught about the African American experience, drilled on how to keep control in the classroom, in addition to taking graduate courses in our majors. We had meetings with the various agencies and community centers in the neighborhood to introduce us as the "new" teachers who would teach in the fall. Community leaders were formal, courteous, somewhat distant, perhaps skeptical of what we were doing in *their* neighborhood, parts of which had been burned during the riots, fires set by oppressed, angry young men inflamed by the racist rhetoric of the Black Panthers. "Burn, Baby, Burn!" had been their mantra.

We were the first group of white teachers to ever teach at Addison, which had a reputation as being the worst junior high in the ghetto. We walked, as a group, through the respective neighborhoods where we would be teaching. We were told there would be a helicopter following us in case of trouble, comforting then, questionable now!

I remember that first day, pulling my white Valiant push-button drive convertible into the old asphalt parking lot, weeds growing through the cracks, smashed liquor bottles in brown bags. I looked up at the ancient, butter-yellow brick, two story building with the broken windows.

"Here we go," I said to myself as I entered the building passing two scowling large adult males stationed at the entrance.

I checked in with the principal, Mr. Findley. Mr. Findley was in his fifties, a heavy-set, muscular black man, who sat behind a large desk. I could tell he had been doing this for many years. He had a soft, Southern drawl, but a man who could be extremely forceful if the occasion called for it.

Outside his office sat sullen looking teenagers, some jiving and carrying on, some with dew rags around their heads, some with agitated parents, usually mothers with babies, angry with their children, angry with the school, angry with life. Mr. Findley explained I would be staying in my own classroom and would not have to move around to different rooms, which was a real plus.

"Glad to have you with us. We need good English teachers in this school," he said, shaking my hand as I left his office.

"There's a red button by the side of the door. Press it once and one of us will come running."

The first week was the most difficult. Just getting the students into their seats and gaining control of the class was the hardest. One of the methods we used was called "Bell Work" in which we would have a riddle or question written on the board in the same place everyday. The students were given points for writing their answers on strips of papers which were passed up after a short amount of time. It was a great technique, usually, for getting them in their seats, materials out, and hopefully, ready to work.

I would stand by my door as each class filed in. They were all very curious about "Miz. Flynn."

"Good Morning." I said to each of them.

"Morning."

"Mornin', Mam."

Some of the students were deferential, respectful and wanted, I thought, to make a good impression. These few were neatly dressed in clean, checkered shirts, belts, jeans or khaki's. The majority wore ill-fitting, dirty clothes. Some wore militant tee-shirts with the black power raised fist symbol, chains, dirty sweatshirts, dew-rags around their heads, smirking, joking and jiving as they sauntered past me.

As I stood at my door, the final student, a tough talking, gum-smacking, heavily-made-up girl with a gold blond streak in her kinky black hair, strolled past me into the room. She suddenly turned and passed her hand lightly over the side of my hair as she walked by.

"My name's *Wanda*!" she informed me. Wanda had the eyes of a woman many years older than the fourteen-year old teenager she was supposed to be, with a short, tight skirt, red halter-top and Afro.

"And I just wanted to see if yo' blond hair was *real*!"

"It's real, Wanda. Please take your seat."

And so it began. They were curious about me and I was equally curious about them. I had up to about 45 students in each class. In those days, many were probably on drugs and/or had fairly severe learning disabilities which we label today as ADD, dyslexia, etc. In my classes, all we knew was that these children could not concentrate. They were noisy and highly interactive with each other.

At the university we had been told that most inner city students suffered from malnutrition. Many of the parents had come to Cleveland from the South or had roots in the South. They were the descendants of slaves, many of whom came to Ohio via the underground railroad in the days of the Abolitionists. In fact, a summer cottage my family had rented in central Ohio when I was a child had a locked basement which the owner said was a "station" for slaves fleeing plantations in the South. The malnutrition these students suffered from was generational and contributed to the high population of learning disabled students. The school's neighborhood was a horrific slum with old wooden houses, rotting with broken windows and sagging front porches. These children had been raised in homes with old lead water pipes and lead-based paint as well. Drugs and prostitution were prominent environmental influences.

One of my brightest students was named James. A large ninth grader, he dressed in clean, plaid, long-sleeved shirts, belt and actual khaki pants, in sharp contrast to some of the more radical members of the class, with their ripped jeans, muscle tee shirts and dew rags. I had never seen him in jeans. Respectful and wanting to learn, he wore his hair short and wore glasses. From the quiet, soft-spoken, deferential way he responded to me as his teacher, I guessed his parents were traditional blacks from the South. Then one day, James, stopped coming to school.

On the third day I became concerned. No one knew where he was. Teachers were encouraged to take an active role when a student was absent, because there was no one else to do it. The one truant officer for the school couldn't possibly keep up with the escalating absence rate. With new, transient students being admitted and large numbers dropping out, it was always quite chaotic.

So I decided to investigate myself. I looked up James's address in the office and set forth out into the neighborhood after school. Aware of neighbors eying me, I pulled my car up slowly to an old wooden house similar to many in the ghetto, built in the 1920's, and literally falling down. Part of the roof had caved in. There were boards across the broken windows. I couldn't believe people actually lived here.

Getting out of my car, I was determined to find this boy. I crossed the cracked sidewalk, littered with weeds and broken bottles and stepped up onto the old front porch, or what was left of it. Many of the boards had rotted and were missing. I peered through the window in the old front door, but could see nothing.

Knocking on the door brought no response. I waited a while and was about to leave, uncomfortable standing around by myself in a neighborhood where I knew I wasn't welcome. Suddenly the door opened a crack and a little black face looked up at me.

"What yo' *want*?? Y'all a bill collector?"

"Why no, I'm not." The little girl was barefoot, very dirty, about five years old. Her braids were natty and her clothes dirty and torn. Her eyes were red with conjunctivitis and her nose was running.

"My name is Miss Flynn and I'm looking for one of my students, James. He's been absent from school for three days now and I need to know why."

"He ain't *here*."

"Well, do you know where he is?"

"No mam. He ain't here no 'mo. He went to live wit his grandma."

"Well, thank you very much." I wondered if this were James' little sister, if she had been left behind and who would take care of her. I would never know.

I never saw James again, but I wished him well wherever he was. He was a sincere student who wanted to learn, a real gift in my classes of troubled students. As I got back into my convertible, I looked back up at the house. I couldn't believe people actually lived there. It must have been a terrible life. But it gave me real insight into the lives these students were living, before and after class. After that when they came to class angry, agitated and wanting to fight, I knew why. I had a better understanding and tolerance for their horrific lives outside school. Who wouldn't be troubled when your home had no electricity, police cars came in the night to break up domestic violence or when gangs, pushers and prostitutes roamed your street?

That first week whenever I called role in the beginning of a ninth grade class, a large, angry-looking black student named "Jimmy" would sit in the back row and bang on a metal pipe he brought with him each day.

"Assume you're not in peril and you won't be," I told myself.

It usually worked well. During the second week, a girl told me as she left the class, "You know, Miz. Flynn, why *that* boy back there *ain't* even *Jimmy*! He's somebody else. He ain't even supposed to *be* here!" I was grateful for that knowledge and the principal's office straightened out the problem.

The first week was extremely difficult. It took all my special training to get control of the seventh and ninth grade classes I taught. They would file into my room agitated, upset, and ready to fight with each other. Luckily, I didn't have to go out in the over-crowded, dangerous halls to change classes. I had my own room for teaching English.

There were guns in the school and other dangers as well. I almost lost my voice the first week from trying to gain control and make myself heard at the beginning of each class. That first Friday I got the class seated and then left for a moment to go down the hall to a water fountain to take a lozenge for my throat as I sounded as if I were getting laryngitis.

I leaned down over the water fountain when I sensed commotion down the hall. Several teachers were rushing into my room from the adjacent classes. I ran down the hall and into my room. The students were all standing up, yelling and pointing. Desks were overturned. The teachers were helping a girl out of my room. There was blood on my carefully-made lesson plan, lying on my desk.

"What happened?" I asked one of the students. "She owed 'em _money_!" a student explained. Members of a neighborhood gang had been in the hall, waiting for an opportunity. They had entered my classroom and stabbed one of the students, a girl I didn't know. They were an extortionist gang. This was a seventh grade class. Somehow I got the students back in their seats, calmed them down and taught my lesson.

At the end of that day, in spite of all my training, I was still shaken by the stabbing. I seriously asked myself if I would return the next day. As I walked slowly down the hall, I saw an older, black teacher alone in his classroom. I walked into his class. He was a tall, thin man with a mustache who looked to be in his late 50's. He wore a bowtie and suspenders. He looked like he had been at Addison for many years.

"How's it goin'?" he asked me politely, in a deep, rich voice.

"It's hard." I said. I was emotionally exhausted and had a terrible headache.

"How do you do it?" I asked.

He looked at me sadly and shook his head. "You know, it never really gets any easier. I've been at this a long time." I noticed he was putting away a group of matchbox cars in his desk.

"Take these here cars." He was holding them in his hand, almost tenderly.

"They like 'em, yes they do. I pass them out to motivate them for doing a good job. It works. Some of these guys are almost old enough to be _drafted_." He smiled, shook his head again, looked sad and then chuckled to himself in that soft, Southern way of acceptance I had come to associate with the black people of Addison.

I wished him a good evening. I had found the strength to return and face my classes in the morning.

If the first week was difficult, the second week was terrifying. Each day I would walk out to my car, wondering how I could possibly go back the next day. Finally, I realized just getting _through_ each day was a victory in itself. In my program back at the university, one of the exercises we had to do the week before starting student teaching, was to practice being stern, to lower our voices. I didn't do very well in the practice session. Most of the young men in the program used body language to convey that they meant business. "You need to look sterner," my master teacher advised me.

"The kids will know right away if you're sincere," the experienced black older woman explained to us. And this was very true. "Don't ever try to be someone you're not. They'll soon figure this out. They'll never accept you and it will be quite difficult."

And try me out they did.

It happened during the second week. I was just getting used to my 7th grade class. I think I was more comfortable with them because they were younger. They were harder to get focused, but not as formidable as the older adolescents in the 9th grade. It was about ten minutes until the bell rang. We had just finished a spelling test.

"O.K. Pencils down. Pass your papers forward. First one in the row pass them across to my desk. That's it. Thank you." Everything seemed normal except for the sudden quiet in the room. It was never quiet in my room.

"O. K. Take out your literature books. Open to page 25. We're going to start a story about life in the Antarctic." I watched as the class took out their books and started to open to page 25. I saw someone turn around and look up at the classroom clock. Suddenly the class of 30 began laughing and shouting and throwing their books at each other. They stood up and overturned their desks, yelling, completely out of control. I stepped back towards the safety of my desk, out of the way as they opened the door and ran, in pandemonium, out of my room. I looked out at my classroom, the overturned desks, papers settling on the floor, books everywhere. I felt faint. Two male teachers came running into the room.

"I...I don't know what happened. All of a sudden....they just..." I couldn't speak. My throat was burning.

"We just found out that they're doing this in each class just before the bell rings at a given signal," one of the teachers explained. Suddenly I felt better. Their actions weren't directed at me personally. Still, I hadn't been prepared for something like this!

"I'm O.K. Just a little scared and shocked. Can you help me with these desks? The next class will be coming in. It won't be good for them to see the room like this."

I knew the importance of order and what they called a "low stimulus" environment for these students. I taught my next class. I was more than a little scared and shocked for the rest of the week.

After a while, the students got to know me. Things got a little better. I think they sensed I loved English and that I was interested in them. I wanted to teach them English, so they would be able to read, write and enjoy literature.

There were actually two categories of students. The first group I would call traditional black southern students. Respectful and polite, they dressed conservatively. Their clothes were ragged, but clean. They were there to learn. A few of these students were very bright. They would someday get out of the Cleveland inner city via education. Some in this group were not very bright, but I was touched with their desire to learn.

Sadly, they lacked fundamental reading and writing skills and would probably take basic labor or service jobs after graduation. They might be considered adolescent versions of "Uncle Tom" blacks, having fourth grade skills in junior high school, but trying to do their best, to please their teacher. They were not angry.

One of these students was Charles. I first noticed him when I was walking down the aisles during a grammar exercise. I had the students do a lot of copying sentences, underlying nouns, verbs and parts of speech. It's the best way, also, of teaching spelling at the same time.

As I passed by, I noticed a boy - about 15 years old, clean pants, belt and plaid shirt, kind of a middle-aged looking kid - not doing the assignment, but working on a comic strip, about dinosaurs, in his notebook. The quality of the cartoons and the dialogue balloons was good enough to be in the *Cleveland Plain Dealer*.

"Charles, what are you doing?" I paused, standing over him. You always had to be very careful in approaching and challenging these students. You just never knew. The boy was shy and looked up at me sheepishly through his thick glasses. "Well, Mam, I jus' workin on my *stuff*."

"Charles, you know these are really very good." As I looked down I could see he had a thick, ragged notebook crammed full of cartoon strips he had drawn, with dinosaurs and other creatures talking to each other. He must have spent hours upon hours creating the notebook. He beamed with the compliment.

"I know you'd much rather be doing these cartoons, but I'll have to ask you to put them away and work on our grammar lesson. I wouldn't be doing my job if I just let you draw cartoons in my class, would I?" To my relief, Charles put the note book away and started copying the sentences from his grammar book. "If you'd like to bring them by after school, I'd love to take a look at them." For Charles, a gifted cartoonist, this would be his way out of the ghetto.

The second group was not so lucky. These were the majority of the students. With no particular talent, and reading and writing at a fourth grade level, they were hostile and angry at life. Most were from broken homes without a father figure. Some had been abused from parents on drugs and/or alcohol. They acted out constantly, fighting, cursing, challenging or interrupting any sincere student who asked a question or tried to learn. Some would become criminals, prostitutes or drug addicts, just like their parents. They dressed like street people.

If all this wasn't enough, they were also under the influence of the neighborhood Black Panthers with their message of hate and "Burn, Baby, Burn!" against white people. I worked hard to gain their respect as a firm, fair teacher who wanted them to enjoy English and improve their reading and writing skills. Many times, after an especially good lesson, I felt I had made contact with them as a teacher and a person, only to see them come in the next day sullen and resentful, ready to fight.

The local Black Panthers did not like having our group of white teachers in the school. We were warned to keep an eye out for them. Some of our older students were members and reported on what was being taught. I knew a few of my students were very much under their influence. I could actually feel it. Many times I felt they wanted to accept me as a person but I was white. These adolescents were dealing first with all the negative historical baggage from their own black family cultures. Then, each day, they heard the intense militant messages of hatred from media Black Panthers such as Eldridge Cleavor and Malcom X on their TV's. Finally, they were being indoctrinated by their own neighborhood "brothers" who had recently set parts of the Cleveland ghetto on fire, to call attention to racial injustices. I could often feel confusion. They were being pulled in two directions. I could feel at times they wanted to like this white teacher but their culture pulled them back and made them ashamed and shame often turned into a subtle, sullen anger towards me.

Sometimes the anger wasn't so subtle. The third week of class, a baby-faced, six foot tall boy named Michael Jones got up out of his seat in the middle of my lesson. He was a good-looking boy, humorous and usually cooperative, but this day he was looking for trouble. Dressed in jeans and a tee shirt and enormous white-topped sneakers, he jumped up on the ancient radiator that hissed and steamed under the long set of windows that looked out over the parking lot from my classroom on the second floor.

"What you *doin'* up there, Michael?" came the calls from the back of the room.

"You *crazy*, boy?"

"What you *doin'*, fool?"

"I *ain't* crazy". Michael's eyes looked dilated, taunting me to defy him from his perch above the class. "I just want a better look at Miz. Flynn's *car*."

"Michael, you need to get down from there. You're disrupting the class." I said calmly. I found that in many situations, if you didn't show fear or anger - *not* giving the expected response - usually deflated a bad situation. And sometimes, on a good day, the class would monitor themselves and their own bad behavior, if I were teaching a really good lesson and someone was acting out or interrupting.

But I sensed Michael may have been on drugs, for he was acting really strange. He was very agitated. I could tell some of the class was afraid. The older boys in the class were telling him to get down from the window ledge and radiator. We were two stories up, above the parking lot. If he tripped and broke through the windows, he would fall to his death.

"That yo' white convertible, down there, Miz. Flynn?" he asked, taunting me.

"Yes, it is, Michael. Why?"

"Sho' would be a shame if somebody messed it up. Sho' would be a shame if someone came by and slashed yo' tires with a knife," he said, "that nice pretty car and all." He looked menacingly at me and then down at my car on the asphalt below, balancing, walking back and forth in his huge white untied tennis shoes along the radiator and window sill.

"Get *down*, fool! You gonna *kill* yo'self, crazy nigga."

"But Michael, the good thing is, now, if anything happens to my car, I'll know who did it!" I said lightly.

"*Whooooo*," came the inevitable low hoot made by the class when someone was put in their place.

"Hey, man, she *got* you*!*" someone called from the back of the room.

"Yo' *mama*!" Michael shot back, the universal phrase used to indicate disapproval or mild contempt.

The class laughed and hooted. I had broken the tension. But you had to be very careful. By my words I had conveyed that I had taken Michael's threat seriously. I would never want to put him down, or worse, make fun of him, especially in front of the class, which could be dangerous.

I remembered my training as well. What had set him off? He was very angry about something. I was concerned as this was a boy who seemed border line. He could be very funny and charming. He was well-liked. He could barely read, but he loved to participate in plays and struggled through the simple dialogue. It was either drugs or something had happened at home. Perhaps he had seen his mother beaten or his father taken away by the police. We had been taught these students were often very emotional as they experienced extreme violence at home, the neighborhood having one of the highest crime-rates in Cleveland.

"Braaaang." Suddenly the bell rang, ending the dramatic interlude. Michael jumped down from his perch along the radiators with a thud and sauntered slowly by me. Body language was everything.

Over time I learned bits of information I would never forget. One day I took my disturbed seventh grade class to the school library to check out books. The librarian, a very large, rotund woman, welcomed the class, explaining the process of checking out a book to them, then turned to me, making conversation while the students milled around, looking for books that appealed to them.

"You know, I wish we had more copies of "PT 109", she said amiably.

"Why is that?" I asked.

"Well, you know, we just can't keep that book in! That's all these kids want to read," she explained, smiling broadly.

"Don't you *know*? John Kennedy's a *hero* to these kids!"

And so he was. In more ways than one. I remembered how it was President Kennedy who had put Title I in place which had funded my masters program if we would teach our majors in the ghetto.

"See that slide projector and tape recorder over there?" she asked emphatically. "Why, we had *nothin'* here in this school before

John Kennedy! Um-*hum* ! These kids *know* what he did, yes indeed!"

In a complicated world, this simple fact made a great impression on me. I admired President Kennedy. To actually see and hear the difference he made in this school-which we were told had virtually *no* audio-visual equipment, no even a record player prior to Title I - touched me, especially coming first hand from the recipients. I watched as the few copies of "PT 109" were quickly taken up from the book shelf. And I resolved I would do *my* part as well.

"You know yo' classroom just don't say *nothin'* to these kids!"

It was late in the afternoon. I looked up to see Leon the art teacher-good looking, but with an attitude-come strolling into my room. He was well-built, muscular and the son of my master teacher, who was very proud of him, so I knew I had to listen to what he had to say.

At first I was really offended. The weekend before, my sister Marianne convinced me that if I put up paper flowers in my classroom it would be "good for the kids" because it would brighten up the room. She had never seen it, but had heard how dingy and plain it was from me. On Sunday we worked with reams of beautiful colored tissue paper up in the attic of our house where my room was, and taught ourselves to make two dozen large, tropical-looking flowers which we attached to green wire stems. That Monday morning I had gone in early and put up the flowers on the bulletin boards in the front and back of the classroom. The old classroom seemed bright and beautiful, a place I was proud to teach in.

"Well, I think it looks *great!*" I shot back defensively.

"As the art teacher, I'm here to critique what you've done for the good of the students."

I was still offended. I thought as an art teacher he would have liked what I did.

"You've put up *flowers* for God's sake. These kids need to see *role models*. Martin Luther King. Doctors. Lawyers. People they can look *up* to!" he said earnestly.

I could tell he didn't particularly like me. Our discussion had been brief and intense. This had been an unwelcome intrusion, but I finally got Leon's point and he was passionate about it. By the time he sauntered out, I had agreed to replace the colorful flowers with collages of famous black role models. Every now and then I got a quick, surprising glimpse into the black psyche, as complicated as it was, and the difficult-and often heartbreaking-enterprise these dedicated black teachers were dealing with. I would be leaving in June, finished my assignment. They were in it for the long haul.

I never got to take down the paper flowers. They were taken down for me. Later in the week, I came down with laryngitis and took a day off. When I came back the next day, several teachers met me at the door of my classroom.

"We just wanted to tell you before you go in, that the Black Panthers broke in last night and ripped down your flowers and did some damage. We got most of the mess cleaned up." I could see the remains of some of the flowers on the floor. Luckily it was Friday. I had the weekend to talk myself into going back.

How did I get through this? I would have to say my mother, who had gotten me into the program, helped me quite a bit. I was the oldest of eight children and I knew she was glad to have me back home after being away at college in New York for the last four years.

Sometimes, especially in the first few weeks, I would drive home, almost in a catatonic state, to our English Tudor home on Berkshire Road in Cleveland Heights. As I drove up the driveway, the familiar gravel crunching beneath my car, I was so glad to be home. The days had been so difficult, trying to gain and keep control of the classes. I often told myself I wouldn't be going back in the morning.

"Don't say a word! I can read your face," my mother would say. "Just go upstairs and take a nice, hot bath and I'll have your dinner ready so you can eat before everyone else." Later as I ate my dinner I would recount the horrors of the day or sometimes I ate in silence if it had been especially bad.

There were five teachers in our program assigned to Addison. One of them, a girl named Mary Carroll Brown taught History. She had the misfortune to be given a study hall to cover, and had a book thrown at her by a student. This item I kept from my mother. I remember many nights staring down at the hot suds as I lowered myself into the tub, wondering how I could back again and get through just one more day.

My husband-to-be, Ed, a pillar of strength to me, was far away in the Navy. But knowing we would be married in August-if I survived my student teaching-was a comfort. There would be an end to this and I would have my masters. Several of the young men selected for the program had an exempt draft status as teachers. They joked that for them it was either teaching in the ghetto or facing the Viet Cong. As the days went by, we became a very tight group and the camaraderie got us through some very tough situations.

In those first weeks the group met each week and shared their stories which really helped. Everyone was going through the same types of incidents at each of the schools. Sometimes we actually laughed, but more often sharing techniques that worked with the students.

Many a Sunday I would go to a large, old church down in Little Italy, away from my beautiful, stately church, St. Ann's, to the crowded five o-clock mass. In the dark recesses of the old church I prayed for the strength to go back in the morning and start the week and always I found the strength.

One afternoon, I closed the door of my classroom, exhausted from the turmoil of day and walked past the rough-looking men, in their black muscle shirts and black pants, arms folded, guarding the heavy metal back door of the building. I nodded to them and they nodded to me. I felt they didn't like me, but I had survived another day. Perhaps they were Black Panthers. Even if they were, we had a common goal: to educate these children, no matter how hard it was, so that they would have a decent chance for a life in their difficult world.

As I drove up Carnegie Avenue, out of the ghetto, up towards the cool, leafy, Cleveland Heights suburb where I lived, I stopped at a red light. Suddenly from out of nowhere, a man in the car behind me slammed on his breaks. He ran up to the car in front of me, pulling a sharply-dressed black man in a shiny grey suit and tie, out from behind the wheel of his car, yelling and swearing, angrily punching the man across the hood of his car. The man in the grey suit was muscular and good looking. There was a girl next to him in the car who jumped out, begging the man who had attacked her driver to stop punching him. I sat frozen in my car. I had never seen two men fighting like that except on TV.

Then I recognized the girl in the car. It was Brenda Watkins, a student in my 9th grade class. Brenda was a tough girl with a mature figure who I could tell, didn't like me, but tolerated me because she wanted to learn. She always wore a white blouse and tight black skirt, her hair styled, lots of make-up.

"You leave her _'lone_ !" I heard the older man, who had pulled the well-dressed man from his car, yell. He continued to punch the man on the hood of his car. The light had turned green and a crowd was gathering.

"*Forget* you, ol' man !" the well-dressed man yelled back.

"*Get* in the car, Brenda," I heard the older man shout to Brenda, pointing to his car behind mine. Brenda was sobbing, her purse and books lying in the street. Finally the police appeared, moving traffic around the scene. I drove on. The term "mean streets" had come to life. I wasn't sure what I had just witnessed. The thought crossed my mind that the man who had leapt from his car may have been Brenda's father and that he was trying to save her from prostitution.

These students had such dreadful, violent home lives. Yet I found one thing they enjoyed was drama. I would ask for volunteers to read a play from a textbook in class and sure enough, some of the "baddest", most difficult young men in the class, wearing dew rags on their heads, would volunteer and actually fight over the best parts. It was very exciting. I would have them read a play for homework and the next day they could volunteer for the parts. They were pretty good actors. They struggled with the words. They could be very funny at times.

"You got any gangsta's in this play, Miz Flynn?" a muscular student named Sam Prevo asked me. "I want to play a *gangsta* role."

"Why no, Sam. But there *is* a king in the play."

Sam was a leader in the school. He was respected by even with the toughest, meanest students in the class. His mother was the head of the PTA and wielded a lot of influence in the school. That first week, Sam had actually helped me gain control of the class, several times. He had stood up in his striped tee shirt, jeans and sneakers, addressing some trouble-makers in the back of the class.

"Sit down and shut up all that shuckin' an jivin', y'all. Don't you see she's tryin' t' *teach*?"

Sam had a deep voice and great presence. Those that were acting out, sullenly slunk down into their desks at his command. I was grateful on several occasions for his intervention. Yet Sam was never friendly towards me. It was usually all business, as if he were on orders from his mother. The students liked and respected him. He had a deep Southern drawl and could be funny and charming when he wanted. He was also temperamental.

"All right then. I be the *King*."

"You ain't no *King*!" came the inevitable challenge from someone in the back of the room.

"You step *outside*, man, I sho you who's *King*!" And so it went. I loved to see these students argue over who would take which part. For a time they left their terrible ghetto lives. In my classroom they could become someone else if only for an hour.

At first I tried very simple plays with easy to understand themes. Eventually I tried the witch scene from Macbeth after carefully explaining the plot. Shakespeare was very difficult for these students, but they boasted they were "doing Shakespeare" and many of the students picked up the humor in Shakespeare immediately.

"Man, this guy's really *funny*!"

These days were the highpoint of my teaching at Addison.

In order to keep the students interested-and survive as a teacher-it was necessary to create lessons that were truly interesting. I found that if you could capture the interest of the class in the beginning, things usually went fairly well. One week I was teaching a lesson on Mark Twain and the Mississippi. I wanted to really capture their interest as some of the students were from the South. I thought the material would be something they could relate to, as so much of what we usually read had absolutely nothing to do with their lives.

I brought in a small prism I found at home, hoping to interest them with the literary concept of "Local Color" in which the literature truly reflects the customs and traditions of the region. Most of them had never before seen a prism. As I stood in front of the class I held it up and a rainbow of color from the sunlight by my window shot across my desk. I heard a low, communal, impressed "Whooo", come from the class.

"How you *do* that?" they asked.

"That *magic*, Miz Flynn?" And truly, those *were* the magical moments when they engaged, if only for the moment, when they were truly impressed with something new and wanted to learn more. During those moments they were mine, no ghetto, no poverty, no Black Panthers. They were mine and I was their teacher. It turned out to be a great lesson. After turning the prism and casting the unique "Local Color" in small rainbows around the room, I passed the prism to a girl in the first row. I watched as each student examined it in their hands as I read Mark Twain to them. The prism never made it back at the end of the lesson. But I didn't care. I was thrilled with how things went.

But there was one time I *did* care, for it was personal. At home I had a set of 6 antique green leather-bound books called "My Bookhouse". I had a first edition published in 1923 by Charles Beaupre Miller. The covers were in colored leather, the pages had a gold gilded effect when closed and had beautiful illustrations done in black, orange and turquoise by Don Crane, a famous illustrator of the day. My seven brother and sisters had enjoyed all the stories and poems from many lands in these books. They had belonged to my father so they had a sentimental value as well.

I remembered a story called "The Ashanti Warriors of Africa" in one of the volumes and decided to teach a unit about it to the 9th graders. I was very excited about the lesson. I could finally introduce them to something they could relate to, something about their history. I xeroxed the story and passed it out.

"By the way, class, here is the book the story comes from. It is part of a set called "My Bookhouse" with authentic stories from many lands. I'll pass it around so you can see the illustrations. O.K., who wants to start?

They seemed to like the story which explained the history of the Ashanti warriors, their superior skills in hunting, how they surpassed other tribes in battle, their daily lives, etc. The bell rang.

"O.K., class. For homework, I want you to write two paragraphs on the Ashanti's, what you remember about their lives, what they were good at."

"Awwwww," was the inevitable response.

"And please, whoever has the book, leave it on my desk." I waited patiently as the class of 35 filed out. Soon there were only 10 students left. Nothing on my desk. Nothing in their hands. I never saw my precious book again. I'd like to think whoever took it wanted to keep it because he or she was inspired by the Ashanti's.

But this was not the end. That evening at my home In Cleveland Heights, I was having dinner when the phone rang. My younger brother got up to answer it.

"Joan Ellen. It's for you."

Pushing myself away from the table, I went to the hall and picked up the phone.

"Hello."

"Is this Miz Flynn?" It was an older black woman, with a slight, soft Southern drawl.

"Yes, it is."

"Miz Flynn, this is Mrs. Prevo. I'm the Head of the PTA at Addison."

"Oh, yes. I have your son, Sam in my 2nd period English class."

"That's what I want to talk to you about."

"Well, Sam's doing very well. He needs to work on grammar, but he always volunteers for play reading and he has a very good speaking voice."

"That's *not* what I want to speak to you about."

"Oh? Well, how can I help?"

"I understand you taught a lesson today on Ashanti warriors."

"Well, yes, I did. I thought the class would enjoy it."

"The reason I'm calling, Miz Flynn, is that the PTA and I would like you to teach them to read and write and leave their heritage to us." I caught my breath for a moment before I replied.

"Well, Mrs. Prevo, if that is how you feel, I'll stick to the basics. I just wanted to make it more interesting for them."

"Just teach them to read and write, Miz Flynn. That's what they need. We will teach their heritage."

"Good night, Mrs. Prevo, thank you for calling."

"Good night, Miz Flynn."

It had seemed so simple. I had no idea the community would know or even react to what I was teaching. Overtime, I would learn how powerful the mothers of Addison could be. It was *they* who held the families together as best they could in spite of extreme poverty, *they* who came to the conferences from their menial jobs, *they* who wanted to know if their young men were acting up in my class, *they* who knew education was their children's only chance for a better life outside the ghetto.

And now I knew the powerful influence behind Sam Prevo and his threatening, glowering-yet very welcome - "Sit down and shut up, y'all! Don't you see she's try'in t' *teach*!?"

"Ain't nobody want to read *my* auto'bography!" Annie stood up from her desk, hands on her hips, her eyes challenging me. By now I knew this 7th grade had a reputation throughout the school as being "disturbed." It was the same class, who, on a given signal, had stood up, overturned their desks and walked out. It had been a frightening experience. However, later, when I heard they had done it in each of their classes that day, I felt better, knowing at least it was not personally directed at me.

"Sit down, girl!" the class yelled.

"Annie, the assignment is to write 5 pages about the first 10 years of your life. Anything you can remember. You can ask you parents, grandparents, brothers and sisters. It will be due in 2 weeks."

"Won't *anybody* want to *read* about it!"

Annie was a wiry, natty-haired little girl, somewhat funny, but mean-spirited, always intervening in everyone else's business, always up for trouble. She liked to verbally spar with her cohorts. She was typical of the girls in the school before they reached the complications of puberty. She was short. Somewhere between the 7th and 9th grade, these girls seemed to grow a foot. Like the other 7th graders, she wore her hair in a short, sometimes messy Afro, a blouse, loose-fitting, flaired skirt, high white knee-high and tennis shoes. She belonged to a clique of girlfriends, intensely loyal to each other, but always either joking or fighting. At times, the humor I overheard among them was very funny, quaint and endearing. This was a crew that could also be angry and violent if aroused. They had significant learning disabilities, horrible home lives and were entering adolescence.

Annie sat down with a thud at her desk, tossing her head and flairing her skirt.

"Forget *you*!" she warned her group of girlfriends. "I ain't *doin'* this, no sir!"

"That's cause yo' got nothin' to write *about*!"

"Yo' *mama*!" The worst insult of all.

I thought the assignment would be a good one. It would make them reflect on who they were, give them practice in journalistic writing, as well as spelling, and involve their families.

Two weeks later I received the assignment from almost all the 35 7th graders. I had not asked that they be submitted in folders, but I was touched at the number of assignments turned in, in colored folders with "My Autobiography" written on the covers. They had taken the assignment very seriously.

What I was not prepared for was the content. Some of the autobiographies were almost illegible. I had to guess at the words. I had no idea their writing skills were so bad. I now knew some of the students were practically illiterate. Yet they had tried.

And the stories they told were horrendous.

"Then he up an' *cut* her an' the po-leece came and took him away."

"My daddy left. I never *met* my daddy but I hope to meet him someday."

"I was born in Arkansas. My momma died. I'm bein' raised by my Grandma."

"They tol' me my daddy's in jail."

"Momma left us. We live with my auntie."

"He broke in and beat her. We tried to pull him off but he kept hittin' her with the pipe. The

po-leece came and took him away."

And on and on and on. Annie's story was especially bad. I could barely decipher her tortuous, penciled script. It sounded as if her mother were a prostitute.

"Good job!" I wrote over and over on their assignments. "We need to work on spelling and punctuation!' "Try to use complete sentences." I knew most of them had done their best. Some of them were truly almost completely unreadable. I was pretty shocked by what they wrote, the lack of spelling skills, yet they had tried, taking the care to put their five pages in colored folders. It was one of the most moving experiences of my time at Addison.

Rain always had an amazing effect on my students. Invariably, when it rained I knew I would have a relatively good day. Falling gently against the ancient leaded windows of my classroom, the scent and rhythm of the rain soothed the students, calming them down. They interacted with each other less, seemed to listen better to the lesson. I always looked forward to these rainy days.

On one such day, I was teaching the 9th grade class a unit on poetry. They were all listening better than usual. I decided to read them a poem on love. When I got to a line in the poem, "You are like a fire in my heart," an unusual thing happened. Michael Jones, of "walking along the radiator" fame, stood up at his desk. He was about six feet tall, a nice-looking boy, handsome with a baby face and wide, expressive dark eyes. But those eyes were angry today.

"What you *mean*, Miz Flynn, 'Fire in the Heart'? Cain't be no fire in the heart! What yo' *mean*???" For a change, the class was very quiet. None of the cat-calling that occurred when someone tried to ask a legitimate question. I think most of the class was somewhat afraid of Michael due to his threatening behavior up on the window ledge that day.

"What the author means is that the person loves the other one so much it feels like a fire in his heart." I was standing in front of my desk. Michael was standing in the row beside his desk, hands on his hips.

"What yo' *mean*?" his dark eyes flashed. You had to be careful because sometimes the students were capable of putting you on, making you think they were serious when they weren't.

"Michael, it's just a phrase, just an expression. He doesn't really mean an actual *fire*."

"Then *why* he *say* it?" Then I remembered something I had learned in my teaching methods class: "These kids have a hard time with abstract thinking. They understand the physical world quite well, but dealing with abstraction can be really tough for them."

So this is where we were, I thought. It was a unique moment. An inexperienced English teacher and an angry young man, struggling to understand the conceit of a love poem describing the intensity of love, the "fire in the heart." He was angry at the author, angry at me, angry because he couldn't understand the poem, angry at life.

"Why he *write* that way if it's not *true*?"

"It's called a simile, using 'as' or 'like' to describe something in a different, more powerful way," I tried to explain.

"Why he don't jus' tell her he *love* her?"

"But he is, Michael, in his own way."

"Seem *stupid* to me. No way she goin' to understand what he be *talkin'* about!"

"What seem *stupid* to *us*, is yo' tall, skinny *self*, Michael!" I knew sooner or later this would be coming from the back of the room. The delicate bubble of teacher and student, trying to understand the material, broke. Michael looked embarrassed and sheepishly lowered his long frame back into his seat, his enormous sneakers extending far under the desk of the girl in front of him.

"Don' matter, no how," he muttered to me.

"You'll *neva* understan' no *luv* poem, Michael!" some girl called from the back of the room.

"*Fo'get* you, girl, Michael retorted. "Yo *mama!*" I knew Michael wouldn't put up with very much catcalling. He had opened himself up to this white teacher and had been embarrassed. The danger of a fight was very real.

The spell had been broken. I will always remember the anguished look on that boy's face, trying to learn, trying to understand the poetic concept of a simile. It was just he and I for about a minute. The class had melted away, but then came back with a bang, calling him down, back into the destructive, ridiculing environment that was Addison. No wonder these kids never opened up.

"Bbrraang," went the bell. The students closed their books and started to file out. I looked at Michael as he shuffled by. His dark eyes peered at me suspiciously from his baby-face. Then his eyes glazed over as he reached out with his long arm, roughly pushing the boy in front of him.

"Yo' shuckin' n 'jivin', we neva get outta this class. _Move_, fool! I got *betta* things to do."

I received my Masters in August of 1969. Many years later I returned to E. 79th St. and Carnegie, looking for Addison. Driving slowly through the all-black neighborhood, I ventured to ask a passer-by.

"Excuse me, Mam," I asked a heavy set woman with a pushcart. "Can you tell me where Addison is?"

"Why, you lookin' right *at* it!" she exclaimed. "They done put up those condos and parkin' lot right where the school used t'be, yes they did!"

I took a good look at the parking lot and condos. Nothing left of what was, the old scarred yellow-brick building, broken glass, brown bags with empty whiskey-bottles - dedicated, talented but tired teachers; gifted, angry, challenging students - the energy, frustration, the gifts and ultimatums - given from both sides, in the heat of the battle, for the minds of the students of Addison.

289

Cleveland Heights, Ohio, 1969

Joan Flynn Beesley

Joan Flynn Beesley

I was now twenty-three. Ed Beesley and I had dated all through late high school and college. Finally, I had my Masters and it was time to marry, which we did, two days later in a big, beautiful ceremony at our local parish church, St. Ann's, in beautiful, tree-shaded, leafy-green Cleveland Heights. I never returned to Addison, but taught English in an average senior high school in Maryland: average white students concerned with proms and SAT's, not particularly impressed with class plays and Shakespeare. A safe environment, but relatively boring compared with the challenge of Addison.

Ed was in the Navy so we lived the next six months near the base in Patuxent River, Maryland until his discharge. Two years earlier he had lost a kidney in a fall aboard the USS Forestall, being air-evacked to Puerto Rico as the carrier was headed for Vietnam. Weeks later the Forrestal was set ablaze in the historic firestorm that destroyed much of the ship and many of the air ordinance men that Ed worked with. I have often thought how perhaps destiny intervened and took him out of the fire and into the frying pan in advance of the blaze.

As we left the wonderful College Club reception that hot August afternoon in our red TR4-A, I really didn't realize I was leaving 2862 Berkshire Rd. for good. In my last minute packing I had been up until 2pm that morning, deciding what to take, what to leave, and cutting a long piece of my hair into braid to work with my veil. I had lived eleven years of my life there. In the excitement and solitude - we were finally alone! - of early marriage, I would only come to miss the lovely English Tudor and the massive leafy oaks that overhung it, years later. After a stint at Time-Life in New York, I would spend the next thirty years of my life in telecommunications in Denver but my thoughts would always return to my home on Berkshire Rd.

How proud I was to become of my parents, Joan and Ed Flynn. Dad eventually retired from his highly-successful commercial window business, The Edward R. Flynn Company, Cleveland successor to The Michael Flynn Manufacturing Company, truly a phoenix rising from the ashes.

True to her roots, my mother, Joan Dillon Flynn, opened the first authentic Irish Import store in Cleveland and, together, she and my father opened eight stores throughout Cleveland, Akron and Hilton Head, N.C. over the years. They took great pains to represent the Irish culture and history faithfully and had a great deal of fun running the business, my father singing the Irish tune, "Was Your Mother Born in Ireland?" on the radio. He would quickly follow with "And even if she *wasn't*, feel free to come visit our shop located at...!" It was an enterprise they loved and when it was finally financially "in the black", my father treated my mother to a beautiful diamond and emerald shamrock ring which they had custom-designed and I still wear today. They ran the shops together for many years. When they closed the last one in their seventies, my brothers and sisters and their families would all go down to the basement of their home in Chardon, Ohio, to select treasures from the wonderful inventory of Irish books, crystal and clothing. My parents were rich tapestries in the Flynn Family's "40 Shades of Green". Their Irish stores are a part of The Case Western Reserve History Annals:

THE WESTERN RESERVE HISTORICAL SOCIETY
MANUSCRIPT COLLECTIONS
REGISTER: Emeralds Unlimited, Inc. Records
MS NO.: 4915
Date: February 1, 2002

Emeralds Unlimited, Inc. (1973-1995) was established to provide
imported goods from Ireland, to promote Irish culture, and support Irish American events
in the Cleveland, Ohio area. The owners, Joan Dillon Flynn, and Dee Keating, who
served as vice president, opened the first Irish import store in Ohio, which was located in
the Flats, on Old River Road, called Emerald in the Flats. Flynn and Keating embarked
on this business venture to introduce an authentic Irish store in a geographical area that
had been settled by the early Irish immigrants to Cleveland, Ohio. Emerald in the Flats
officially opened on October 13, 1973.

Emeralds Unlimited Inc. was the first import business to participate in the Irish
Cultural Festival at the Berea Fairgrounds in Cleveland. A second store was opened in
Akron by Flynn's son, John Flynn. It ceased operations one year later, when John Flynn
moved out of state. *Emeralds Unlimited Inc.* imported Irish stone and turf jewelry,
sweaters, woolens, crystal, and art work. Bernadette O'Brien, native of Dublin and
costume designer for the Cleveland Play House handmade "bainin" skirts and purses for
the store. Natives of Brooklyn, New York, of Irish parents, Joan Dillon Flynn and her
husband Ed moved to Cleveland, Ohio in 1958. Emeralds Unlimited Inc. in total
consisted of eight stores, including one located in Lakewood and another in Euclid. The
operation ceased in 1995.

The Emeralds Unlimited Inc. Records (1979-1993), consist of a catalog, history of
the company, and newspaper clippings. The collection is arranged alphabetically by
document type, and then chronologically.

This collection is of value to researchers studying the history of Irish American
businesses in Cleveland, Ohio. The records contain Irish recipes, information pertaining
to St. Brigid, the Flats, and the histories behind Irish jewelry pieces, including the
Claddagh Ring and Irish clothing. The collection includes genealogical data pertaining to
the Flynn family. Those interested in traditional Irish clothing created by an Irish
woman will find the information pertaining to Bernadette O'Brien's work to be useful.
All photographs have been removed to the photograph collection.

Brooklyn, New York, 1970

It was like a dream come true. A fairly-new high school English teacher, I sat at my kitchen table in Patuxent River, Maryland, pausing from correcting papers to read The New York Times. Recently married in Cleveland, my husband was now stationed in the Navy. The year was 1970 and the nation was in the midst of the Vietnam War.

Help Wanted
Time-Life, Inc.
Administrative Assistant
Personnel Department
New York, New York
Interviewing in Washington, D.C.
February 14 and 15

I had received my Masters Degree in Teaching English to Disadvantaged Adolescents in Cleveland, 6 months prior, 2 days before my wedding. As part of my student teaching I taught in Cleveland's Inner City at Addison Jr. High School, a tale in itself. Teaching now in a white suburban senior high school was a lot safer, but the students, many of whose fathers were stationed at the Naval Base, were fairly ordinary, not as complex as the challenging inner city students. About twenty-five percent of the students came from poor sharecropping families and were noticeably absent when Maryland's tobacco crop was harvested.

My dream was always to be a writer. It had always been what I did best. I stared at the ad. A toe-hold at Time-Life! Before I knew it I dialed the phone and set up an appointment, Washington, D.C. only a few hours drive from Maryland. Ed would be discharged from the Navy in six months.

Monday morning, Time-Life was interviewing in a hotel near the capital. I entered the suite and met with Muffin, the Head of the Personnel Department. Muffin was about 5 years older than I. She wore a conservative grey business suit, white blouse, black heels, like I did, but gave the impression of wearing a girdle that was too tight. She also had a starched professionalism about her personally, as if she were looking right through me.

"How fast can you type?" she asked, reviewing my application. I had never been asked this question before.

"You know, I don't really know!"

"Then I'll need you to take the typing test before you leave."

The actual interview proceeded well once we left the topic of typing. I told Muffin about my Masters in English, how I had read "Time" and "Life" magazines my entire life and how much I would love to work there.

"When could you report for work?"

"What?"

"How soon could you come to our office in Manhattan?"

And so it began. Fortunately it was a week before the end of the semester and I was able to turn in my notice. It was decided I would live with a host of relatives in Brooklyn until Ed was discharged from the Navy in 6 months. It would be especially difficult living apart as we had only been married 6 months. Soon I found myself at the Dulles Airport saying goodbye to Ed and several of his friends who accompanied him.

The last six months as a Navy wife had been so carefree and fun. We truly enjoyed our new independence from our large families of 9 and 8 siblings! There was a major eclipse of the sun that day and we all took turns peering at it through a pinhole in a sheet of paper. I hugged Ed tightly and said goodbye to the handsome young sailors.

It was very cold in New York. I hailed a cab to take me to Brooklyn where I would stay the first two weeks with my mother's mother who was diagnosed with cancer. My great adventure had begun.

"So you're moving to New York?" the leathered cab driver asked me, as we drove from JFK down to Brooklyn on a cold late Sunday afternoon.

"That's right. I'm taking a job at Time-Life in New York, starting tomorrow. I have several relatives here in Brooklyn who've agreed to let me stay weeks at a time. Hopefully I don't have to stay too many rounds before I can locate an apartment."

"Do youse have any pets?"

"Yes, we have a black French poodle named Pierre and a grey Maltese cat, "The Maltese Bippi".

"Get ridda dem."

"What!?"

"Lose 'em before youse move up here. And yer car, too."

"What!?"

"Youse don't want pets or a car in Brooklyn!"

"Why?"

"Just remember what I told ya!"

On that ominous note, the cabbie pulled into a circular drive and up to large apartment building on Flatbush Avenue, close to Avenue M. I tipped the driver and walked under the blue canopy and into the lobby. It was an older building, well kept but also well worn. A muffled sound of strange voices. Strong aroma of heavy ethic cooking permeated the halls.

My mother's mother, Eleanor Dillon, had made it to my fabulous wedding in Cleveland but was undergoing chemotherapy for throat cancer and had worn a wig. When her husband John died, she had moved into her apartment from their home of 40 years on Avenue M with the magnificent horse-chestnut tree that took up most of the backyard.

I rang the bell.

"Aaaaraaank."

"Who is it?"

"It's me, Grandma."

"Oh, Joan Ellen! Just push the buzzer and come up!" The familiar voice sounded pleased, but weak and strained. Apprehensively, I trudged down the dark carpeted hall on the third floor and rang the bell, trying to peer in through a tiny peephole hole in the metal turquoise door.

Eleanor Dillon was much smaller than I remembered her. She embraced me in her flowered house dress and slippers. She was wearing a lifeless short brown wig, but her beautiful porcelain skin and dark brown eyes, just like my mother's, were as beautiful as ever. She had been very pretty as a young woman and somewhat vain as she grew older. I knew wearing a wig was very difficult for her.

Grandma Dillon was known for her difficult temperament, cranky and critical. She had always been nice to me, however, in spite of many explosively memorable visits to my parents when I was little. Frightening to a small child, she invariably called for a taxi to take her to the airport and home to Brooklyn after picking a fight with my father by saying something belittling and nasty to him under her breathe. The command "Joan, call the taxi!!", after some perceived slight, signaled the conclusion of each visit. It was inevitable as clockwork. My Dad and I often shared the secret anticipation of "*When?*"

As we sat at her small table in her tiny kitchen, she served me a welcome dinner. She was a great cook and marvelous housekeeper with remarkable Victorian standards of cleanliness. As we talked, she opened a can of Ensure, swallowing it with difficulty, coughing into her handkerchief.

It dawned upon me that I was out in the world now, alone, without Ed or my parents, seeing the world as it really was, without any protective veneer. I could see my grandmother was very sick and very alone.

Tomorrow was The Big Day, the day I was to report to the Personnel Office at Time-Life. Grandma Dillon gave me instructions on where to catch the subway on Flatbush Avenue and take the IRT into Manhattan to Time-Life on 52nd Street. It was all happening so fast. I couldn't believe I was really in New York!

"I'm glad that you'll be staying with me awhile," she said softly as she made up a bed for me on the living room sofa. After she went into her room, I read the "Apartment for Rent" sections of The New York Times and New York Post, circling some possibilities. Finally, I laid the paper on the radiator, hissing softly near the sofa, and fell asleep, missing Ed's strong arms safely around me.

The next morning I strode forth from my Grandmother's apartment in my best suit, walking down Flatbush Avenue at 7 am, a conquering hero. I have always loved to write. It has always been my passion and I was always told I was very good at it. Therefore, landing a job at Time-Life in Manhattan, -any job-was like winning The Nobel Peace Prize.

My administrative position on the 32nd floor was in Personnel. "Muffin" Berry, my boss, was one of two abrupt and trendy young women who ran the office. My main job was to type and send out one of several template rejection letters, mainly to hopeful young college students like myself, who had submitted their resumes in hopes of working as writers there, which was my dream as well. For a time I was psychologically speechless just to be working there.

I actually worked in a small closet with the door closed. Over time I discovered the wonderful Time-Life Bookstore on the 7th Floor where I often spent my lunch hour. Employees could enjoy nice discounts on excess inventory of Time-Life Books and beautiful coffee-table books like "The Coaching Days of England", a huge oversized book with colorful lithographs, which I bought from money saved from my very small paycheck.

I was within walking distance of St. Patrick's Cathedral and 5th Avenue and usually went over to Rockefeller Center to eat a hot dog from the ever present Savarin umbrella stands for lunch. Sometimes after work I would attempt to find an apartment for Ed and I to live in as soon as he was discharged from the Navy in Maryland. While my grandmother in Brooklyn made every attempt to make me comfortable in her tiny apartment on Flatbush Avenue, she was losing her battle with throat cancer and could now only drink Ensure. As bad as she felt, she was always up to encourage me every morning as I left in the frigid February snow for the subway into Manhattan.

The first Sunday I was there she instructed me on how to find the closest Catholic Church as she could no longer attend. As I started to walk that winter morning, following her directions, I realized Avenue M, her lifelong home and the home my mother grew up in, was not far away. Soon after my grandfather died, she sold the home and moved into the apartment.

I found myself walking past the church, soon standing in front of the modest, dear little home in the "All in the Family" style that meant so much to the Dillon side of my family, complete with the wondrous horse chestnut tree that lovingly spread its boughs over most of the backyard. As a little girl I knew many of the secrets of that house, including its basement with a ping pong table in the small rec room with high school pennants, simply resting on compressed earth, always very cold and damp down there.

I remember returning after what I thought was about an hour, my grandmother asking me how the service was. I've very rarely lied in my life, but glibly told her "It was fine," not wanting to risk her disapproval of my not going to Mass. I felt bad about that for a long time.

Muffin Berry and her co-boss turned out to be very difficult, cold people. The soft-spoken young black secretary who patiently put up with Muffin's ego, once confided to me that her boss sometimes put half-eaten apple cores in her out-box for the secretary to empty.

Over time I was asked to deliver certain resumes to the upper floors of Time Magazine, Sports Illustrated and Life. I realized these were "approved" resumes of candidates for open positions. How I wished I were one of them!

Then one day, alone in the elevator, I decided to look at one of the resumes in the manila envelope I was delivering. How odd, I thought. This fellow has only a B.A. I have my B.A in English and a Masters in

Teaching English and have taught English at two schools. Although I felt lucky to have my administrative position, as I looked at more and more resumes, I realized I was better qualified than the all-male B.A. resumes sent up to the executives for consideration.

As the months went by, I made several weak attempts to let it be known to Muffin that over time, I would like the same consideration. I remember her looking at me as if I were a two-headed giraffe.

Several weeks passed and I was told that now part of my development would be to go on rotational assignments until I was placed in a permanent position. I was sent to be a temporary replacement executive secretary for a Mr. Brumbaugh, the VP of Finance, who was retiring. His was an amazing office with a private master bath, Chinese Mandarin décor and antiques. Answering his phone, making appointments and serving coffee from a sterling silver service were my main duties.

My next assignment was working for Mr. Pitt, VP of Public Relations, who had been given a pink slip. I was to be the temporary secretary while he was allowed to keep his office and look for another position. Mr. Bill Pitt was a patient, lovely and gracious man, even in the midst of his dilemma. I enjoyed working on the tail end of several projects he was winding up, including his fund-raiser for the Schaumberg Museum in Harlem. I also stood in for him, taking an inner city girl to lunch and up to the top of The Empire State Building where we both breathlessly looked down on the isle of Manhattan.

Finally I was awarded a permanent position. I was to be the administrative assistant for the Editor of The Time-Life Gardening Series, Bob Jones. Yes! At last I would be getting close to the field of writing!

Bob's Head of Research, Joan Mebane, introduced me to the various researchers and writers for the Gardening Series. In the hall I could see the morning's copy, neatly distributed in metal cubicles with everyone's name. The facts would be checked by the researchers and then the writing submitted to the Editor, Bob, for his rewrite or approval. I was simply beside myself to be *that* close to the process of creating a book series.

Then it was time to be introduced to Mr. Jones, a small owlish man with horn-rimmed glasses and a sweater, exactly as I pictured a successful Time Life Editor to be. I shook his hand heartily.

"Glad to have you aboard, Joan. You'll be sitting right here outside my office."

"I'm very excited to be here, Mr. Jones."

"Did you just hear that?"

"No, I didn't," I said, staining my ears for what he had just head.

"That little bell. Do you know what it is?"

"Why no, I don't."

"That's the sound of the coffee wagon. I like mine black with a little sugar."

I found myself speechless. Suddenly the excitement of the morning evaporated and I found Joan Mebane steering me away from Bob Jones to my desk. A little voice inside me wanted to escape and run back into Bob's office explaining:

"Wait! She has a Masters in English! She's a talented writer! Get your own coffee!"

I bitterly knew I was sorely miscast. But I also had to make money for a deposit on an apartment.

I worked on the editorial staff as administrative assistant for about a year. Every one was pleasant, but in the way you would speak to a commodity. Tortured to be so close to the book series process but not permitted to do any real editorial work was very difficult for me. Yet I was determined to do my best in whatever they gave me to do. The day would eventually come when I could ask to be given a chance to be a writer. I knew it would.

Being regarded as an administrative secretary in a community of editors, researchers and writers was extremely painful every day. Perhaps I overrated my abilities but I felt like a neuro-surgeon doing the work of a candy-stripper.

I recall the day the regal Evelyn, lucky young wife of one of the established male writers, sauntered over to my desk.

"Sweetie, do you sew?" she simpered.

"Why no, I don't, "I replied. "Do you?"

She gave me an odd look and walked away from my desk.

I did meet many memorable and talented people there. There was the art team, a somber graphics lead named Leonard and his charming, humorous, gay assistant, Murray, an artist who loved to show you his latest illustrations on his large draft board.

Helen was a very old researcher who had been on staff many years. I often noticed a heavy scent whenever I was in her office. She seemed befuddled and confused at times and I eventually learned she was an alcoholic.

Joan, the head researcher, was a no-nonsense, detailed person who managed the whole process very efficiently. I mostly did her bidding, distributing the morning's finished copy of the Annuals and later the Roses volumes in the series. I got to meet the outside consultants on the Series, a lovely woman, illustrator of the Roses Book, and a master horticulturist, another great expert in his field, who met frequently with Bob Jones.

Towards the end of my time there I was sent out to meet a photographer at The Brooklyn Library who needed assistance (holding the page open while he lowered his extensive lenses!) photographing old advertisements of vintage gardening tools for the book. I later picked up the proofs from his studio in Manhattan. It was wonderful to step out of the clerical role, close to the art of creating a book, if only for a moment!

One afternoon I was sent to the TIME-LIFE Photo department. I met with a woman, actually named "Minnie Magazine" who was looking at photos through a large magnifying glass. How exciting it was to be there, researchers searching the massive and famous archives for requests like mine. Everyone there dressed in black! I was told they'd have to look back through the archives for specifically what the Gardening Series needed and they'd contact me in the morning. How exciting it was to be close to the inner workings of some of the world's most excellent magazines.

One day I took some time to stop on one of the actual floors where the magazines were produced. There was the TIME MAGZINE floor, the LIFE MAGAZINE and the SPORTS ILLUSTATED floor. I choose the LIFE MAGAZINE floor. Getting off the elevator, I knew I was in a very special place. In the lobby outside the small bank of elevators, I looked up at the ceiling to see the "plates", the metal templates used to print the famous covers of LIFE Magazine. There were about 50 of these, covers of Marilyn Monroe, the Kennedy's, Eisenhower, all of which had been used for notable LIFE Magazines of the past. It was thrilling.

And it was equally thrilling to be close to the tremendous talent getting off those elevators with me, the writers, editors and researchers of LIFE. How proud they must be to work on the great magazine, pleasant men for the most part, in Brooks Brothers attire. I ventured through the glass doors emblazoned with the "LIFE MAGAZINE" logo. I held my breath. In 1971 you could go virtually anywhere in the building if you were an employee. I, however, felt as if I were walking on sacred ground.

Inside the door was a small exhibit of photographs. "Alfred Eisenstadt", it read. I ventured around a corner and read the name "Gordon Parks" on a small cubicle. I just knew a net was about to be lowered on my head at any moment and security called. There were many photos of a ghetto neighborhood spread out on his desk. Mr. Parks wasn't there. I don't know what I would have said if he were. Suddenly I found myself passionately writing him a note and leaving it under one of the photos. It read:

Dear Mr. Parks,

I am an employee here at TIME-LIFE and want you to know how much I admire your work. I also want you to know that I taught in the ghetto in Cleveland for a time. It was very difficult but I came in contact with some wonderful and very special inner-city students.

Sincerely,

Joan Flynn Beesley

Although I never heard from Gordon Parks, I remember returning furtively to my seat outside Bob Jones' office that afternoon, knowing I had been near greatness.

Then there was the tall, handsome Greek correspondent, Eric, with a last name that used almost every letter of the alphabet. He would occasionally walk by my desk in his shiny Armani suits, always most pleasant and courteous, typically wishing me a good morning.

There was a nasty older researcher named Jane, skinny, with a tightly pulled-back blond pony-tail, always in the requisite black trousers, who actually had a type of fit when an invitational memo I sent out for one of her meetings, went out on the wrong memo form. I had to be careful of her.

Marion was Bob Jones' assistant editor, a very nice and dedicated woman whom I respected. It was Marion that I would make my career aspirations known to at the proper time.

Then there was Louise Solomon, an older researcher who told me sadly she had just received a pink slip, three months before her 30 years retirement. I was getting a fast education in the ups and downs of the corporate world.

I was about to learn quite a bit more. It was 1971 and I slowly became aware of Gloria Steinem and the Woman's Movement. One afternoon I received an invitation addressed to the women working at Time-Life. A meeting was being held that evening at the loft of one of the researchers from another department. It had a clandestine feeling to the wording, inviting women to discuss their views on "certain practices" at Time-Life.

Recalling my frustration upon opening the resumes of male college grads and how these were quickly being sent up to the editorial departments of TIME, LIFE and SPORTS ILLUSTRATED, I found myself hurrying up from the subway after work one cold winter night to the meeting in Greenwich Village.

I went up several flights of stairs to a loft apartment where about 40 women sat, drinking coffee and talking quietly among themselves. I had never seen exposed water pipes, industrial fans high up in the vaulted ceilings and exposed brick walls in a home before.

As the meeting began, the TIME-LIFE researcher thanked the group for coming and announced the purpose of the get-together was to discuss certain unfair practices towards women that seemed prevalent in all departments at TIME-LIFE. These included unequal pay for the same jobs done by men and women and limited promotional opportunities for women, among others. These same practices were being documented by the women from NEWSWEEK and in fact, a lawyer was going to represent the unfair practices at both TIME-LIFE and NEWSWEEK in a civil suit.

We were invited to give our viewpoints. A woman started speaking, extremely hesitant at first, about her observations. Then older researchers, some very close to retirement, described how they had been mere "fact-checkers" their entire careers, while male counterparts quickly moved into the coveted "writers circle."

After about an hour, I decided to join the group and describe the Personnel practices I had witnessed firsthand and how angry and frustrated they had made me. I was also aware I could possibly lose my job if my testimony got back to my employer but in the excitement of the meeting I felt I was making a contribution to better workplace practices and I was. It was very obvious at the end of the meeting that "discrimination", as they called it, had been prevalent for a long time at TIME-LIFE and NEWSWEEK.

Those who had witnessed unfair practices in their departments were asked to stay at the end of the meeting. A lawyer took our names and asked if we would be willing to come down to his office next week and go "on record" with our testimonies. I figured why not, I had nothing to lose. There was also the encouragement and excitement I felt at the meeting, so many frustrated and talented women joining together to tell their stories to affect change.

The following week there was the now-historic march of women, led by Gloria Steinem, down 5th Avenue. It was to end at a small park next to The New York Public Library where Gloria would address the marchers in a rally following the parade. I recall gingerly leaving work somewhat early that day, curious about the parade and the exciting-and revolutionary-message of this growing group of women.

Walking up to 5th Avenue, I was unprepared for what I saw. Thousands of women, just like me, had also apparently left work early. They were marching down 5th Avenue, closed to traffic, with many different banners raised high, calling for the end of "The Glass Ceiling", which I knew nothing about, and the like. As I watched, the women called to onlookers on the side, both women and men, to join the march.

"March with us!" they cried. "Don't be afraid!"

There were very well-dressed women in business suits and heels, administrative workers like myself, blue-collar women, medical personnel, postal workers, so many women from different job titles. Yet they all had one thing in common and were uniting to fight it: discrimination in the workplace. I watched as women stepped gingerly, and then enthusiastically, proudly, from their sidelines on the curb.

I knew their cause was right. I had seen it first hand. I found myself picking up a poster someone had discarded. It was a blank sheet, nothing had been written on it. I saw the group protesting "Equal Work for Equal Pay" coming down the street. That was the issue I wanted to protest. I had seen the cover of a new book earlier that day at Barnes and Noble, entitled "The French Lieutenant's Woman". Hastily I wrote the title of the book on the poster board and stepped out into the street, holding what I thought to be a sexist title, high over my head. I seemed to have the approval of people I marched by, cheering us on.

It was quite an exciting afternoon, the enthusiasm of the marchers, the applause of the crowd, the policemen on their huge brown horses, protecting the marchers, letting us express our point of view. I had an inkling of how the suffragettes must have felt, marching for the vote.

We finally made it down to the park next to The Public Library. The massive concrete lions guarding it seemed to glower at me:

"What do you think you're doing? Get back to your typing!"

I tried to make my way near the distant podium where Gloria would be addressing the crowd. There was no way I could get near. My feet ached and I longed to now be home. I had been feeling unusually tired and sometimes nauseous in the morning. As I turned down into the subway stairs, I heard Gloria's confident, firm voice begin her address to the crowd.

"Sisters, today is a very special day!"

In retrospect I wish I would have stayed to hear her speech. I walked up to our apartment in Brooklyn that night with a new perspective on life.

"Hi, honey, you're late."

"Yes, I know."

"Wow, did you hear about that Women's Lib March down 5th Avenue today? The news said there were several thousand women marching for equal rights today."

"Yes, I know."

Ultimately, the management of TIME-LIFE and NEWSWEEK listened to the testimony and settled out of court. They agreed to begin moving women into the writing field by giving them tests to determine their writing skills, a big victory and breakthrough to researchers and perhaps even low-level administrative assistants like myself.

But I was never to take the test which might have changed my life forever.

One month later I was sitting at my desk. It was 9 am and, yes, I was listening for the sound of the coffee wagon, to retrieve Bob Jones' morning coffee and roll.

My phone suddenly rang. It was Bea Dobie, the Head of HR, who had given me my orientation for my position at TIME-LIFE BOOKS. She wanted to see me. Were they finally going to offer me a chance to take a writing test or position as entry-level researcher?

Bea, a woman in her 40's, was sitting at her desk, white blouse, black suit, professionally-coiffed blond hair. She got right to the point.

"Joan, it's been noticed that you are expecting a child."

"Yes, I'm so excited. Ed and I are thrilled. It will be our first."

"Well, I'm sorry, but I must ask for your resignation. Pregnant women are not permitted to work here when it becomes obvious that they are with child."

As I signed the papers she had prepared I was in shock. I knew I was planning to tell the department at some time that I would need to be off for a while but that was it. I really hadn't thought too much about it. It was company policy, Bea glibly explained. But I knew my dreams of being a writer or researcher at TIME-LIFE had come to an end.

I had about two weeks to wrap up my work before my replacement was hired. In a way it would be a relief to end the close association with TIME and the pain of being in daily contact with a field I loved, but couldn't get near.

The last week of work, I was startled to see a new researcher proudly take her seat in the row of researchers' offices. She looked familiar. It was an English major from my college, one year behind me, eagerly introducing herself, long brown hair, high black boots and long skirt-the uniform-to the researchers around her.

I don't believe she ever saw me, the office administrative assistant, trying to conceal the ever-growing miracle inside my now-snuggly fitting red wool pantsuit!

Suddenly, my priorities were changing. Ed and I would soon move to Denver-starting our family-to begin a new life, in a new city. I would work the next 30 years of my life in telecommunications, happily writing many strategic and operational plans after being one of the first women Outside Plant Engineers in the Company and being designated a company spokesperson on a controversial new policy called "Affirmative Action". I eventually enjoyed my cake-and the icing on it tasted great.

Part 6: The Visitor:
Brooklyn, New York
September 11, 2001

Michael Flynn

I saw her, standin' in front of 230 Baltic, starin' at me dark red brick brownstone. She was clearly listen'n for the past. Search'n, as if by braille, try'n to hear the old conversations, the laughter, the struggles, the life of the Flynn Family she's found on the 1900 Census:

"Michael Flynn. Age 45. Born in Ireland. Paper Stock.
Mary A. Flynn. Age. 42, Wife, Born in New York.
Anna C. Flynn Age, 9, Daughter, Born in New York.
Frank F. Flynn, Age 7, Son, Born in New York
Charles Flynn, Age 6, Son, Born in New York"

She won't be find'n me on Ellis Island. 'Twas opened to receive us in 1892. And I'm not listed among the earlier immigrants arriving at Castle Garden in the Bowery either. I arrived in 1854 and The Castle opened in 1855.

I was born in County Leitrim, high up in the north of Ireland, next to County Sligo, the wild country. I was put on a ship for America when I was 3 years old. I'm told they gave me cousin, Oonie Farrell, a hundred dollars to take care of me.

Too late she be, my great-granddaughter Flynn, too late she be in this life. Lifetimes away. Too late.

Joan Flynn Beesley

It's chilly this early morning. I've finally used part of my vacation-with 25 years in telco I've accumulated lots of vacation days!- this year to come to Brooklyn to see where Michael Flynn actually lived and worked. The early sun shines on the ancient faces of the red row houses, trying in vain to awaken them, the sun filtering through the green leather leaves of the many oaks and maple trees that line these narrow streets.

This old Brooklyn street is just like a stage, now intensely quiet, the play over, the drama enacted, the actors gone, just the props and stage set, the rustling curtain poised to quietly close. But not just yet.

So still and quiet, as if waiting, the gentle breeze stirring softly in the feathery golden locust trees and red maples above. Waiting. Waiting for what? For me to come and finally tell the story.

I'll take one last look around this neighborhood, the neighborhood of Michael Flynn, and I'll be on my way. If only I could have been a part of it then, to know them…. So quiet, ancient almost, silenced. True, there are other people living in these red brick row houses now. Young professionals with brief cases and business suits, headsets, water bottles, armed with the requisite "New York Times" tucked confidently under one arm, heading for the subway into Manhattan to do battle.

I'm now standing here at the intersection of Congress Street and Columbia, mesmerized by the stunning panorama of the East River and lower and mid-Manhattan beyond, under the clear blue autumn sky. To my right the magnificent Brooklyn Bridge arches its historic back, cat-like, spanning the two islands. Married in 1880, Michael and Mary Ann would have watched its completion from this waterfront neighborhood. What an extraordinary time to be alive! I'm writing a book "40 Shades of Green" about Michael Flynn and his times. How wonderful to be here where it all took place. So entirely different from my world of telecommunications and conference calls! Yet I feel I am deaf. I can see but I can't hear, how it was, what actually went on then.

My father told me how he had navigated a Liberty Ship out of New York Harbor in WWII as a new lieutenant in the Merchant Marine, the very waters I see now, probably out of the Brooklyn Navy Yard. Perhaps Michael Flynn, my grandfather, my father and I, all have saltwater in our veins. Funny how everything comes together when you're older.

Knowing my great-grandfather Michael saw this same breathtaking view every morning is the only tie I really have with him, but it is real. The then bustling waterfront is where Brooklyn Port Authority now stands, unapproachable behind a chain link fence, secured tighter than a drum.

But the old docks and warehouses beyond, remain. How exciting it was to see this in a satellite image. Columbia Street, parallel with the water, intersected by Congress right across from the huge docks No. 7 and No.8, with their associated old warehouses. The satellite image of the address of the Michael Flynn Inc. warehouse places it right on the docks there.

Yesterday I found 230 Baltic where Michael Flynn and his new bride lived in 1880. After walking up and down the elegant old street and silent row houses, I got in my car, thinking there must be a Catholic church close by. It would have been the one he was married in and had his three children, Anna, Charlie and Frank, my grandfather, baptized. Around the corner on Clinton Avenue, sure enough, was an enormous Catholic Church, "St. Paul's", it read. "Second Oldest Catholic Church in Brooklyn." What a find it was.

I pulled into a small space between two large black limousines. Suddenly a thin young man dressed in black handed me a sign that said "Funeral".

"Put this on your dashboard," he said, opening the door with a flourish and doing the job himself, firmly planting the sign on my dash.

Suddenly I found myself being escorted up the massive stone steps into the largest church I've ever been in. The interior looked was a deep ornate cave, as big as a city block, beautiful old statues on the traditional alter, small private shrines, large marble baptismal fonts. It smelled very old. It felt larger than St. Patrick's Cathedral in New York

There in the vestibule were the funeral attendants, all older gentlemen dressed in black, sitting together on chairs in a circle, waiting for the mourners to arrive. A casket lay in the aisle ahead of me. I approached the men in black.

"I'm sorry for your loss," a younger man said as I approached.

"Actually, I'm not here for the funeral," I explained awkwardly.

"I told you, Joseph, we only say that to the older ones!" one of the older gentlemen said to the younger man who was sorry for my loss.

They all smiled at me. Even at a funeral, the wonderful old Brooklyn humor!

"I came here to understand the life of my great-grandfather, Michael Flynn, who lived around the block at 230 Baltic Street. He came here in 1854."

"Well you came to the right place, Miss. This is where he would have come. They all came here to St. Paul's. The Irish were all baptized, married and buried here."

I thanked them and let myself once again take in the ancient beauty of the magnificent old church and the fact that Michael and Mary Ann were surely married in this very place.

As I was getting back into my car, the young man in black suddenly appeared at my window again. I felt I owed him an explanation. I handed him back the "Funeral" sign he had given to me.

"Thank you, but I'm really here researching the life of my great grandfather who lived over on Baltic Street in 1880," I said.

"It's all right. Glad you got to see the Church. You can park here a while. I want to show you something."

He led me to the side street of the Church where there was a garden and a very old small stucco building behind the high, black wrought iron fence and gate."

"The Chapel is actually older than the Church. It's been here a very long time."

How I longed to see it! Perhaps this is where they were really married.

"Can I see it?"

"It's locked today. When the Church is open, the Chapel is locked. When the Chapel is open, the Church is closed. Today the Chapel is closed because of the funeral in the Church. When one is open, the other is closed. Open...closed. Open...closed."

The young man in black seemed slightly simple-minded, but was clearly proudly devoted to his duties and routine at the Church.

As I slid once again into the driver's seat of the rental car, I tried to hand the "Funeral" sign back to the helpful attendant, but again he handed it back, planting it firmly on the dash of my car.

"Anywhere in Brooklyn," he was saying to me. "Anywhere in Brooklyn."

I stared at him.

"Put this sign up on your dash and you can park in front of any church, anytime, anywhere in Brooklyn!" he explained proudly.

Captivated, I slowly pulled away, waving goodbye to the young man. There is no place like Brooklyn! If only for a short time, it was good to come back.

I decided to drive around for a bit, then park and get out and walk. Where there's a Catholic church, I reasoned, there has to be a Catholic school close by. Starting back from the Church I decided to walk around the block and suddenly there it was, in the middle of the block.

It dominated the whole street once you saw it was there. A massive dark red building, built of large, smooth stone blocks, all silent and dark inside, so quiet and unobtrusive I would have missed it if I hadn't been looking for it! I stood on the smooth, weathered front stoop of the school and looked up. "1882" was carved in massive lettering at the top.

So this is where Michael and Mary Ann Flynn probably sent my grandfather, Anna and Charlie to elementary school, I thought. As I stood in front I tried to peer into the front corridor through the windows in the heavy doors of the school, but it was all dark, yet immaculately well-kept, preserved almost. Sleeping, just like the church. What life and activity there once must have been here, resting now.

Suddenly the door opened and a young man in a black suit hurried by me. He had the look of a seminarian. I would have liked to ask him a few questions but I could see he was in a hurry. The door closed with thud and locked shut behind him. Suddenly I felt like an intruder who didn't belong there, a playgoer who arrives at the end of the play.

But that night in my dreams I could see the enterprising young Irishman taking his children to school to be educated, then hurrying down the three blocks to his scrap warehouse at Congress and Columbia Streets, across the street from the docks. Every morning he hurried to haul back the discarded heavy rope hawsers from immigrant and cargo ships that cast off during the night. It will be hard to go back to my world of meetings and milestones tomorrow.

The next morning I check out of the small hotel I am staying in. It's 6:45 am. I know it's time to say goodbye. I would have loved to have met you all. What a wonderful experience this has been! But I have one more stop to make before I catch my plane back to Denver at 2 this afternoon. I want to visit Ellis Island and check for Michael Flynn in their database. I won't have a lot of time to linger and mustn't get lost in my National rental car on the way to lower Manhattan.

I walk up the street towards Clinton Ave., following the steady stream of early commuters who disappear down a subway entrance to Manhattan. I pause by a small newsstand by the subway stairs. Besides the stacks of newspapers, I see a small map of Brooklyn.

"Can I help you, Miss?"

A young man with olive skin addresses me. He is wearing a turban, has a heavy black beard, gold ring in his ear, complete with a colorful caftan top and blue jeans.

"I'll take a *New York Times*, and do you happen to have a map of lower Manhattan?

"Sorry, I'm out. But they might have one down there in the subway."

"Now then, might I just happen to have one for the young lady?"

An old man came forward from the back of the tiny newsstand where he had been sitting on a stool. He had painfully eased himself off the stool, slowly, map in hand.

"Just the stiffness of the early mornin' mist in me bones, wouldn't y'know!"

He wore a tidy but very dated suit. He peered at me with blues eyes, apparently amused at his joke. He had a mustache. Something prompted me to speak further.

"I've actually been doing research on my family. They lived here in the neighborhood at 230 Baltic from 1900-1920."

"A fine block it is."

"I hated to leave the street. I'm on my way back to Denver where I live, trying to write a book about Michael Flynn, my great-grandfather from Ireland."

"A fine name."

"I'm hurrying into New York this morning. I want to take the ferry over from Battery Park to look for him on the Immigration List, to get a feeling of what it must have been like to land at Ellis Island in those days so I can write about it."

"Quite a place, I hear." He was a wiry old gent, thick mustache, somewhat balding, with thick glasses.

"My plane leaves for Denver at 2 so I'm trying to catch the 9 am ferry. That's down by Wall Street, isn't it?"

"It is indeed."

"I've actually been spending most of my time right here in this neighborhood, researching the book."

"You don't say."

"Yes, they lived on Amity Street and then at 230 Baltic."

"Beautiful streets, grand, right by the water."

"He had a junk and later a scrap metal business at the corner of Congress and Columbia across the street from the docks."

"Yes."

"I'm hoping to catch the ferry over to Ellis Island. I want to look at the exhibits and photos of the passengers. I understand many of their belongings are on exhibit."

"They are."

He seemed hesitant to contribute much of his knowledge about the area which I guessed must be substantial, considering his advanced age. And then:

"May I ask when it was that your great grandfather arrived here?" he asked pointedly.

"Why yes, 1854. That's what was entered on the 1900 Census they took at the house on Baltic over there. I've been told he was three when he was sent over from Ireland. That's all I know."

"Well, then. I can certainly save you that trip over to Ellis this cold morning!"

"How is that?"

"Bein' a longtime resident of the neighborhood, I can tell you that Ellis did not exist in 1854. Someone writin' a book should surely know her history a bit more accurately now. It was opened for the immigrants in 1892. Your Irish relative certainly did not arrive here in Brooklyn through Ellis Island!"

"Oh no. All this time I've imagined how he crossed the ocean and arrived here with his cousin, standing in long lines, being processed, like I've seen in the movies."

I was astonished. My whole life I had pictured my great grandfather as a 3 year old, accompanied by an older cousin, being processed through Ellis Island.

" 'Tis grand to imagine it happened that way, missy, but 1854 was long before the formal processin' they did at Ellis and one year before they opened Castle Garden. So many people believin' their ancestors were processed through Ellis! The Coffin Ships, as they called 'em, landed wherever they could, Boston, Philadelphia, even North Carolina. There were, in fact, hundreds of ships arrivin' each day. It was chaos. People were sick, dyin' enroute, dyin'soon after they arrived from typhus. They were starvin. Families torn apart, children from their parents. No work for 'em when they arrived!"

He looked at me sternly, somewhat angrily even.

"So you're writin' a book about Irish immigrants, are ye? Have you, in fact, taken the time to actually read about The Famine, Miss? I suggest you read some of the older firsthand accounts. "Paddy's Lament" or "Trinity" would be a good start. Hard readin'. Then you'll understand."

He seemed to turn away from me for a moment, somewhat impatient, miffed. Cranky in fact! He was, indeed, quite old. Clearly, I had upset him. Then his original cordiality returned.

"If you're to be leavin' at 2 o'clock, missy, I'd suggest you do your researchin' in the Brooklyn Library up in Prospect Park. 'Tis there you can read about 'em in The Brooklyn Eagle and The Brooklyn Standard Times. 'Twas what they all read. I wouldn't be goin' down to Battery Park. Lower Manhattan will be very crowded today." The old gentleman looked at me sternly.

"Do you have the time now, sir?" I asked. "I'm afraid I left my watch in Denver!"

We had spent longer than I had anticipated talking about my book, the neighborhood and its history.

He reached across his chest and there I saw a flash of brass. No, it looked like gold. It was a watch fob, more functional than ornate, about 3 inches long, criss-crossed into an intricate interlocking pattern, chain-like, supporting a gold watch that he pulled from a small pocket in his vest.

The old, knarled fingers slowly pried open the watch.

"'Tis 7 am already!" he announced proudly.

"Are you sure?"

"Surely, she's never wrong!" he winked at me as he lovingly fingered the old watch, lowering the gold chain and fob neatly into the worn vest pocket.

So much for my trip into the city, I thought. There's always my vacation next year. I had decided to heed the old man's advice and spend my limited time up at The Brooklyn Public Library near beautiful Prospect Park and Grand Army Plaza.

"Miss, if you're not in such a hurry now, there's a beautiful old church you might wish to visit down the block from Baltic St. It's St. Paul's Catholic Church, the second oldest church in Brooklyn, built in 1832. 'Tis quite likely the Irish Catholic Church where all your relatives went."

"Why yes. I found it yesterday. And also the old school, around the block from Baltic Street. In fact, the date at the top of the school said "1882". My great grandparents were married here in 1880. The school had just been built and the Brooklyn Bridge near completion. Can you imagine all that was going on in this neighborhood at that time?

"Yes."

"Thank you so very much. You'll never know how exciting all this is to me. How do you know so much history about this place?" I asked him.

"Brooklynites know their history," he said proudly," And newsagents know even more!" he said with a twinkle in his blue eyes.

Finally, it was time to go. My rental car was parked about three blocks away. I decided to walk pass 230 Baltic Street one more time. I would probably never be back here again. I wanted to absorb all the details of this marvelous old Brooklyn block for my book, the huge, shading trees, mysterious old brick row houses and the secrets they kept, silent and dark, like a museum piece. A stage the actors had left, the play over. Once full of life, now resting. Stately red maples and lofty, feathery green locust trees, danced above the street, embracing deep red, weathered russet brick row houses, each a mere 30 feet wide. Resolute, profound, radiating oldness and age.

There was a sense that many lives lived here before today. How to peel back the layers. You could hear it in the stillness. You could see it in the worn slate sidewalks and front stoops. You could smell it in the moist shade of the tall, dark row houses, in the damp, dancing sunlight of the stately trees softly feathering the street, as if to gently say:

"There were a great many lives and stories here before today." A sense of the very old, powerfully guarding the past. Stillness itself.

"He walked up and down this street every day when he went to work as a junkman in his warehouse on Congress Street," I thought to myself. I took several pictures of the neighborhood, from each end, knowing none of them would do justice to the presence I felt there.

Then, standing in front of the stone steps leading up into the parlor entrance of 230 Baltic, I was taken in by the dark, lower level street entrance below the stairs. All the row houses had a small, enclosed wrought iron patio off the sidewalk leading to their lower entrance. 230 Baltic was no exception.

Bravely, I opened the black, rusty, creaking gate, stepping down onto the slate slab patio, one step below the sidewalk, hoping no one from the stoop above would come out. I peered into the lower level entrance under the stairs through the black wrought iron door. All was dark inside. In the old days, the lower level was rented out to boarders or used for servants. It had this private entrance to the street, so as not to bother the inhabitants and owners above.

Now it really was time to go. As I turned from the doorstep and started towards the patio and sidewalk, I tripped and suddenly felt myself falling through the air. What's happening, I thought? I had been so focused on the mystery of the house I hadn't seen the small step up. Painfully, I landed prostrate, my right knee now bleeding, aching with the weight of the fall on my bruised bare hands, my brown leather Daytimer and airline itinerary spilling across the tiny courtyard in front of me.

"Oh, my God," I thought. "How embarrassing!" I gathered myself up, inspecting my painful, bleeding knee.

I looked around, hoping no one had seen me, but a well-dressed black woman pushing a stroller several homes away, was making her way up the street. She had witnessed the whole thing, a haughty, disdainful look on her face, as she made her way past.

But half way down the block, out of my range, the woman suddenly looked up, her eyes riveted on Brooklyn Harbor. Transfixed like Medusa, she watched the first billows of oily black smoke roiling insidiously from the wound in Tower I. Soon a monstrous cumulous cloud, spewing dead white ash, would lurch hungrily along Wall Street.

Back up the block, unaware of the sight, I tried to collect my dignity and belongings as I rose slowly on my bleeding knee. Then I saw a glint in the corner of the patio by a small shrub. I reached for my glasses lying where my Daytimer and purse had emptied their contents.

Something metallic, glimmering in the early morning light. My knee was really throbbing now! A flash of heavy brass. No, it looked like gold. It was a watch fob, more functional than ornate, about 3 inches long, cris-crossed into an intricate inter-locking pattern, chain-like, that folded neatly on itself, supporting a gold watch. I reached for it, prying open the stiff, crusted 24k gold lid enclosing the old watch:

"7 a.m."

A cranky old Irishman with a curious timepiece, no stranger to terrorism himself, had saved my life, leaving his precious calling card.

Examine the cracked white porcelain of memory
Holding it up to the light of today's reality
Yes, these things really did happen
And, it was wonderful!

Acknowledgements

I'd like to thank Ancestry.com for many wonderful nights of breathlessly searching old Census Records, The Brooklyn Eagle, Brooklyn Directories from the 1800's, birth, marriage and death certificates, passport records, etc. seeing relatives I'd only heard about, come to life!

It was through an inquiry I made for "Michael Flynn" in Geneology.com that I met Diane Brook of the UK, a descendant of Peter Flynn, Michael Flynn's uncle, who fled to Scotland during the Famine and later lived on Amity St. in Brooklyn. My distant cousin Diane introduced me to another cousin, Carol Langer and her mother Eileen Bagley of Boston, also descendants of Peter Flynn.

In 2009 they arranged a wonderful, touching phone call with Eileen, who was then 93 years old. Eileen recalled a visit with Michael Flynn in the 1940's at his Brooklyn home on 5th St. when he was very old and bedridden with arthritis. She was introduced to him with many of her young cousins. She remembered that he was very crippled, bed-ridden then most of the time and taken care of by a male nurse and "that it was supposed he had a lot of money!" She recalled him growing impatient with the many noisy young relatives and suddenly announced "Huummph!!! Too many people!!!" and memorably shooed everyone from the room!

It was such a surprise meeting an unknown branch of the Flynn's dating back to the mid 1800's!

About the Author

Joan Flynn Beesley

Joan Beesley was born in 1946 in Brooklyn, New York and has had a lifelong fascination with her great-grandfather, Michael Flynn, the "Scrapman of Brooklyn" and the empire he built.

"I spent my summers in Brooklyn, at 587th 5th Street, near Grand Army Plaza and Prospect Park. We were the Flynns, my father being Edward Flynn who went to St. Saviors's and later Brooklyn Prep, then King's Point. He was born in 1928. My grandmother shopped on 7th Avenue. My family is originally from County Leitrim and my mother, Joan Flynn, opened 7 "Irish Emerald" stores in Cleveland, the first of its kind to both import Irish goods and teach about the Irish traditions. Danny Green, of the movie, "Kill the Irishman", once came into her shop, wanting her to order IRA rings!"

This is a compelling story of an immigrant who arrived with nothing, rising from "Junkman" to industrial millionaire. Michael Flynn came to America at age three in 1854, rising from a scrapman on Amity Street (lots of Flynns lived there!), collecting hawsers from the immigrant ships, starting a business at Columbia and Congress, a block from the East River. He bought the legendary David E. Lupton & Sons window company during the Great Depression, shrewdly dismantled and scrapped "L" trains, many WWI and WWII destroyers, buying the USS Normandy and other ships, then selling them back to the Brooklyn Navy Yard for salvage!

An active member of the old Brooklyn "6th Ward", he was "A friend to statesman and politicians". His 1942 obituary mentions ties to members of the notorious Democratic Brooklyn Ring including New York delegates to the Democratic National Convention James Kane and James Ennis, Justice of the New York Supreme Court James Dunne, and New York State Senators Michael Coffey and Bart Cronin. He was a lifelong member of The St. Patrick's Society of Brooklyn, The Brooklyn Lodge of Elks, The Emerald Association and The Knights of Columbus. His company, The Michael Flynn Manufacturing Company, continued by his sons, installed the windows in many New York City sky-scrapers, becoming global, building the locks for the Panama Canal and hangers in Peru. At one time his company was the third largest metal company in the United States after Alcoa and Reynolds Aluminum. There were so many stories!"

Joan currently lives in Denver, Colorado with her husband of 45 years, Ed Beesley, children Robert, Rosemary and Kimberly and grandchildren Tyler, Dillon, Ellen and Ashleigh. Other books by Joan include *Hot House Flowers, I Just Wanted to Be Here When You Called My Name*, a novel about pediatric cancer survival. Joan has also published two poetry collections, *Lot's Wife* and *Poems Along the Path*, and *Witchbox: A Collection of Short Stories,* all available on Kindle and most recently a memoir entitled "Through the Looking Glass."